To Patrice —

Thank you for joining us at the Waterfront Hilton for the " Alliance Directors Conference."

Best Wishes,

Bob Mayer

6-17-10

WITHOUT RISK THERE'S NO REWARD

TALES, TRIALS AND TRUISMS

FROM THE AMAZING LIFE

OF A PIONEERING

SOUTHERN CALIFORNIA DEVELOPER

WITHOUT RISK
THERE'S NO REWARD

STORIES FROM MY LIFE'S JOURNEY

ROBERT MAYER

WITH

PETER WEISZ

SEVEN LOCKS PRESS

SANTA ANA, CALIFORNIA

Seven Locks Press
P.O. Box 25689
Santa Ana, CA 92799
(800) 354-5348

Individual sales: This book is available through most bookstores or can be ordered directly from Seven Locks Press at the address above.

Quantity Sales: Special discounts are available on quantity purchases by corporations, associations and others. For details, contact the "Special Sales Department" at the publisher's address above.

Printed in the United States of America

Jacket photo of Bob Mayer and portrait photo of Bob and Maya Mayer by:
Phillip Stewart Charis of Charis Fine Portraiture, San Juan Capistrano, California

Design by Kira Fulks • www.kirafulks.com

Library of Congress Cataloging-in-Publication Data is available from the publisher

ISBN: 0-9801270-9-2
        978-0-9801270-9-6

DEDICATION

In memory of my parents, Bert and Betty
and
Marcie and Mary Ellen
and
to my children, Linda, RJ and Michael
and their children and their children's children

❦

ACKNOWLEDGEMENTS

I am grateful to the following people for their assistance in the preparation of this book:

To my cousins Jim, Roger and Mike Mayer and Annette Kutilek, and my sister, Dolores, who, collectively over many years have been caretakers of our family's history. They provided not only ancestral background but also many of the photographs and newspapers clippings in this book. And to the valuable assistance of another member of the family, Juanita Licher, who over many months digitally scanned those photos to give us a pictorial glimpse of our ancestors.

Many thanks to the Blue Earth County Historical Society in Mankato, whose mission statement "to collect, preserve and promote the history of Blue Earth County for present and future generations" is generously supported by its dedicated staff of volunteers.

To Peter Weisz, who made this book come to life with all of his editing skills, his historical knowledge of facts and his extraordinary sense of humor.

And to my wife, Maya, who not only encouraged me to write this book but laid out its concept. For her invaluable input, the long hours she's spent editing, researching, gathering photos, creating profiles and taking care of the many countless things that go into producing a memoir such as this—she has my deepest gratitude.

CONTENTS

MY LOVE OF FLYING

MEMORABLE MOMENTS

FAMILY VIGNETTES

WITHOUT RISK THERE'S NO REWARD

STORIES FROM MY LIFE'S JOURNEY

INTRODUCTION

Where I'm going has no end, what I'm seeking has no name.
No, the treasure's not in the takin', it's in the lovin' of the game.

Pat Garvey

Perhaps it's due to my heritage, to my personality, or to my general lack of common sense, but I have, throughout my business career, always warmly embraced risk as fortune's accomplice. As a builder and developer I have been fortunate to make numerous successful runs around the Monopoly board, repeatedly passing "Go" and managing to avoid "Going to Jail." In real life, just as in the board game, however, every property acquisition is preceded by a roll of the dice. There is no other way. Without the risk there simply is no reward.

How many times—in business or in everyday life—have you heard the expression "Risk vs. Reward?" It's a common equation we all use to evaluate any contemplated course of action. Will the value of what you may gain offset what you may lose in order to gain it? Common sense tells us that to move ahead, the expected reward should exceed the risk, or, at the very least, it should be "worth the risk." In business we are constantly presented with calls to "reduce the risk" or "manage the risk," and are encouraged to precisely identify our "risk tolerance." Actually, I have never regarded risk in this fashion. Once the deal makes economic sense, that is the time to forge ahead and welcome whatever risks you are required to accept. To me, risk is simply a four-letter way of spelling opportunity.

I've asked myself many times, am I being foolhardy by throwing caution to the winds? Do I embrace risk because of some kick or adrenaline rush I get by living on the edge? No, actually, not at all. I have found that in real estate, as in real life, all risks must be weighed and measured carefully. From the stories I present on the following pages, you will see that I have been blessed by such opportunities many times over the course of my 60-plus year career. In reflecting back, I can honestly say that I derived the most pleasure and satisfaction, not from eventually owning and operating whatever properties we acquired, but rather in the risky process of navigating all the twists and turns of the deal that got us there. That was, and continues to be, the true fun part for me and even though we didn't always emerge successful, the lure and excitement of that risky road always kept me coming back for more.

So, just as the journey is the destination, I can honestly say that in my experience, the rewards have been worth the risk. It is the sharing of this point-of-view that has prompted me, among other reasons, to record the following life episodes assembled on these pages.

This is essentially a book filled with personal memories, stories chronicling an assortment of my life's unexpected and sometimes amazing adventures. While most memoir books are usually organized into chronological chapters, this book is different. Each chapter here is meant to stand on its own, independent of the others. Although they all share a common thread that connects them, you are invited to read these chapters in any order you choose. Each one is designed to recount an encapsulated event and does not require your having read any prior chapters to follow the storyline.

While some chapters recount amusing incidents, others are testaments of tragedy. And, just like real life, they don't come at you in any particular order. Before embarking, however, you may want to make Chapter One, titled The Foundation, your starting point. The Foundation provides a brief background timeline about my life's journey. By acquainting yourself with the Foundation chapter, you will be able to place the events in the ensuing chapters into their proper context.

I've tried to model this book on the structure of a high-rise apartment building or possibly a hotel. After coming in on the ground floor (The Foundation), you're then free to get on the elevator or climb the stairs and get off on any floor you choose. The Building Directory (Table of Contents) in the front of the book should help you decide where to go next. No matter what floor you get off on, I'm confident that you'll find something there that will amuse you, move you, or even enlighten you.

Why I decided to build this literary high-rise at this particular time of my life is really quite simple. The ancients built the Pyramids and Stonehenge and the Taj Mahal for one reason. They wanted to leave something behind that would endure. That's what I want to do as well, but not with massive monuments such as those. That's not my style. I would rather build an enduring record of my life for the people I care about most.

I'd like to know that long after I've been laid down into that same earth I've built upon so often, that my great-grandchildren, for example, will be able to pick up this book years from today and learn something about who I was. I hope they'll discover some of what their great-grandfather believed about risk and reward, and will gain some insight and understanding of how I've lived a life that, in turn, has had an impact upon them.

Secondly, my stories are also written for my friends and colleagues, as well as the occasional stranger, who may get a chuckle from some of the more humorous segments, as well as an education about the trials and tribulations of a developer's life.

And, there also exists a third major reason I decided to write this book. The world I live in today is very different from the world of my ancestors, my grandparents and even my parents—yet I feel intimately connected to their history. But, alas, we have no first-hand diaries or journals. I have been able to weave together only the barest threads of some of the events of their lives. Other than a few newspaper articles written about the Mayer Brothers and my grandfather, Fred Pizzo, there are no first-hand journals, diaries or personal correspondence to speak of. I was, however, able to locate the names of family members on ship passenger lists documenting their journey to America from Europe.

As I read the ship logs containing my ancestors' names on the manifest, I could visualize them leaving their homeland behind, crossing the Atlantic, and settling in an unknown world with an uncertain future. Even in the absence of any written records, I can picture them in my mind's eye, carrying all of their worldly possessions, small children in tow, trudging down the wharf as they became absorbed into the noise and congestion of late 19th century New York City. It is a powerful vision that conveys only a fraction of their dauntless pioneering spirit. How much I would enjoy reading or even listening to their personal stories as passed down through an oral history. All of us today—me, my children, and my children's children—are their future generations and we are the beneficiaries of their bravery.

I came from modest beginnings, starting as a young construction worker earning one dollar an hour, and eventually was fortunate to enjoy the recognition as one of the nation's major multi-family housing developers. I have been the architect as well as the developer who took the risks, brought the deals together by securing the land, arranging the financing and putting the thousands of pieces into place to complete the final project. As the years roll by, the homes, the buildings and the hotels I've built may outlive me. But those structures will not endure forever—they're only made of clay. But this book is here to stay.

Like everyone, I hope that the legacy I leave to my family will allow my children and their children to live richer and more contented lives. But beyond that, it is my hope that this memoir will form a bridge connecting us across generations through the sharing of our genealogical history with our ever-expanding family tree.

Just as my grandfather, Lorenz, and his brothers, Louis and Conrad, followed their father into business, I too am heartened to observe that an ensuing generation of the Mayers' lineage has chosen to follow my path into this industry. I extend my family mantle to them and rejoice that they share my life-long affection for this work as they continue building upon their success. While I still take an active part in the management and growth of our company—a pursuit that was all-consuming over the past 60 years—the pace has now slowed and it permits me a bit of time to reflect. I have dearly loved what I've done over my career as a developer and have never considered it to be work. From Baltic Avenue to Boardwalk, my life on the Monopoly board has been more like a grand game I have always enjoyed.

This Introduction is about the only place in this book you'll find any sort of philosophizing. All the other chapters were written to give you a down-to-earth glimpse of my life and times. Just as with any building project, a book project also comes with its share of risks. "What if no one reads it?" "Will my family and friends enjoy it?" It's another throw of the dice. With a building project, measuring success is a straightforward and simple matter. Is the building fully occupied? Does it generate sufficient cash flow to justify the construction costs? But how will I know if I should count this book as a success or not? I've concluded I'm not going to wait for it to appear on the New York Times bestseller list before making this judgment. Actually, the success or failure of this book project all depends upon you. Or, to put it another way: "My life is in your hands." If you come away with a heightened appreciation of our family's amazing ancestors; if you find a chuckle or two in what I've written; if you find my tales of triumph and tragedy to be engaging and informative, then I will honestly be able to say that the reward was worth the risk.

And, finally, as with any development project, the best prize is the process. The very act of writing these stories has allowed me to reflect upon my own past and has provided me with fresh insights into understanding my own life's journey. Moreover, sharing these stories with you has given me a chance to strengthen the structure of our family tree as I learned about our predecessors upon whose shoulders we all stand. And this, to me, has been the greatest reward of all.

—**Bob Mayer**
Newport Coast, California
Spring 2008

WITHOUT RISK
THERE'S NO REWARD

CHAPTER ONE

THE FOUNDATION

Come and grow old with me, the best is yet to be.

Robert Browning

Welcome to my world. As I explained in the Introduction, this is the chapter where you "get in on the ground floor" of my life. The episodes you will explore in subsequent chapters should be regarded in the context of the overall course of my life's voyage. They are my personal memories. This chapter, then, is a short roadmap for that journey or, if you prefer, the foundation for the structure that is to follow.

The "Ancestry" section at the back of this book recounts my family history before I arrived on the scene. I urge you to have a look, especially if you are a member of our family by blood or by marriage. Introducing you to our proud heritage is one of my primary purposes in sharing these memories. But even if you are not a family member, you will find the story of the Mayer Brothers, for example, to be an uplifting and exciting embodiment of the American Dream. To understand who I am, I feel it's helpful to become acquainted with those who went before. You may discover a bit more about who you are in the process. But for now, this chapter starts with a little bit of personal history about my life.

I was born in 1926 in Madison, Wisconsin, the only son of Bertram Joseph Mayer, of German-Austrian descent, and Benerita Pizzo, the daughter of Sicilian immigrants. My sister, Dolores, came along a few years later. Shortly after I turned eleven, because of my mother's health, our family moved from Madison to the warmer and dryer climate of Los Angeles.

Upon graduation from Huntington Park High in 1944, I enlisted in the Army Air Corps in hopes of becoming a pilot and serving my country in the war effort. Shortly after my tour of duty ended in 1946, I returned home and entered community college. I later met and married Marceline (Marcie) Ann Correa, a 19-year old daughter of a Portuguese immigrant and my sister's co-worker at a Los Angeles Bank of America branch. For our first home, Marcie and I rented one of the tiny apartments my parents owned in Huntington Park. We later moved to, and managed, another of my parents' properties in Lynwood.

Soon a baby was on the way and I left school to find work. By this point my father, a trained engineer, had found employment designing heat exchange systems with the C.F. Braun engineering firm in Alhambra, where I also found work during the first few years of our marriage. In 1949, not long after our daughter Linda was born, I lost my job at Braun and was again on the hunt for new employment. That hunt led me to an opportunity that would alter the course of my life forever.

During this critical phase, there were three stalwart men who each had sufficient faith to provide me with the "leg up" I needed at the time. Collectively, their confidence in me provided the ballast that launched my career in construction and real estate development. I have been, and will forever be, in their debt. The first of these men was my father.

Dad had saved a bit of money and, hoping to cash in on the post-war housing boom, decided to invest in a small apartment building in Lynwood. He contacted a man named Claude Howard, owner of Howard Construction Company, who had built a number of such buildings for various owners. My father and Claude successfully negotiated a deal, but not before the builder threw in a "sweetener." He agreed to give a job—at $1 an hour—to the buyer's destitute out-of-work 23–year-old son … me!

In the years that followed, Claude, the second of the stalwart men I mentioned, became my boss and trusted mentor as I received valuable on-the-job training about the many complex ins and outs of the construction business. I spent the early 1950s working hard, pushing wheelbarrows, and was caught up in an ever-expanding apprenticeship that soon introduced me to the fast-forward world of real estate development. In a few years I became the company's general manager. I also acquired a broker's license and successfully sold a number of the properties that contributed to our company's status as the largest developer of apartment buildings in the Los Angeles area.

By 1955 I felt that I had enough experience under my belt to strike out on my own. I was headstrong and convinced that I knew all I needed to know about construction and the real estate game. By this time Marcie and I were the parents of three children and I soon discovered that there was one very important thing I did not know: Where to get the start-up capital to start my own business.

I decided to set up shop in the garage of our little house in Whittier, and succeeded in getting some small home remodeling jobs, kitchen modernizations and the like. As long as the homeowner paid me on time, I was able to pay my subcontractors in turn and we managed to eke out a small living. But amassing enough cash to buy land or launch a new construction project was still out of the question. Despite my lack of a bankroll, I kept my hopes high and my eyes open for attractive opportunities, and in 1956 I found just the one.

Open land was plentiful in L.A. in those days and the demand for low-cost housing seemed unlimited. An ideal lot in Lynwood, perfect for a two-unit duplex, became available for $3,500. I had the knowledge, the experience, and the foresight to recognize this as a terrific opportunity. What I did not have was the $3,500. That's when I turned to Johnny Nisser, my neighbor and the third of the stalwart men who demonstrated their faith in me early on. Needless to say, this successful deal marked the beginning of a prosperous friendship and business relationship that has endured to this day. It also marked the full-fledged launching of my first business venture outside of remodeling by the Mayer Construction Company.

By the 1960's I had earned the title of the largest apartment developer in Southern California, but this time it was different. I was an entrepreneur, not a manager working for someone else. During the rest of the decade, Mayer Construction took on larger and larger building projects, including a hotel in Palm Springs. That job led to my lifelong love affair with the desert resulting in our decision to purchase a Palm Springs condo there. In the decades that followed, I continued to yield to the arid lure of the desert via active membership in various Country Clubs such as The Springs and Morningside in Rancho Mirage.

With Marcie at my side rearing our children, handling the bills, the accounting and payroll, Mayer Construction prospered and we decided to relocate our family from our small Whittier garage. What started as a "mama-papa" operation soon took on the trappings of a "real" business when we opened our first office in Downey in 1959, and soon became accustomed to dealing with the substantial risks associated with the construction business. In fact, I began to view such risks as an integral part of our enterprise and, rather than dread, I began to welcome them. Fortunately, and more often than not, the rewards we collected exceeded our expectations and kept us coming back for more.

As a result of our hard work and the blossoming prosperity we were beginning to enjoy during those years, Marcie and I indulged in the purchase of some grown-up toys such as sports cars, boats and private planes. We deployed them to create some very special good-time family memories including a run-in with a massive steamship during one unforgettable boat cruise off of Catalina Island.

It was also during this period that our success gave me the needed confidence to consider some more adventuresome business ventures. For example, in 1965 some buddies and I hatched the notion that we could establish a state lottery in Nevada as lottery fever was starting to sweep across the country. This unsuccessful foray convinced me to stick to the business I know best.

In 1967, Marcie and I flew to our special retreat in the Palm Springs desert for a get-away weekend. By the time we were to return home, a storm had blown in and Marcie opted to drive back to Downey on her own while I flew back. Tragically, Marcie was fatally injured after her car inexplicably drove off a high overpass in Colton, California. The loss of Marcie, just at the point we were reaching the sweet spot of our lives, was then, and remains today, the most unbearable experience in my memory. But, as it must, life moved on.

Almost four years would pass, when in 1971, my attorney, Al Fink, introduced me to a wonderful young lady who was working at a bank at the time. After a false start, Mary Ellen and I began dating and within a year were married. This juncture marked the end of my extended mourning period and, with Mary Ellen at my side, enabled me to enter a truly golden period of my life—both personally and professionally.

Also about this time, I partnered with a newly formed REIT (real estate investment trust) to establish a chain of some of the very first "extended stay" hotels in the country. The first of these pioneering Ambassador Inns was built off the Strip in Las Vegas. The venture nearly went up in smoke when a construction fire demolished the 343-unit complex just as it was being framed. Fortunately, we pulled through and eventually wound up building twelve Ambassador Inns, containing over 2,600 units, in twelve different California, Nevada and Arizona cities. In the late 1970s I struck a deal with the REIT and wound up as sole owner of the successful chain.

After a few years, I decided again to re-focus my professional life by devoting all of my time and energy to the construction and land development business. I decided to sell off all the hotels in the Ambassador chain to individual investors—almost all of them, that is. I surmised that the original Las Vegas Ambassador enjoyed great future profit potential and decided to hang on to it. And it was through this avenue that I somewhat reluctantly found myself in the role of a licensed Las Vegas casino operator during the 1980s.

After years of securing financing for various building projects, I had gained an appreciation for the advantages of being on the other side of the loan committee table. I decided to leverage some of my financial equity and in 1979 I helped to co-found Metro Bank. The bank focused primarily on new business development and was successfully sold to Comerica Bank in 1996. I also became involved with another business bank, Prime Bank, which was recently sold to East West Bank based in Southern California. While I certainly enjoyed and profited from my forays into the financial services zone, I would invariably miss the rough and tumble of the real estate development world.

It was also around this period that I acquired an interest in the Waterfront property in Huntington Beach that would play such an important role in my business activities during the 1990s and beyond. 1980 was the year I sold off most of the assets, including the name, of the Mayer Construction Company to renowned

Canadian financiers, the Belzberg brothers, and began what I thought would be a time for me to slow down and relax, but that was not to be. After a few months of retirement, and with little improvement in my golf game during this unusual transition from my normal active life, I felt idle and so began to devote some of my extra energy to a few real estate ventures and then a great deal of time in my negotiations with the City of Huntington Beach regarding the Waterfront Project. I felt strongly that the City was ready for a renaissance and that our property could be the catalyst that would elevate Surf City, USA to the crown jewel of Southern California. The trick was convincing the City leaders to invest in my dream.

To accomplish all of this required starting up a new business. Since I had sold the name of my previous enterprise, Mayer Construction as an asset of the company, I had to now rename my new venture. I decided to call it: "The Robert Mayer Corporation." Although it didn't quite describe the business, it was an accurate name since I was at that point pretty much running the operation myself.

By 1985 I was joined by Steve Bone, as Operations Director of The Robert Mayer Corporation. Steve shared my vision of bringing a world-class destination resort complex to life along Pacific Coast Highway. Our first priority was to tackle the Waterfront development in Huntington Beach in earnest. At about that same time we also decided to remodel the Ambassador Inn in Las Vegas and add a small casino that we inherited after the casino operator was unable to carry on its management. We had named the casino "La Mirage," and this fact led to negotiations with famed Vegas impresario, Steve Wynn, over the use of the Mirage name. The outcome was truly a Wynn-win situation.

Thanks to over twenty-five years of diligent effort, we finally came to terms with the City of Huntington Beach relating to the development of the 50-acre Waterfront property. During the course of the 1990s, we were able to construct and operate the 300-room Hilton Waterfront Beach Resort along the beachfront. The project also includes 25 acres of luxury condominiums, the 184-unit residential communities of Sea Cove and Sea Colony. By 2003 the project was enhanced by the opening of the magnificent 517-room four-star Hyatt Regency Resort and Spa. The Hyatt is home to the largest oceanfront conference facility in California. A third hotel is being planned and final development of the Waterfront Project should wrap up in 2011, after over thirty years of planning and development.

From a family standpoint, the 1990s were both the best of times and the worst of times. I took great joy in watching the growth of my children's families and the arrival of the first of my great-grandchildren. Likewise, the first twenty years of my marriage with Mary Ellen had been wonderful, however, by the mid-90s we had grown apart and I watched with sadness and dismay as our relationship unraveled. As the millennium came to an end, so did our marriage. Our divorce was granted in 2000 after a three-year separation. The stress during this period may have had some effect on my health. In 2001 I underwent a six-way cardiac bypass. Happily, the operation was a success and afterwards I felt terrific. Over time, I also succeeded in transitioning my marital relationship with Mary Ellen into an enduring friendship that lasted until she passed away in 2005 at the young age of 68.

At age seventy-five and single again, I felt like a young man, and ready to re-conquer the world. It was then that Maya walked into my life. On the dance floor during our first date, I had an epiphany: "My goodness," I said to myself, "this bundle of dynamite could have a profound influence on the remaining years of my life." She has brought me into the digital age, and today, at the age of 82, I feel I'm growing younger as I grow older. I have learned to surf the

Internet and enjoy many of the benefits of this computer age. Maya and I married on the island of Maui in October of 2006.

So, there you have it in an over-sized nutshell. The timeline of my years—so far. Years filled mostly with blessings, for I do count myself as a very fortunate man. Through the years I have been blessed with relatively good health, a wonderful family, good friends and the joy of intensely loving my work. As a result I have no intention of withdrawing from the arena of life just yet. I still join my son and grandson when I report to work at the offices of The Robert Mayer Corporation in Newport Beach. And there's no reason to believe that I will stop collecting amusing vignettes and true-life anecdotes over the coming years.

Armed with this chapter's foundation, you are now prepared to place the memories that follow into their proper context. Please understand that what you've read so far is merely preamble. A setting of the stage, if you will. In the episodes that follow you will meet and get to know the many people mentioned in this chapter whose lives were, and in many cases still are, so deeply intertwined with my own. I'm confident that you'll find these stories entertaining and, perhaps at times, amazing and uplifting. And, some are also quite humorous.

I believe that there's very little risk, and ample reward, in your reading of the remaining chapters of this book. So, I invite you to do as the poet Robert Browning suggests: "Come and grow old with me. The best is yet to be."

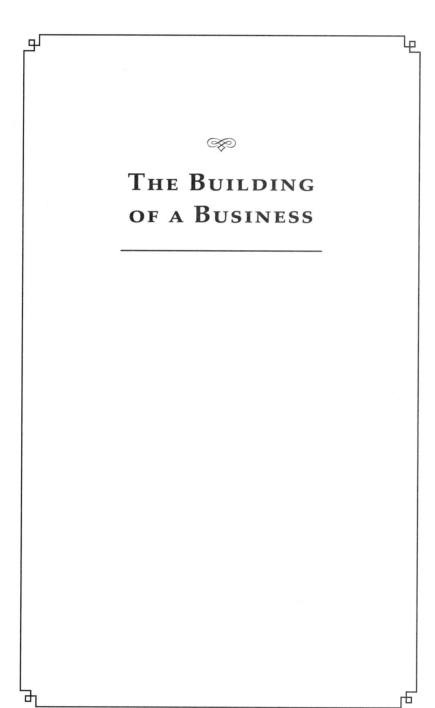

THE BUILDING
OF A BUSINESS

CHAPTER TWO

THE RENT MAN COMETH

*A man builds a fine house; and now he has a master, and a task for life; he is
to furnish, watch, show it, and keep it in repair, the rest of his days.*

Ralph Waldo Emerson

The year 1950 saw the establishment of the Kefauver
Committee to investigate organized crime in America, the
Great Brinks Robbery in Boston, and the outbreak of a shooting war
in Korea. But as stories of these and other world events filled the
pages of the L.A. Times, I remained focused on my new duties at
the Howard Construction Company. I was given the job as part of
a real estate deal my father had worked out with Claude Howard,
my new boss, and I was hard bent to prove my salt. I was earning
the princely sum of $1 per hour and my job description could
pretty much be summed up in a single sentence: "Do whatever the
boss tells you to do."

The Howard Construction Company was, as the name indicated,
in the building business—primarily apartment development across
Southern California. Los Angeles County, along with the rest of
the nation, was undergoing a post-war housing boom that was
not going to be defused by the Korean conflict or anything else.
Urbanization was progressing on a grand scale as America's cities

swelled with an unending population influx—flowing mostly from the country's rural areas. From 1945 to 1950 the population of Los Angeles rose by nearly twenty percent. Affordable housing was the order of the day and Claude Howard was there to fill that order.

I soon found myself serving as Mr. Howard's gopher, although I sometimes felt like more of a pigeon. I didn't mind, I told myself, because every day I was learning more of the ropes. I learned how to obtain permits, how to get the best deal from vendors, how to select reliable sub-contractors and, of course, how to actually produce well-built apartment projects as cost-effectively as possible. Claude Howard was twenty years my senior and knew his stuff. I counted myself as very fortunate to be able to gain such a valuable education from him. Eventually, Claude introduced me to no-lien contracts and all of the intricacies of the building trade.

Little by little, Claude increased my scope of responsibility and before long I was handling many of the day-to-day construction duties on my own. The assignment I received that summer of 1950, however, was something completely alien and unexpected—and one that would dramatically shape my life and my career.

In addition to being a tradesman, a teacher, and a talented businessman, Claude was, above all else, a compassionate and caring man. When he learned of the availability of some low-cost vacant lots, stretched across a mile of industrial tract in a section of L.A. known as Watts, he immediately recognized the inherent opportunities. By acquiring the lots and erecting low-cost rental units, he would be providing housing for those most in need. At the same time, if the apartments were properly managed, they would provide a steady income stream for the company.

The 50 by 125 foot lots were located along 108th Street between Avalon and Central Avenues; areas surrounded by flagging factories and light industry, that had, for the most part, fallen into disuse after the war. In addition to the bargain bin price tag of only $600 per lot, we were able, in those days, to obtain a building permit in under two hours instead of the typical two years of waiting required to obtain a permit today. Of course, today it would be unthinkable to even apply for a residential building permit for an area zoned for industry—unless the neighborhood had been targeted for "gentrification" by the army of urban planners who, in those days, occupied the mayor's office. But in 1950, it was wide open and "anything goes." Zoning considerations were not given a second thought as communities did all they could to promote new home construction.

In no time at all we had gotten underway, building either four or five units on each 50-foot lot. Sometimes Claude was able to purchase three adjacent lots and we would erect from twelve to fifteen units on such a "super-site." Over a period of two years, we constructed twelve freestanding apartment buildings comprising 120 new housing units. Once we began placing them on the market, we soon were delighted to discover that they were a smash sell-out.

No one had seen new housing go up in this area for generations, so the project enjoyed widespread attention. The fact that the apartments were located in an industrial section of town did not diminish their appeal. As soon as the buildings were ready and a "Now Renting" sign was erected, prospective tenants stood in line for hours just for a chance to rent one of these shiny new units.

After the first apartment building was completed, Claude soon realized that constructing and leasing out these units was one thing, but effectively managing them was quite another. That's when he called me into his cramped office.

"Bob, we've got all the Watts apartment buildings ready to rent," he began.

"Yes, sir, I know," I replied. "That's great."

"It sure is, but now we're going to have to hire someone to manage them," he explained.

"Manage them?" I asked.

"You know," Claude said. "Go around and collect the rent each week. Stuff like that."

"That's no big deal," I shot back. "We don't have to hire anyone extra. One of our people could do that with no problem."

"We'd need somebody honest and responsible," Claude admonished and then walked around his desk looking pensive. "And I think I know just the guy."

"You mean....?" I was afraid to finish the question.

"That's right, Bob," he said with a broad grin. "You're going to be our new rent collector. You'll go door to door every Saturday and collect all the rents and then bring them in here on Monday morning."

This would add an extra day to my work week and I sure could use the extra cash, but I really had no experience at this sort of thing. I was a builder, not a door-to-door salesman, I told myself. But it didn't take long for me to admit that all my reservations didn't matter one bit since I was not about to say "no" to the boss.

"Sure thing, Mr. Howard," I chirped. "When do you want me to start?"

The following Saturday I began my pavement pounding rounds and soon became affectionately (for the most part) known as "Mr. Bob, the Rent Man."

At first, the job was a trivial one. After all, we were only operating one small building with a handful of units. The whole affair took me twenty to thirty minutes each week. But two years later, with 120 doors to knock upon, it took me the better part of a full day to make it all the way around the neighborhood.

Weekly rents ranged from $13 for a one-bedroom to $17 per week for a two-bedroom unit. Each week I learned a bit more about the living habits of our tenants. Most were working class, blue collar, and almost all collected their weekly paychecks on Friday. Collecting the rent, therefore, on Saturday made sense, because by Sunday morning, a good portion of those paychecks had been consumed. The rent was easily affordable and still provided an adequate return on investment for Claude who had expended about $10 per square foot in building the apartments. To give you some basis of comparison, similar apartments today would cost roughly $80 per square foot to build and fetch between $800 and $900 per month.

As I trudged from door to door, my swelling collection envelope in hand, I soon garnered a whole library of often-inventive excuses as to why the rent money was not going to be paid this week. Some of the more popular entries:

"My auntie died and I needed the money to take the family to the funeral." I was amazed at how many sickly old aunties some people seemed to have.

"My kids got sick and I had to pay the doctor." This was before the advent of Medicaid.

"My car payment was due and I had to pay the repo man." Evidently he was more intimidating than I was.

"You know, I had the rent money for you here this morning, but now I can't seem to find it." This excuse was often accompanied by the sounds of tumbling dice in the background.

Most tenants didn't stay behind in their rent for too long. All it took was a reminder that there were at least five other families ready to jump into their apartment if they did not make things right. Those who simply couldn't manage to scrape together the rent, would usually slip out in the middle of the night, leaving behind a trashed apartment and no forwarding address. We soon began demanding an up-front damage deposit from all new tenants.

While I was certainly not the most welcomed visitor for whom our tenants opened their doors, and despite the fact that I at times was required to be firm and direct, I always tried my best to treat everyone with respect and courtesy. I addressed everyone as Mr. or Mrs. and tried to remember the names of each family's children. I saw myself as a representative of the landlord and I attempted to always conduct myself in a professional manner. As a result, I feel, I earned the respect of the residents. I'm pleased to say that for the duration of the time I pounded this beat, I never experienced a single security problem—even though, by the end of the day, I was carrying around about $2,000 in cash in one of the roughest neighborhoods in L.A.

Eventually the reality of this situation began to take its toll. Being the Rent Man, on top of the expanding scope of my regular responsibilities, was becoming more and more of a chore. After three years, my position in the company, as well as my confidence level, had risen sufficiently to allow me to request a meeting with Claude.

"Mr. Howard, I've been collecting the rents in Watts for three years now," I stated, "and it's starting to get to me. I've got a family now and I'm nervous about carrying all that dough around that neighborhood every Saturday."

"I can understand how you feel, Bob," Claude said sympathetically. "Have you had any trouble?"

"No, sir. Not a bit," I responded. "I've been lucky and I try to be careful. It's just that I think I can be more useful doing something else. And besides, Marcie wants me around the house on Saturdays." By this time I had earned a few pay increases so my financial needs were not as urgent as they had been three years earlier.

Claude was disappointed and he said so, but in the end, he understood how I felt and agreed to hire someone to replace me. After a two-week search, he located two off-duty detectives from the 77th Street police precinct located a few blocks from the apartment complex. The following Saturday I went on my rounds with the two detectives, introducing them to the tenants as the new rent collectors and saying my farewells. I had grown close to a number of the families on my route and some of these good-byes became emotional. Finally, at the end of the day, I hung up my "Mr. Bob" hat and said good-bye to being the neighborhood Rent Man. And, as things turned out, just in the nick of time.

The following Saturday — the day the two new Rent Men made their first collections — was a true day of infamy. Claude phoned me at home just as I was starting in on some overdue yard work. He instructed me to meet him right away over at the 77th Street police station. Once I arrived, I spotted Claude shaking his head as he listened to the two rent-collecting detectives, both wrapped in blankets, as they recounted their sad tale:

"We had just finished collecting at the last stop and had about $2,000 in the envelope as we got into the car. We stopped at a traffic light at 108th and Central when two guys ran up to the car and put their guns to our heads. They got in and commandeered the car. One of them drove while the other held a gun on us in the back seat. After a few miles they pulled into an alley where they had evidently pre-arranged to meet the rest of their gang. They told us to get out and then proceeded to take everything we had. The money, our guns, our car, our wallets, our badges, and even our trousers. They didn't hurt us, but boy, we had a heck of time getting back to the station without our pants."

On top of taking a serious financial loss, Claude was faced with another problem since the two police detectives decided on the spot that they had had enough of rent collection and turned in their notices. Fortunately, Claude succeeded in finding two other officers to replace them and the collections continued smoothly.

I learned, some time later, that in order to convince them to take the job, Claude was required to pay the off-duty cops considerably more than the flunkey wages he had been paying me. This is what we used to call a "Hazardous Duty Bonus" back in the service. Fortunately, during my duty round, I must have enjoyed an "angel on my shoulder," because I was never once intimidated, threatened, or harmed. This, despite the fact that every person living in those apartments knew who I was and understood that I carried large sums of cash around every Saturday.

I don't think I'm flattering myself too much when I say that my demeanor contributed to the fact that I operated in safety for over three years. I'm not suggesting that the two replacement cops were robbed on their first day because they acted disrespectfully to anyone. But I do believe that I managed to build up a relationship based upon trust and respect among the residents and this fact served to shelter me from harm as I trod the mean streets of southwest L.A.

Claude eventually tired of being the landlord and decided to donate the apartments to a local Baptist Church, enjoying a substantial tax write-off for this magnanimous charitable contribution. Some ten years later, on August 11, 1965, on a corner not far from the apartments, a California Highway Patrol motorcycle officer pulled over a drunk driver and sparked one of the worst urban race riots in American history. When it was all over 34 people had been killed and over 1,000 injured. Also, over 1,000 buildings across Watts were destroyed. Sadly, these included some of the 120 rental apartments built by Claude's company in the 1950s where I had served for three years as Mr. Bob, the Rent Man.

CHAPTER THREE

JOHN NISSER
A TOWERING CEDAR

*A friendship founded on business is better
than a business founded on friendship.*

John D. Rockefeller, Jr.

The ancient world cherished the mighty cedar trees of
Lebanon whenever it came to matters of construction. The
prized cedar logs were used to build ships by the Phoenicians,
tombs by the Egyptians, and by the Israelites to construct King
Solomon's Temple in Jerusalem. They unquestionably stand as the
world's oldest known high quality building material. It is fitting,
therefore, that my own career in construction was helped thanks
to one man I consider likewise to be of the highest quality—a true
cedar of Lebanon, my best friend, Johnny Nisser.

I met Johnny in early 1950 when Marcie and I moved to
Lynwood where we managed a six-unit rental property that my
parents owned. Johnny and his wife, Rosalie, bought a three-
unit building right next door to us that they likewise lived in
and managed. Although Rosalie and my sister Dolores went to
high school together, since I was a couple of years older I really
never knew Rosalie until she married Johnny and we all became
neighbors. As struggling landlords, we had much in common and

we soon became fast friends and shared much of our time together. Our families became so close that we were named godparents to their daughter, Denise, and they served as godparents to our son, RJ.

There were many times, in the cool of the evening, when John and I would relax around the kitchen table stirring our dreams and ambitions along with our scotch and sodas. "There are so many housing opportunities popping up around here," I would often point out to Johnny, "that any man who's willing to work hard could make a killing." Johnny would always respond by voicing his confidence in me.

"Well, why not you, Bob?" he would offer. "You're a licensed contractor. You've got the construction experience. You've made a lot of money for Howard. You could do the same for yourself someday." Someday was about to arrive.

As I continued cranking out the bathroom and kitchen remodeling jobs over the summer of 1956, I heard about a parcel of land that had come on the market that might just be the ticket I was looking for. It was zoned to allow for the construction of a two-unit building and could be purchased for $3,500. While this price was certainly attractive, it was still more than I had available. With some trepidation, I decided to call upon Johnny.

"If you could loan me the $3,500 to buy the land, I'm sure the bank will give me enough to cover the construction of the duplex," I explained. Johnny listened and nodded.

"It will take me six months to build it and then we'll put it up for sale. I know we'll turn a good profit." I next laid out a plan that would form the basis of our business relationship and would be replicated countless times over the many real estate deals we put together over the coming years.

"Once the duplex is sold and the bank is paid off, you'll get back your $3,500 in full and we'll split whatever's left." That was it. Sweet and simple. Johnny nodded thoughtfully and responded with "Okay, Bob. Let's do it." He filled out the check right there on the kitchen table and handed it to me.

The project was a success and it became the first speculative business venture of the Mayer Construction Company. As I had projected, the duplex was finished in six months and sold immediately. After paying off the construction loan, we had earned a $5,000 profit above our original $3,500 investment. Johnny received half, a return of $2,500 in under six months for having invested only $3,500. That equates to an annualized return of over 140%! Not surprisingly, my friend was impressed and delighted.

My situation was even more positive. I had invested nothing, other than my "sweat equity," and pocketed a cool $2,500. All of my kitchen table philosophizing about grand opportunities in the real estate business had been proven correct and both Johnny and I understood that we were standing on the verge of something big. We immediately set to work figuring out how to best duplicate our initial success. It was the beginning of a long and prosperous business relationship that has endured to this day.

During the years I ran Mayer Construction Company, whenever I encountered a downturn in the construction industry and money got tight, I knew I could always depend upon Johnny. Time after time, he provided unsecured loans that would help get me through those lean years. All I had to do was make a phone call, and Johnny was there on the spot. But who is Johnny Nisser? His life story is a fascinating and inspiring one. It deserves to be told.

John Nisser and I were both born in 1926—a mere ten days apart. But we entered the world on opposite ends of the Earth. The town of Batroun, Lebanon where John was born and raised, some fifty kilometers north of Beirut, has perched on the sunny Mediterranean coast since the days of antiquity. Nestled in the foothills of Mount Lebanon, Batroun's sandy beach-rock has been

used as a quarry since the town's founding by the Phoenicians.
From that rocky soil, John emerged as an educated and tough
Maronite Catholic just as the war in Europe engulfed North Africa.
As a Christian, and fluent in Arabic, French, Spanish, and English,
John was recruited by the British forces in Lebanon and soon sent
to serve under Field Marshal Montgomery, first as a translator and
then as a disbursement officer.

Shortly after the war, an unexpected event in faraway Los
Angeles took place that would change the course of John's life
forever. The event was recorded on the obituary pages of the Los
Angeles Evening Herald Express under the headline: "Wife of
Herald Express Founder Succumbs."

The wife in question was Johnny's aunt who had, many years
before, sallied forth from Batroun to escape the ongoing Islamic
persecution Maronite Christians had endured there for centuries.
She made her way to the United States during the late 1920s where
she wed the son of a newspaper publisher. The Evening Herald
Express had been founded in 1871 and, by the 1920s, was one of the
more than a dozen broadside tabloids that catered to the working
classes of Southern California. Late in that decade, newspaper
tycoon J. Randolph Hearst arrived in Los Angeles determined
to consume the newspaper business, just as he had done in San
Francisco and New York.

In 1931 John's aunt and her husband sold their interest in
the Express to the Hearst syndicate for an attractive sum. Hearst
operated the paper for the next thirty years until it was merged in
1962 with the L.A. Examiner, a morning newspaper, to form the Los
Angeles Herald Examiner, which came out in the afternoon. This
move created a vacancy that was soon filled by the Los Angeles
Times, the City's only surviving major newspaper today. When
John's aunt passed away in 1947 her will stipulated that a portion of
her estate be directed to her family back in Lebanon. Her attorneys

made contact with the family and requested that a representative be sent to Los Angeles to help carry out the settlement of the estate. Since John was single, in his early twenties, and spoke English well, he was elected by the family to represent them during the probate proceedings.

John had faced forces in North Africa, but nothing in his experience had prepared him for wrangling with American lawyers in the wilds of L.A. County as they sorted out the estate of his late aunt and the publishing interests she had left behind. Despite his youth and lack of experience, John comported himself with aplomb and succeeded in fairly distributing the inheritance to all the proper parties.

During the course of the proceedings Johnny discovered that he had not only fallen in love with America, but that he had also fallen in love with one very lovely American lady named Rosalie Barhoush. John and Rosalie were soon wed and became our Lynwood neighbors. Although John and Rosalie would travel back to Lebanon occasionally, Lynwood became their permanent home. John used the inheritance money he retained to purchase a small grocery store in Bell Gardens that he wound up operating successfully for many years. They moved to Downey at about the same time we did and as our family grew, so did John and Rosalie's. Their three daughters, Alanna, Denise and Mary Lee grew up side-by-side with our three kids, Linda, RJ and Mike, and his daughters continue to refer to me as "Uncle Bob" to this day.

John has always been quick on the uptake. After our initial joint venture described earlier, it didn't take him long to appreciate the upside potential of apartment building development in Los Angeles. He quickly jumped into the game on his own and, over the following years, built and operated numerous highly successful rental properties.

During the decades of promise and prosperity that John has witnessed in America, he has never forgotten his Lebanese heritage and his devotion to the Maronite Church. This lifetime of devotion was recognized in 2007 at the annual St. Maron's Feast Day celebration, held at Our Lady of Mt. Lebanon Cathedral. Following the liturgy, and before 700 guests in the Grand Ballroom of the Biltmore Hotel in downtown Los Angeles, Johnny was awarded the Lifetime Achievement Award by his church for his many contributions to the Maronite community. Throughout his life, Johnny has continued to channel financial support to his home church, St. Stephen's, back in Batroun and has donated generously to the poor and needy throughout war-torn Lebanon. Countless Lebanese transfer students coming to L.A. have been housed free of charge in one of Johnny's apartment buildings for the duration of their studies. His generosity to youth summer camp programs and other Catholic charities is something only his closest friends know about since, in keeping with his beliefs about modesty and humility, he prefers to make such donations anonymously.

Like many who have come through the crucible of immigration, Johnny is a firm believer in the virtues of hard work. While some might chalk his success up to luck, and perhaps his initial inheritance could correctly be considered a lucky break, Johnny sums it perfectly when he proclaims: "In America, the harder I work, the luckier I get."

Certainly luck—both good and bad—played a key role in one of the most memorable of many stories Johnny recounts about the days when he, like me, worked as a door-to-door rent collector at one of his housing projects.

Johnny had just finished making all the collection rounds and had stuffed the day's receipts into a black bank bag that he set on the rear seat behind him as he drove straight from the property to the closest Bank of America branch. He pulled his car into the parking lot directly behind an old junker. He didn't pay much attention to the fact that the driver of that car, along with two very agitated passengers, was desperately trying to get the ignition to turn over but having no luck in doing so. Just as Johnny put his car into "Park" and was reaching into the back seat to grab the black bag, he came face to face with a blunt-nosed Saturday Night Special in the firm grip of a hand stuck angrily through the passenger side window. He looked up to see that the driver of the uncooperative vehicle was clutching several bags stuffed with cash in his other hand. His partner, equally laden down with booty, opened the driver's side door and ordered Johnny out of the car. Johnny quickly surmised that these two assailants had just completed robbing the Bank of America branch and found that their getaway car would not "get."

"Get out and shut up," barked the bank robber and Johnny did as he was told. Two of the men jumped into the front seat and the third into the back seat where John had placed his rental collection money. If there had only been two bank robbers they might have overlooked the black bag in their haste to make their getaway and meet up with a fourth accomplice who was waiting for them in another car down the street. As it was later discovered, after the car was recovered a few blocks away, the thieves obtained more money from John's black bag than they had from robbing the bank.

To this day, Johnny recounts this story to demonstrate how the saints from St. Stephen's back in Batroun have continued to watch over him. "Those guys could have killed me," Johnny explains with great passion, "but I guess they were just happy to get a ride out of the parking lot."

I liken Johnny to the cherished cedars of Lebanon that provided great strength and support to the builders of the ancient world. When I consider the many times in my own life that I received his support, I feel fortunate to have known John Nisser. He continues to be a true and enduring life-long friend to this day.

CHAPTER FOUR

HI-YO SILVER STATE LOTTERY

The lottery is a tax on people who flunked math.

Israel Gallegos

Of all the states in the nation, a mere eight—or 16%—bear the listing "No State Lottery" next to their names. And of those eight, only one, the great state of Nevada, takes things a step further by adding the following stern footnote: "Lottery Constitutionally Prohibited." In other words: "Don't even think about it in Nevada, buddy!"

These days it probably would not come as a surprise to anyone familiar with the term "special interests" that the financial well-being of the moneyed few at times overrides the wishes of the masses. But back in 1965, when the power of legal entities such as the NRA and Halliburton to bend the course of mighty legislatures had yet to be exerted, a few of us innocent souls dared to suppose that an idea would succeed if only enough of "the everyday people" got behind it.

In 1965, I, and several of my friends, for reasons now unclear, hatched an interesting idea. We determined that the silver state of Nevada would be a great place to start a statewide lottery similar to the one that had been recently launched in California. Based on the overwhelming success that the California Lottery was enjoying in our home state, and buttressed by the spread of state lotteries across the nation, we arrived at the conclusion that "The Silver State Lottery" would be one helluva good idea.

While lotteries are most often operated by an agency of the state, there exist numerous ancillary opportunities when a new one is established. Such areas as printing of the tickets, point-of-sale terminals, advertising and marketing are usually farmed out via exclusive contracts to private concerns. As members of the initiating consortium, we would be able to board the Lottery Elevator on the proverbial ground floor and ride it all the way to the top.

Of course, at the time, our little group didn't realize that we'd be paid in Silver State Certificates—promissory debentures issued by the State of Nevada—which eventually wound up as totally worthless.

Our first step was to retain counsel. One member of our group was buddy-buddy with a high profile Las Vegas lawyer. After a get acquainted conference, the lawyer agreed that our hare-brained idea held some merit and that with his influence among Vegas VIPS, he would be the ideal "go-to" guy for this project. So, we took the bait. Hook, line….but, fortunately, not the sinker.

The next six months were a blur of back and forth jaunts to Las Vegas and the state capital, Carson City. On top of the travel costs, we piled up massive expenditures at the direction of our Las Vegas lawyer who claimed the money was needed to "grease the wheels." We lobbied legislators, schmoozed state senators and cozied up to union bosses and corporate toadies throughout the gaming industry.

"We'll put the name of your casino on the lottery tickets," we told the casino owners.

"A lottery will deliver millions into your state and county coffers. You'll be able to lower taxes. Your constituents will adore you!" we told lawmakers and politicos.

"Every gas station clerk in Nevada will become a dues-paying gaming worker," we told the unions.

Alas, nobody was listening and nobody was buying what we were selling. It was as if everyone in the state was behind some impenetrable wall and could not be reached with simple reasonable logic. That wall was called "fear of competition" and not even our well-paid legal beagle could manage to surmount it. We eventually wound up telling our "go-to" guy exactly where he could go to.

After six months of futility, we came to the implacable conclusion that no matter how you sliced it or diced it, if more money was going to be wagered on lottery tickets, then less money was going to be wagered in the casinos. Although we vaguely understood this "minor obstacle" to our grand design, it took a special sort of messenger to bring the problem into truly sharp focus for our little group.

In the era bracketed by Bugsy Siegel on one end and Steve Wynn on the other—let's say from the forties through the seventies—Las Vegas ran on one highly sought after energy source: Juice. In that pre-corporate era, before Treasure Island and Circus Circus became "family fun destinations," real power in Las Vegas hinged upon "being connected." The more connected you were, the more Juice you could exert.

We were aware of all this when we were contacted by "a friend." I'm not going to reveal the identity of the messenger, but let's just say he was well connected and very, very "Juice-y." From his 2-lb diamond pinkie ring to his hand-tailored Korean suit, our guest visitor exuded "Essence de Cosa Nostra." His card read: General Secretary, Nevada Casino Owners Association.

"You guys should simply forget about it," he advised our little group. "Any more dough you pour into this deal is gonna be good money after bad. Cut your losses, pick up your marbles and go back home to California. There ain't gonna be no Silver State Lottery. That's all there is to it." To underscore his point, our guest went on to inform us about the untimely death of the previous wise guy who tried to start a State Lottery in Nevada.

"I guess you could say his number came up," he intoned with a knowing sneer. We got his drift, packed up our tents, and vanished into the desert dust like a mirage (hmmm....now there's a good name for a casino, don't you think?).

Evidently, our foray into lottery land had its impact on the powers that were. Within a few short years the Nevada state constitution had been amended to outlaw any form of statewide lottery. Despite this Powerball Prohibition, the citizens of Nevada have consistently indicated their desire to enjoy the benefits afforded by a statewide lottery. A bill to overturn the constitutional ban and introduce enabling legislation for a lottery has been introduced every year in Carson City since 1982. The most recent public opinion survey revealed that 72% of Nevada voters favor a statewide lottery. So what? Who cares? Some things are just too important to leave to the chancy democratic process. Not when millions are at stake.

Nevertheless, every year, in undaunted gestures of futility, a few populist Nevada state legislators continue to introduce bills to overturn the prohibition and launch a state lottery. Bills that they know will fail, but that serve to impress voters back in Sparks and Reno when these public servants pat themselves on the back at election time with: "I fought against the big money interests to set up a state lottery that would rebuild our schools and lower your taxes."

Debate about proposed lottery legislation brings about some of the most bizarre manifestations of "democracy inaction" imaginable. A visitor to the gallery of the Nevada General Assembly would be astounded to see a representative from Las Vegas, of all places, stand and, with a straight face, rail and rant against the pervasive evils of gambling. All in an effort that will eventually succeed in quashing some doomed pro-lottery bill. It's the kind of outrageous hypocrisy that hasn't been seen this side of Al Gore's home heating bills.

In the end we were persuaded that there "ain't gonna be no" Silver State Lottery and I'm just as convinced today that there will never be one. Not as long as the slots keep jingling and the Juice keeps flowing in old Las Vegas.

CHAPTER FIVE

SUITES AND REITs

A first-rate hotel is like a first-rate marriage: expensive, but worth it.

Mignon McLaughlin

By the late 1960s, as I surveyed our company's growth over the prior fifteen years, I was able to proudly proclaim that Mayer Construction was the largest builder of apartment buildings in Southern California. We were focused on conventional multi-family housing units that were rented out unfurnished and typically bearing one-year leases. Those leases were both a blessing and a curse. While on the one hand they provided us with the ability to accurately project our residency levels, in most cases, they really did not offer the security of bankable commercial leases. If tenants chose to move out before their lease had expired, they did so with little consequence beyond forfeiting their damage deposit. We were not about to track them down in an attempt to collect the three months' rent still due to us. Instead we would quickly fix up the unit and lease it out again as quickly as possible—usually at a higher rent level.

In a rising market, like the one we faced in those days, where demand outstrips supply, strange things can sometimes happen.

I noticed, for example, that our ROI (return on investment) from those rental communities with a higher turnover of tenants was considerably greater than what was being generated by our more stable communities. In other words, by being able to increase rents more frequently, we were making more money on the "short stay" or "fly-by-night" apartments than on the ones occupied by traditional long-term tenants. This revelation got me to thinking.

If I carried this notion to its logical conclusion, I'd soon find myself in the hotel business, I surmised. And then I asked myself: "Why not?" As the concept took shape in my mind, I envisioned a sort of hybrid. Half apartment, half hotel. A place to live, not merely to stay. Units would be designed as small suites and contain a built-in desk, kitchenette, bathroom, wardrobe closet and extra storage space. They would be offered to the public by the day, the week, or the month with payment collected at time of check-in. Such an "extended stay" operation would enjoy the keen competitive advantage of flexibility in a shifting market. Unlike conventional apartments, I would not be required to wait for a lease to turn over before adjusting the rent levels. I could quickly match my prices to the market and thereby maximize profits while maintaining my competitive position.

The more I thought about the "extended stay" idea, the more enthusiastic I became. I determined that there existed an enormous untapped market of people in need of affordable temporary housing. My market research identified a huge need for this type of product among corporate residents who were being transferred to new locations by their companies. Typically, transferred executives in this situation would be put up in an expensive hotel until their permanent living arrangements could be found. The idea of an "extended stay" facility was met with warm enthusiasm among every corporate travel department I spoke with.

Of course, the key to making the concept fly was affordability and that meant keeping our costs down. For example, we would offer maid service, but only on a semi-weekly or weekly basis unless the guest wished to pay for more frequent visits. In a short time I had put together a basic business plan describing the concept. Now all I had to do was find someone willing to underwrite the financing.

My first stop was at the doorstep of Union Bank where I had established a strong financial relationship over the prior decade. I knew it was going to be a tough sell. Bankers are, by nature, leery of innovation and overly cautious when faced with any departure from the norm. And this certainly was a departure. Is it a hotel? Yes. Is it an apartment? Yes. Has this ever been tried before? Uh... no. It is an everlasting testimony to the courage and confidence displayed by the lenders at Union Bank that they agreed to extend both construction and permanent financing to an experimental project of this type. They understood that we had found a "niche" and were well prepared to scratch it.

As was so often the case, the risks we were required to take by staking a claim in uncharted territory were accompanied by a stroke of good fortune. It was precisely at this point in time that the residential and commercial real estate industries entered a period of great change due to one very powerful force: The Rise of the REIT.

A REIT is a Real Estate Investment Trust and is a business entity descended from the old Massachusetts Trusts that enabled corporations in the 19th century to circumvent the law that prohibited them from investing their assets into real estate. REITs officially came into existence in 1960 when the Eisenhower administration enacted laws that allowed for the creation of stock companies whose sole purpose was investing into real estate ventures. All profits had to be distributed to the stockholders and could not be retained by the REIT. The attraction here was that, unlike in the case of a conventional corporation, earnings generated by a REIT would not be taxed until they were distributed out to the stockholders.

While initially used to raise money for home mortgages, REITs took off in popularity in the late sixties because of high interest rates and tight money. Banks now found themselves unable to lend out C&D (construction and development) money to people like me because of regulatory restrictions. These restrictions did not apply, however, to REITs. Hence REITs began blossoming all over the country as a source of funding to fuel the still booming real estate market. Between 1968 and 1970, REIT assets almost quintupled from $1 billion to $4.7 billion.

Another advantage enjoyed by REITs was that they were not limited, as banks were, on the returns they could pay out to their investors. As a result, REITs were able to pay the higher interest rates required to secure funding for riskier real estate development projects while banks could not do the same. Many banks, in order to keep from being frozen out of the real estate game, decided to set up their own in-house REITs, but that's not what happened at Union Bank. All of the bank's top real estate people—the true best and the brightest—resigned their positions and started their own business: a new REIT called The Mortgage Investment Group, known as "MIG."

MIG quickly got to work putting together public offerings and succeeded in raising millions from investors anxious to cash in on the burgeoning real estate market. They soon faced a shortage of suitable investment-grade opportunities and that's when we entered the picture. MIG looked to me as an opportune investment vehicle. Not only were the former Union Bank officers familiar with our company's long-standing track record of bringing in many successful projects, they were also very supportive and enthusiastic when I described my "extended stay" concept. We needed a non-traditional funding source and they needed a non-traditional real estate venture. It was a matter of being in the right place at the right time.

So, MIG and Mayer Construction formed a 50-50 joint venture in which MIG provided the dollars, and Mayer Construction provided the expertise to build and manage the properties. It was a marriage made in heaven. The terms we arranged were simply another iteration of the very first deal I put together with Johnny Nisser many years before. MIG would issue the construction financing and then convert it to a permanent loan upon completion. Earnings were used to service the debt and build up equity with both parties splitting the profits whenever a property was sold. In addition, I was granted a position by MIG as an advisor. This role entitled me to a fee based upon all the projects in which I was involved. It was a marvelous opportunity for me that would allow me to acquire a fifty-percent equity position in what I felt would soon become a major hotel chain, with absolutely no cash outlay on my part. We needed something with a touch of class to identify our new venture. So, while it was still in the planning stages, I decided to name our fledgling chain the "Ambassador Inns of America."

In 1972, the first hotel we built in the Ambassador chain was in Las Vegas where I believed an extended stay hotel would be warmly welcomed. I had visited Las Vegas over the years and had often attended some of the lavish showroom productions the town was famous for. While everyone is aware of the Dean Martins, the Elvis Presleys, and other big name headliners, not much thought is given to the hundreds of other musicians, dancers, stage hands, extras, and behind-the-scenes production workers who make these magnificent shows possible. While the superstar is put up in the hotel's finest penthouse for the three to four week run of the show, where do all the other associated people stay, I wondered? After doing some research I found that housing for cast and crews was spotty and oftentimes non-existent. When Sammy Davis Jr. played Vegas, his stage director stayed in a mobile home park outside of town. I felt that an extended stay hotel would meet the needs of this group perfectly and, as things turned out, I was correct.

There was another demographic that I felt would be attracted to an affordable apartment/hotel hybrid. Las Vegas, in those days, had some of the most liberal divorce laws in the country, but to take advantage of them a person had to be a Nevada resident and that meant living in the state for at least six weeks. Marketing our services among the Las Vegas legal community helped us spread the word and made our establishment the premier spot to sit it out while waiting for a divorce decree to be handed down.

Added to this mix, would be the tourist visitors who filled almost every hotel room in Las Vegas on the weekends and provided added occupancy during the week. Once the financing was in place, we secured a site near the Las Vegas Strip and quickly got to work constructing the first 343-unit Ambassador Inn complex.

The entire future of the Ambassador Inns of America almost came to a disastrous end when early in the construction process the newly built wood framing caught fire due to an accident involving a welder's torch. At that time, it was the largest fire in the history of Las Vegas. That unenviable record was later surpassed by the MGM and Hilton fires in later years.

If the Las Vegas Ambassador Inn was our only hotel at the time of the fire, I believe MIG could have easily decided to end our new venture by concluding that this business was not for them. Fortunately, our company had already started construction on two other similar hotels, one in Tucson and one in Phoenix. Once those projects opened, they immediately proved to be successful. They were doing so well that their combined cash flow offset the losses we incurred due to the Las Vegas fire. Over the years that followed, we would build a total of twelve different hotels with MIG throughout the San Francisco Bay area, Sacramento and Southern California including the Inns already built in Las Vegas, Phoenix and Tucson. The entire chain consisted of around 2,600 residential units, averaging a little over 200 rooms per project.

The concept of extended stay hotels, which we pioneered with the Ambassador Inn chain, was soon picked up and emulated by some of the major players in the hospitality industry. In 1974 another lodging visionary, Jack DeBoer, opened the first Residence Inn in Wichita, Kansas employing a concept identical to our Ambassador Inns prototype. The Marriott purchased the Residence Inn chain in 1987 and there are over 450 locations operating in the U.S. today. Since its inception, the extended stay model has achieved fantastic growth across the country. The common definition of an "extended stay" hotel in today's market is one where guests typically stay for five nights or more. Today twenty percent of all hotel stays are five nights or more and this growing trend helps to fuel a market that has become more and more segmented. There are typically three types of extended stay hotels operating in today's market: The All-Suite Hotel, the Apartment hotel or "aparthotel," and Serviced Apartments. There are close to thirty extended stay chains in the U.S., each with seven hotels or more, including Staybridge Suites, MainStay Suites, Extended Stay America, and InTown Suites.

As the extended stay concept gained momentum during the 1970s, the same could not be said for the growth of REITs. Squeezed by more rigorous accounting requirements, and faced with cash flows that did not live up to expectations, many REIT managers discovered that the need for a project to constantly be generating cash was not being met. They began to re-cast their roles back to that of a lender, rather than that of a developer. MIG, in 1979, agreed to sell me their fifty percent interest in the Ambassador Inn chain.

They pocketed the cash and retained all the loans in place, but any gains enjoyed at the time the properties were sold would now all flow to me. Like all good deals, it met the financial expectations of all the parties involved.

Over the coming years I did indeed sell off each Ambassador Inn—except for one—to individual investors and enjoyed the fruits of our efforts in building one of the world's first extended stay lodging chains. I decided to hang on to our original Las Vegas location, but that's another story.

CHAPTER SIX

LAS VEGAS IS BURNING

Fire, water and government know nothing of mercy.

Anonymous

There's a story that real estate developers like to share about two former landlords who meet for the first time in a Florida retirement community. When asked, the first gentleman explains: "Yeah, I owned a 250-unit garden apartment complex in Minneapolis. One night it burned to the ground and the insurance paid me enough so I could retire here in Florida."

"Same by me," responds the second developer. "I had a 600 room hotel that got wiped out in a flood. The insurance paid it off and here I am."

"Hmm," says the first fellow. "How do you start a flood?"

Disaster was no laughing matter as I stood surveying the damage at the intersection of Flamingo and Paradise Roads, just blocks from the famed Las Vegas Strip. It was 1972, a few days before the Memorial Day holiday. The superheated desert wind carried the odor of charred pine to my nostrils as I absorbed a scene of utter devastation. Just one day before, this property had been the site upon which our future dreams were being erected.

Construction of the first of our "extended stay" hotels, the 343-room Ambassador Inn, was nearing completion. Everything about this project represented new ground for me and for Mayer Construction.

This was our first venture into the fast-growing hospitality and lodging industry. It was our first project in conjunction with our new REIT financial partners, the Mortgage Investment Group ("MIG") and now, it was our first major property destroyed by fire. I had flown to the scene as soon as I got the call and now my heart was sinking as I peered across the smoldering remains of what had been the largest hotel fire in the history of Las Vegas to date. There was nothing to do now but pick up the pieces and try to figure out what had gone wrong. An investigation revealed the following facts:

The fire apparently began with a small spark from an iron welder's torch. He had been installing ornamental iron railings along the balconies of each of the three-story building's hotel rooms. Only sixty-six of the rooms had been plastered, leaving the wood framing of the other 277 rooms completely exposed. The wood had been baking in the intense desert sun for weeks and was now as dry as kindling. The fire spread with the thrust of a slow-motion explosion—engulfing everything in its path and leaving a mile-high tower of smoke in its wake. Construction workers were forced to leap from the building's second and third story balconies in order to escape the swiftly spreading inferno.

The fire department arrived on the scene in a flash, but they were unable to prevent the flames from devouring all of the structure's non-plastered areas. Adding fuel to the fire, their efforts were hampered by large piles of lumber and other building materials blocking the hallways and making interior access next to impossible. Thanks to the heroic efforts of those brave public servants, two fire trucks managed to get through the flames and gain access to the rear of the building. They soon found themselves trapped and the fire trucks incurred severe damage when a portion of the edifice collapsed around them. Fortunately, there were minimal injuries. This situation resulted in extensive damage to the water lines. Hence the availability of precious water to fight the fire was greatly limited and there was little to do but watch the fire rage out of control. This created yet another serious problem.

Today, most piping and plumbing lines are made from PVC, but at that time galvanized metal was the material of choice. The intense heat of the fire caused the galvanization inside of the pipes to melt. Once liquefied, the oozing metal ran down into the plumbing under the building's concrete foundation slab where it cooled and solidified within the pipes. Had this not happened, the slab itself could have been re-deployed when the hotel was re-built, since the foundation had not been severely damaged by the fire. Because of the clogged pipes and mass of cooled metal, much of the foundation had to be jack-hammered out and then replaced.

It was a nightmare drawn from hell and I was the one destined to pay the devil his due. I consoled myself by offering thanks that there had been no loss of life or serious injury, but I knew that the financial implications of this loss could be crippling. Like many subcontractors, the welder who had caused the fire carried only $100,000 in liability insurance and our losses were in the millions. Eventually, I would have to sit down with our insurance carrier representative who extended the company's heart-felt sympathies and, at first, not much else.

While this was my first (and, hopefully, last) property loss due to fire, I had learned that it is after the flames have gone out that the real fire fight usually begins. The insurance company representative explained that under the terms of our policy they were obligated to pay for only the building materials that were lost in the fire. Such a sum would come nowhere close to off-setting the millions my new partners and I had invested in this project. I glumly considered the implications of this loss. It would not simply effect the erection of this particular Las Vegas hotel, but it would likely cause MIG to pull the plug on our entire grand plan to construct a chain of Ambassador Inns across the southwest. The most ambitious and expensive project ever undertaken by Mayer Construction was now facing a near certain doom. What on Earth could I do?

As I rolled things over and over endlessly in my mind, suddenly I remembered something that might just be useful. Since MIG was providing the financing, and since they were made up of some very conservative former members of the banking community, they had insisted that certain safeguards be put into place to protect their interests in case of a fire. One such safeguard was "loss of rents" insurance. They insisted that we purchase this type of "exotic" coverage that is similar to business interruption insurance. It is designed to compensate a property owner if the flow of rent revenue is suddenly disrupted, thereby making the business owner capable of still making his loan payments even when there's no money coming in the door. We had never purchased this type of insurance in the past, but, if the lender was insisting on it as a requirement, I certainly wasn't going to make it a deal-breaker, so we went ahead and bought the "loss of rents" insurance.

The specific terms of our policy required that the insurance carrier compensate us for loss of revenue because of a delay in opening our doors due to fire. The insurer was required to pay us 100% of the projected rent revenue from the day of the hotel's planned opening until the day it actually opened for business. It didn't take long for the insurance claims adjuster to do the math. The fire had destroyed nearly all the construction we had completed to date. We would have to start from scratch. This meant an eight-month delay in getting the place opened to the public. Three hundred and forty-three rooms, with an average rate of $75 per night and an overall occupancy rate of 80% came to just over $7.5 million in projected lost revenue. In addition, they were still responsible for the cost of rebuilding all of the structure lost in the fire. Suddenly, the insurance company became much more understanding of our position. They could not wait to get the claim settled and we were able to arrive at an acceptable figure through negotiation in very short order.

It was thanks to that "exotic coverage" policy that our bargaining position was strengthened. Hence, we received enough money to rebuild the Las Vegas Ambassador Inn, which operated successfully for many years. The entire Ambassador Inn project, although derailed for several months, quickly got back on track and turned into one of the most successful ventures of my career to that date.

Thinking back about the way I felt as I stood looking across the blackened twisted desolation of what had been the new Ambassador Inn of Las Vegas, it seemed, at the time, that my entire future had gone up in flames. I was overcome by a penetrating sense of loss that was symbolized by the cinders and ashes that surrounded my feet. But, I did not permit that feeling to linger for long. All I had to do was to consider how fortunate it was that no lives had been lost in the wake of such a devastating disaster. Moreover, I was grateful for that turn of good fortune—the "loss of rent" clause—that saved my financial hide. It was focusing on these two miracles that enabled me to overcome my despair, rise from the ashes, and start all over again.

CHAPTER SEVEN

THE MIRAGE, THE MONEY, AND MR. WYNN

For you and me, today is all we have;
tomorrow is a mirage that may never become a reality.

Louis L'Amour

In 1972, during those hopeful early days of the new decade, I set down stakes in Las Vegas by building my first modest hotel at the outlying intersection of Flamingo and Paradise Roads. The hotel eventually became part of the Ambassador Inn chain that, at its peak, included twelve inns scattered throughout California, Arizona and Nevada. By the end of the decade I was ready to sell out and move on, but I could not bring myself to give up my original establishment, particularly since by 1979, Las Vegas was considered the fastest-growing city in America. So, while I sold off the other eleven hotels, I hung on to the Las Vegas property for, shall we say, sentimental, as well as economic, reasons. I had a hunch that this place had potential and would enjoy a special destiny. My gut feeling, in fact turned out to be accurate—but not in the way I could ever have imagined.

The Ambassador Inn did a steady business during the 1980s, housing conventioneers and tourists looking for a quiet, clean and affordable night's sleep. We finally succumbed and added a small casino as part of an extensive remodeling program. It wasn't too lavish, but it wasn't exactly a "sawdust parlor" either. The casino soon earned an affectionate reputation as a "local's joint," since it catered for the most part to casino and hospitality workers from the major hotels who wanted to relax and unwind during their off hours. Unlike the big "tourist mills," we offered an intimate atmosphere where "everybody knew your name" and nobody tried to hustle anybody.

At that time, I was disinclined to go through the rigorous and time-consuming process of getting myself licensed, a process that would have allowed me to operate the casino. So, instead, I decided to lease the space to a third party for a flat monthly rental rate and limit myself to managing only the lodging end of the operation. I had no profit participation in the casino whatsoever. If my tenant was savvy and ran a good operation, he could pay me the monthly rent and still make a healthy profit all for himself.

Unfortunately, the original tenant was anything but savvy. In fact, he was a total disaster. Although he had some talent at marketing and promoting the place, he failed to comprehend the particular peculiarities of running a cash-based business. Cash, he soon learned, has a tendency to vanish mysteriously — kind of like a mirage. The original casino operator made the critical mistake of not implementing stringent cash control procedures. This essentially amounted to issuing a license to each of his employees to steal him blind. Which is exactly what they did right up to the day he mustered enough of his remaining vision to look up the phone number of the nearest bankruptcy attorney.

Ultimately, his demise left me holding a rather unpleasant bag. If you've ever seen a dark, empty, abandoned casino then you know it's a pretty depressing sight. Well, that's exactly what my hotel guests were now forced to gaze upon as they made their way from the front desk to their rooms each day. Nobody likes to be around a decomposing corpse—especially in the Vegas heat and especially when they're on vacation. I had to fix this quickly, or face seriously hurting my hotel traffic. Luckily that's when I met Nick Robone.

Nick knew all about running a local's joint. He had all the right connections and was very savvy when it came to managing the casino cage, the counting room, and all the financial aspects of the business. There was only one thing Nick did not have—money.

We needed start-up capital for new equipment, signage, marketing, etc. in order to get the casino back on its feet again. Since I had no gaming license, the money could not come from me—at least not directly. I took a big gulp and decided to loan Nick the funds needed to refurbish the place. He used it wisely to purchase new crap tables and slot machines as he began to give the place a real Vegas-style facelift. I viewed the venture as simply protecting my investment in the hotel. Without a functioning casino, the market value of the business itself was greatly diminished. I needed a thriving casino and it looked as though Nick was the right guy to pull it off.

One day during the remodeling, Nick approached me with a proposal.

"You know, boss, this place has gotten a pretty bad rap because of the bankruptcy and all," Nick started. I had to agree.

"People associate the name 'Ambassador Inn' with trouble," he continued. "What do you say we change it?" Not a bad idea, I agreed. New face, new casino, new name.

"Sure. Why not?" I said. "But what should we call it?'

"Well, I've been thinking about that and I've always liked 'La Mirage.' It fits in with the desert thing and sound pretty classy to me."

"Hmm… 'La Mirage Hotel and Casino?'" I tried the name out loud a few times just to see how it felt rolling from my lips.

"To tell you the truth," I said. "I'm not wild about the name, but you're the guy who will have to live with it here in Vegas. I'll be spending most of my time back in Orange County. If you like it, it's okay by me." And so it was christened the Las Vegas' original "La Mirage" casino. Or so we thought.

Over the next few months we poured hundreds of thousands of dollars into the complete renovation of the property. Actually, I poured the money into Nick's bank account and he then proceeded to pour it into the pockets of contractors and suppliers all across Nevada. Finally, we were poised for the "Grand Opening" of the new "La Mirage" as awareness of our marketing initiatives announcing the event (mostly via billboards and print ads) succeeded in penetrating the city's cumulative consciousness. Evidently, the word reached one fellow who did not take the imminent opening of "La Mirage" as very good news at all. I received a phone call from this unhappy chap a few days before we were set to re-open.

"Hello, my name's Rosoff and I want to speak with the owner of the Ambassador Inn," said the testy voice on the line.

"Well, that would be me," I responded, "although we're operating under a different name now."

"That's what I heard," he intoned, "and that's the reason I'm calling."

"What do you mean, Mr. Rosoff?" I said, genuinely puzzled.

"Well, you see I own the Mirage Motel on the old Las Vegas highway." Suddenly I understood. I knew the place he owned. It was a tiny 50 room "no-tell motel" on the edge of town.

"You can't open your doors using that name," Rosoff insisted. "I've been operating under that name for many years and it belongs to me."

"With all due respect, Rosoff," I blurted. "You're nuts! Places use similar names all over this town and you know it. There's three

Golden Nuggets, two Silver Slippers and a dozen Lucky this or that. Why do you care if we call it the Mirage? Will our doing so cost you any business?"

"I don't care," he shot back sounding like a petulant child. "The name belongs to me and you can't use it. If you do, I plan to file suit. So just find yourself some other name. Good-bye."

I immediately called my attorney, Grant Sawyer, who was a former Nevada governor. I had run the name by him before we adopted it and he had given us the green light. He was as surprised as I was that anyone would object to its use. Grant advised that in intellectual property cases such as this it was necessary for the plaintiff to prove that the alleged infringement actually resulted in measurable damages. We all agreed that there was no way that Rosoff could convince anyone that our use of the Mirage name had hurt him in any way financially. In fact, we could probably make the opposite case: by applying the name to an attractive, modern hotel casino near the Strip, we would be enhancing the image of his rundown establishment, thereby generating additional business for him. Based on Grant's advice, we continued financing the renovation and opened as scheduled under a new sign that read: "La Mirage Hotel and Casino."

Rosoff, we discovered, was not bluffing. Shortly after our re-opening, we were named as defendants in the first lawsuit in Nevada history to complain about "name infringement." Next came an endless stream of depositions as the discovery process ran its course. Did I know of Rosoff's prior usage? Should I have known about it? Did I have constructive knowledge? Was Rosoff guilty of laches by failing to effectively enforce his rights? For three long years the legal wrangling over the Mirage moniker raged on, generating a mountain of legal fees over a molehill of a dispute.

We had hoped that we could better weather the lawsuit financially than could Mr. Rosoff. Eventually, we told ourselves, he'd tire of the expense and give up the ghost. But in those days, you could rent out almost anything on weekends and he managed to stay afloat during those long years despite his mounting legal bills.

We eventually learned how to live in the never-ending shadow of the Rosoff lawsuit and managed to let it just percolate on the back burner as we went about our business. This was all about to change thanks to a phone call I received one afternoon in my Newport office.

"Hello, is this Bob Mayer?" said an energetic voice I did not recognize. I said that it was.

"Hi, this is Steve Wynn in Las Vegas," said the voice. "I've got something I need to discuss with you."

"Steve Wynn? Really?" I replied in mock awe. "Not THE Steve Wynn, the famous casino owner? Who is this? Really."

"No, I'm not kidding. This really is me. I'm calling from my office at the Golden Nugget and I want to talk to you about your place, La Mirage. You are the right guy I need to speak with, aren't you?" By this point, it had started to dawn on me that this really was Steve Wynn and I had just made a complete ass of myself.

"Uh, listen, you'll have to forgive me, Mr. Wynn, but I just thought this was some crank call."

"Forget it. I get this all the time," he said quite kindly. "Maybe I should introduce myself as Donald Trump instead, huh?" We both chuckled and I then asked what I could do for him. Like everyone in Las Vegas, I knew Steve Wynn by reputation as a real mover and shaker. He was the dynamic developer of the Golden Nugget who had barreled out of Atlantic City in the 1970s determined to make his name synonymous with the "New" Las Vegas. He had already transformed Downtown Vegas and had now set his sights on the City's prime real estate, the famed Las Vegas Strip.

"I've been following that little brouhaha you've been having with the other guy about the name of your casino," explained Wynn.

"No kidding?" I responded, genuinely surprised. "Why does our lawsuit interest you?"

"Well, you might have heard that I'm planning to put up a place on the Strip next year," he said. "It'll be right next door to Caesar's."

"Yes, I know. I saw the model under glass at the Nugget last week. It's very impressive." The maquette represented as stunning a piece of architecture as I had ever seen. The exterior's sleek lines and endless corridors gave it an almost other-worldly appearance. "It's magnificent and I see that you're going to call it 'La Rêve,'" I commented.

"Naw," said Wynn. "That's just a fake name. The real name is going to be 'Steve Wynn's Mirage.'"

I hung my head in disbelief. "How did Nick Robone ever come up with a name that so many other people want to own?" I asked myself silently.

Nevertheless, I smelled an opportunity and decided not to waste any time before pursuing it.

"I could fly over tonight and be in your office tomorrow morning to talk this over," I suggested.

"See you at 8" he responded before saying good-bye.

Piloting my Cessna towards McCarren airport that night, I began to assess the strength of the hand I'd been dealt prior to sitting down at Mr. Wynn's poker table.

I concluded that while it was no "lock," I held a moderately strong hand, but with a bad kicker. The kicker was a wild card named Rosoff. How could I sell whatever rights I may hold in the Mirage name to Mr. Wynn while my legitimate claim to those rights was being challenged by Mr. Rosoff? Whatever Wynn might be willing to pay me would have to be reduced by the fact that, along with the name, he'd also be buying a nuisance lawsuit.

I finally arrived at a number I considered realistic. I expected that Wynn would offer me between $25,000 and $30,000 as just plain "get lost" money. He'd probably reach a similar deal with Rosoff and that would be the end of it. If that was the offer, I decided that I would take it. And take it gladly. I never liked the name in the first place.

As we stepped out of the elevator, Steve shook my hand and beckoned me to have a seat in his exquisitely appointed office suite. After a bit of small talk, Steve got to the point.

"Here's the way it is, Bob," he began. "Wynn Enterprises is already a force here in Vegas and we pay millions in taxes. We're going to call our hotel Steve Wynn's Mirage whether you decide to sell us the naming rights or not. There is not the slightest question that we would prevail in any sort of legal action you might bring to bear."

This was pretty much the strong-arm spiel I had anticipated. So I just sat there taking it in and still expecting that he'd throw around $25,000 on the table once his little speech had concluded. When he stopped for a breath, I popped in with: "Okay, Steve, I get the picture. Now tell me, what's it really worth to you?"

"I'll tell you, but first you have to understand, I'm going to give you just one week to take it or leave it. We go public with 'Steve Wynn's Mirage' seven days from today come hell or high water." I indicated that I understood the deadline.

"And another thing," he added. "You and this Rosoff fellow have to agree and both sign off. Without his okay, there's no deal." So that's how he was going to deal with the lawsuit. He wanted me to neutralize Rosoff. Okay, I thought. I can do that. But I still needed to know the bottom line.

"You and Rosoff can continue using the Mirage name until we're ready to open our doors," Steve elaborated, "but once we're operational, the signs come off at your places and the naming rights revert to me."

"I understand, Steve," I said and then I asked again: "So, what's it all worth to you?"

"Well, I've added up how much I'd have to pay to the attorneys if one or both of you guys sued me, in order to make this go away, and I figured why not just give the money straight to you and save everyone a lot of headache. Here's what I came up with. Six hundred."

"I'm sorry, how much did you say?" I said shaking my head.

"Six hundred thousand split between you and Rosoff," said Wynn. "Either way I'm going to have to pay it to somebody. Might as well be you two instead of those legal people. Do you think you can let me know in a week?"

I shrugged and tried to act blasé using my best poker face skills not to reveal the fact that inside I was jumping up and down like an excited kid who just came upon an overturned ice cream truck. $600 Grand. That's $300,000 each or more than ten times what I was expecting when I walked into the room. I was sitting there holding a pretty weak poker hand and Steve Wynn had just gone "all in" with over half a million. All I had to do was fold my hand and take the money. What could I say?

"Okay, Steve," I finally got it out after I was sure I could speak without a tremor in my voice, "I'll get with Rosoff right away and have an answer to you ASAP." With that I stood up, shook hands and said my good-byes.

I ran directly from the Golden Nugget down to the Mirage Motel to call upon Mr. Rosoff who lived with his wife in one of the rooms of his establishment. He agreed to listen to what I had to say after I explained that I had just been with Steve Wynn and I bore an offer that could settle our dispute and benefit us both. I relayed the content of our conversation that morning, sat back with a broad smile and waited for what I was sure would be Rosoff's overjoyed response. Boy, was I ever mistaken.

"No!" finally erupted from his tightly pursed lips. "No. No way. Not Bob Mayer. Not Steve Wynn. Not even Jesus off the cross. Nobody is going to buy my name. That's all there is to it."

"Now I know you're nuts," I told him right to his face. "Your whole damned place here isn't worth $300,000 and this guy's going to write you a humongous check just so you'll put up a new sign out front. What is wrong with you, mister?" Rosoff did not like hearing the truth and became infuriated. "You'd better leave now, Mr. Mayer," advised Rosoff's wife, who appeared to be a bit more reasonable than her mulish husband.

I returned home to Newport under a cloud of bitter frustration thanks to this obstinate man and his decrepit motel. Without his cooperation, the whole deal would go up in smoke. My dreams that night were in the form of an animated cartoon. I was crawling on my hands and knees across the desert when I spotted an oasis straight ahead. Once I reached it, there was a genie who resembled Steve Wynn, offering me buckets filled with cool, cool cash. As I reached out my hand to accept a bucket, a voice cried out "No! Never! Not a chance!" as the entire oasis dissolved into the dust before my eyes. It had all been a mirage, I realized, as hundreds of thousand dollar bills with little wings flitted off into the sunset. I woke up in a cold sweat.

The next morning I phoned Rosoff again and tried to reason with him. We only had five days left before Wynn would announce the official name of his new pleasure dome and we'd be forced to sue him in order to collect anything. Rosoff insisted that we could do much better than $600,000 by waiting until Wynn began using the name and then filing suit against him.

"Is that the same strategy you used when you decided to sue me, Rosoff?" I was beginning to get agitated again and decided I'd best hang up. I was plagued by more weird dreams that night and by the next day the stress was beginning to take its toll. This process went on for four more days during which time I was unable to budge Rosoff one inch or in any way overcome his inexplicable obstinacy. Finally, I recalled our conversation—or should I say, confrontation—in his hotel room during which time I came away feeling that his wife might be the more rational of the two. I decided to call her. I knew that Mr. Rosoff liked to trawl the downtown card rooms at night, so I called his room that evening and was able to speak to Mrs. Rosoff without her husband within earshot.

"Why is he being so stubborn, Mrs. Rosoff?" I implored. "Offers like this don't come along every day, you know."

"You've got to try and understand my husband," she pointed out patiently. "This motel's all he's got besides me. He's had a pretty rough life, without much time for the finer things like music or art, you see. The one single creative thing he's ever done in his whole life was to come up with a name for this place. So you see, Mr. Mayer, it's not about the money. There's more involved than just that."

I didn't know what to say, but I was starting to get to the root of the problem at last.

"Well, does he listen to you, ma'am?" I asked softly.

"Sometimes. Yes, he does," she replied.

"Do you think you could persuade your husband to accept the offer?" She said nothing for a long time after I said that.

"I'll see what I can do, Mr. Mayer," is all she said at last and then hung up the phone.

I was not plagued by any nightmares that night for the first time in four days.

The next morning I received a call from Mr. Rosoff. With less than 12 hours remaining before the deadline, Rosoff said that, although it broke his heart to do so, he'd be willing to accept the offer just to keep his wife happy. He would agree to drop the complaint against me and to sell whatever rights he believed he held in the Mirage name to Steve Wynn Enterprises for $300,000. It was over at last.

As a postscript, Steve Wynn announced the name of his new establishment as Steve Wynn's Mirage Resort and Casino in a press release the following day. He constructed a destination showplace where a live volcano erupted on the hour and Siegfried and Roy performed world-class magic amidst white tigers and lions every night. From there it was on to Treasure Island, the Bellagio, and the fabulous Wynn Las Vegas, as Steve proceeded to swiftly and dramatically change the face of the Strip and lead an unprecedented expansion boom—a boom that can still be heard to this day.

Mr. Rosoff managed to dredge up a bit more creative talent and re-named his property The Glass Pool Motel after his unique above-ground swimming pool with its big glass portholes in the side. The place remained in business a few years more and finally collapsed after Mr. Rosoff's death.

As for us, I decided to hook up with the Quality Inn people to manage the hotel side while Nick Robone came up with the name: Key Largo Casino, named after one of his favorite fishing spots and the classic Bogart/Bacall movie. The new sign out front read "Quality Inn and Key Largo Casino." Sadly, Nick fell ill several years later and was no longer able to operate the casino. I finally relented and decided to enter the gaming business and operate the casino myself. My son, RJ, Steve Bone and I all went through the licensing procedure together. We ran both the gaming and the lodging operations as a team for the next few unforgettable years. That amazing experience is recounted elsewhere in this book.

The Quality Inn and Key Largo Casino was finally sold in January 2005 to several wealthy real estate developers from Mexico. They had planned to demolish the building and construct a 40-story high-rise condominium tower alongside a hotel tower containing 344 rooms. As of today, however, the property remains vacant, fenced and shuttered.

Oddly, the area around the vacant site today bustles with resort communities, restaurants, and thriving businesses. It is truly one of the "hottest" areas in town. Unfortunately, the market for luxury condominiums has grown soft over the past few years. I suspect that the current owners are biding their time and reassessing how to make best use of the property.

I guess you could still call me sentimental. I invariably drive by the site of the old Ambassador Inn whenever I find myself in Las Vegas, before going on to marvel at what visionaries like Steve Wynn, Kirk Kerkorian, William Boyd and yes, Donald Trump, have achieved to secure Las Vegas' place as the premier resort destination of the 21st century. What these and others like them have built in Las Vegas is very tangible, very real and permanent—and in no way a desert illusion. The Las Vegas of today is no chimera. And the Las Vegas of tomorrow is certainly no mirage.

CHAPTER EIGHT

GETTING PERMISSION
FROM THE COMMISSION
OR WELCOME TO THE
INQUISITION!

The gambling known as business looks with austere disfavor upon the business known as gambling.

Ambrose Bierce

Nineteen-ninety-seven was a time of cross-current change in Las Vegas. Over 100,000 people per day flocked through the doors of the newly-opened New York-New York Hotel Casino on the Las Vegas Strip while, amid hurrahs and hoopla, Sherman Adelson broke ground for the vast Venetian Hotel Resort on the grounds of the old Sands Casino. Feeling the heat, mega-resort developer Steve Wynn, publicly called for a "take it slow" approach to future Las Vegas expansion. And, after a lengthy deathwatch, the Aladdin was finally put out of its misery. It was the best of times for some, the worst of times for some others.

As the year dawned I, along with my son, RJ, and Steve Bone, found ourselves operating the lodging side of the Quality Inn and Key Largo Casino at the corner of Flamingo and Paradise Road.

Our partner, Nick Robone was in charge of running the casino operations. Sadly, Nick fell ill and could no longer perform his duties. As a matter of necessity—and after resisting the inclination for many years—our team saw no choice but to take over control of the gaming activities on our premises. This decision carried with it a highly distasteful downside. We would all—Steve, RJ and me—be forced to undergo the surgical scrutiny of the legendary Nevada Gaming Control Board before we could be granted a license to conduct our business.

We were aware that obtaining a Nevada gaming license was no walk in the park, but we were not prepared in the slightest for the proctologic periscopes that we were about to endure. We retained the services of a consulting firm who advertised that they would hold our hands and guide us through the process. I'll never forget my initial conversation with the fellow assigned to our case.

"They'll need to see your educational records, Mr. Mayer," he advised me.

"Sure thing," I replied agreeably, trying to recall where I had stuck my high school diploma. "How far back?"

"Um…actually, all the way, sir," came the reply. "You do recall the name of your kindergarten teacher. Right?" I suddenly understood where all those former KGB agents had found employment after the Cold War ended.

People had been gambling in Nevada since before there was a Nevada. From the thimble-rig games that skinned hapless emigrants passing through the newly formed U.S. territory in 1861, to the Chinese "green tables" where prospectors gambled their daily gleanings, Nevada enjoyed a long-standing tradition of separating the saps from their savings through "honest" games of chance. As the Comstock Lode, and later the construction of the Hoover Dam, poured riches into the state, the controversy over the legal status of gambling began to build. By the thirties—just in time for the Great Depression—the matter was settled in favor of legalized gambling as the Nevada legislature assigned the job of policing the state's saloons and sawdust joints up to the Tax Commission and its toothless enforcement arm, the Gaming Control Board.

It was into this environment of lax law enforcement, dusty carnival games, and penny-ante poker, that a New York Jewish wise guy experienced an epiphany in the desert during a 1939 drive from Los Angeles to Chicago. The man's name was Benjamin Siegelbaum, better known as Bugsy Siegel, and he would go on, some eight years later, to establish the Flamingo, the first lavish Las Vegas hotel casino, before meeting his demise because he failed to keep an eye out for a mob hit man.

The 1959 Nevada Gaming Control Act completely overhauled the state's control machinery and gave birth to the Nevada Gaming Commission. The newly formed Commission was empowered to put teeth into the enforcement powers of the Gaming Control Board. The Board now enjoyed nearly unlimited power in auditing, analyzing, investigating and interrogating anyone wishing to legally obtain a Nevada gaming license. With a mandate to "keep gaming clean," the Board continues, to this day, to leave no stone unturned as it exercises its power to grant or to deny the state's highly treasured gaming licenses.

By clamping down on the corporations that set up shop in Las Vegas during the 1960s and 70s, the Commission mostly succeeded in removing the stigma of organized crime from the gaming industry. The perception that money wagered and lost in Las Vegas was now going into the coffers of regulated corporate entities, rather than into the pockets of Mafioso-types, has helped to boost public confidence and contributed to Las Vegas's continuing growth as a premier holiday destination.

As our application process got underway, we began to gain an understanding of how the game was played. Absolute truth and absolute thoroughness were the watchwords as we embarked upon the Vegas vetting process. We had heard the common wisdom: "The Commission doesn't care if you've killed someone, as long as you tell them about it," and learned that this was only a slight exaggeration. The Commission demanded a complete accounting of all our prior sins, no matter how trivial, and insisted that any positive points we claimed in our favor be fully verifiable.

None of this surprised us since we'd been hotel operators in Las Vegas long enough to have "learned the ropes." We were amazed, however, at the depth to which the Commission saw fit to dig into our pasts and the vast police state style powers they enjoyed. Below is a checklist of some of the aggressive investigative measures employed by the Commission as they conducted their due diligence. I offer it as an advisory to anyone contemplating applying for a Nevada Gaming License.

Ten Things You Should Be Prepared For Before You Apply For A Nevada Gaming License:

1. Having your secretary's computer and rolodex reviewed and every personal and professional contact—both yours and hers—questioned.

2. A complete securitization of every dog license, zoning permit, lien filing and library book late fee that you have ever registered with any government agency at any time in your life.

3. An audit of all your state and federal tax returns, both individual and for any business in which you have ever enjoyed an interest, going back to the beginning of time.

4. An unannounced knock on the door by a gaming inspector who will order you to bring your keys as he drives you to your safety deposit box and then instructs

you to open it for a surprise inspection. Any unreported loose cash, loose diamonds, Kruggerrands or Whitey Ford baseball cards in mint condition will spell the end of your chances.

5. Questions about every piece of real estate you've ever bought or sold. Who did you buy it from? Who did they buy it from? Who did you sell it to? Who did they sell it to? And so on.

6. A thorough audit of every transaction conducted by you, your company, your wife and your kids over the past five years. That means being able to explain every single checkbook entry, every line on every credit card statement, and the reason for every single cash withdrawal and wire transfer.

7. Providing not only the office space for a four-person team of Commission agents to camp out on your premises for at least nine months, but also paying the cost of their travel, housing, meals and other expenses for the duration. No, you cannot later claim them as dependents.

8. Impounding of your personal and company computers, Blackberries, iPods, etc. as the agents sift through your files in search of illegal movie downloads, software piracy and other evidence of bad behavior. Better close that Facebook account.

9. A complete scan of all your phone records to learn if you've ever spoken to anyone in New Jersey with an Italian last name.

10. The subpoenaing of your Blockbuster Video rental history to see if you repeatedly rented movies like *Scarface, Goodfellas* or *The Departed*.

The above descriptions are only a slightly embellished account of the actual licensing process. The fact is that the Gaming Commission left no stone unturned during its investigation. You may be assured that any person who currently holds a Nevada Gaming license is one "squeaky-clean" individual.

In addition, the Commission will strongly encourage you to attend a class at the University of Las Vegas in order to learn how easily crooks are able to cheat honest, hard-working casino operators. Some of the techniques you'll study include:

- Marking face cards at the Blackjack table.

- Manipulation of electronic and mechanical slot machine payouts.

- Misdirection and distraction of your employees while theft takes place elsewhere in the casino.

- Placing of late bets as the roulette wheel comes to a stop.

- The placing of Blackjack bets after some of the cards have been dealt out.

- Use of loaded dice.

- "Third base" Blackjack players peeking at dealer's hole cards.

- Use of mirrors and other "cheats" to view concealed cards.

- Signs of collusion between players and pit dealers.

Of all the techniques ever employed by casino cheats, the most effective was not entirely illegal. It involved the use of a team of Blackjack card counters and a so-called Big Player. Keeping track of the cards already dealt out has been a method used for years by Blackjack players wishing to improve their chances. Since, in those days, the game was dealt using a single deck that was not reshuffled until most of the cards were dealt out, it was possible to deduce what cards were left in the deck by keeping track of those already exposed. In this way, a shrewd player could determine when the remaining cards in the deck contained an abundance of aces and face cards. This produced what was termed a "hot deck" and would prompt the card counter to dramatically increase his or her bet now that he or she enjoyed a better than average chance of hitting a winning Blackjack hand.

There were two problems with this situation from the card counter's point of view. First, it required great patience as the player waited through dozens of repeated shuffles for a deck to turn "hot." Secondly, pit bosses had trained dealers to alert them whenever a player dramatically upped his or her bet. Doing so would bring on the heat (casino scrutiny). The "Big Player" team approach effectively eliminated both of these drawbacks. It worked like this:

A gang of highly trained card counters enters a casino together, each one taking a seat at a different table in the Blackjack pit. There they would sit, making minimum bets, watching and waiting for a deck to turn hot. Once it did, the team player would signal the "Big Player." The Big Player would roam up and down pit with a (fake) drink in hand and lots of high value chips. Once he spotted the signal from a member of the team, he would sit down at the "hot deck" table and place as many bets as possible at the highest level permitted. His behavior would not arouse suspicion since he was acting exactly like a typical drunken "high roller" or "whale" — the bread and butter player of the casino industry. The only difference was that this high roller would win and win big.

After a good run at one casino, the team would withdraw and hit another. Using this guerrilla approach, a nine-person team managed to win over $1 million in two weeks from a dozen small to mid-size casinos in 1984. They were never apprehended, but based upon their success, casinos today have instituted a number of protective procedures including the use of six-deck shoes, shuffling machines, and digital facial identification methods.

After learning about the rigorous ordeal prospective Gaming License holders are put through and about all the hazards an operator is exposed to at the hands of professional casino cheats, why on Earth would prospective casino operators voluntarily put themselves through all that? The answer is a simple one: Financial opportunity or, to put it simply: Money!

Despite the higher limit of pit games like Blackjack, Craps and Roulette, the banks of what were once termed "fruit machines" or "one-armed bandits" — the venerable slot machine, represent a casino's ongoing revenue stream. With a mere 250 such machines, in the five to twenty-five cent range, our Key Largo Casino was regarded as a small to mid-size operation. Yet in those days we generated over $100 million per year flowing through those slots. This might sound like a lot, but you must bear in mind that in order to remain competitive anywhere from 95% to 97% of that cash was paid right back to the jackpot winners. The remaining three to five million was hardly net profit. Those funds were used to cover the costs of operation including equipment, payroll, free liquor, advertising, insurance, debt service, etc. After all the expenses were covered, our profit margins in the casino end were pretty much the same as on the hospitality side.

To get some idea of the scale of today's large casino operations, take our numbers and multiply them by a factor of at least ten thousand. You'll begin to approach the billions of dollars that are involved in a modern luxury casino facility. Even with razor thin profit margins, the revenue represented by that sort of volume is unmatched in any other industry and accounts for the willingness of prospective casino owners to undergo the risks and burdensome rites of passage I've outlined.

Was it worth it? Was the reward worth the ordeal? On balance, I'd have to admit that it was. In my case, I was buoyed by the knowledge that I really had nothing to hide. I knew that no matter how deeply the Gaming Commission dug into my background looking for dirt, they would consistently come up empty. Hence, my advice to anyone contemplating applying for a Nevada Gaming License is this: "Clean all the skeletons out of your closet, buckle up your seatbelt, grit your teeth, and go for it." In the end, you'll be very glad you did.

CHAPTER NINE

THE MAN IN THE
WHITE ROLLS ROYCE

Finance is the art of passing money from hand to hand
until it finally disappears.

Robert W. Sarnoff

B y 1995, I had fallen into a routine when it came to managing our sole Las Vegas property, the Quality Inn and Key Largo Casino, a few blocks from the famed Strip. As we did each week, Steve Bone, RJ and I conducted our regular inspection of the premises and then sat down in my office to review the property's operational performance. While the hotel was not wildly successful, it did earn enough to cover expenses and provide us with a modest return on our investment. I felt that by continuing to operate the place we were building long-term equity and also providing some of our people, who worked out of Newport Beach, a perk opportunity to spend a little fun time in Las Vegas.

Just as we were discussing what the hotel might fetch were we to put it up for sale, I was informed that there was a Mr. X waiting to speak with me. "He pulled up in a big white Rolls," my secretary quietly informed me when I failed to recognize my visitor's name. I asked her to show him into the office.

Mr. X turned out to be a dashing, smooth-talking real estate developer who expressed a determined interest in purchasing the Quality Inn. When we got around to price, I was amazed that his offer exceeded the sum that we had just been tossing around. Although I really had no specific desire to sell, I simply could not pass up the price being proffered. Once I indicated my willingness to consider selling at the specified price, Mr. X explained that he did not have the cash or the financing available to make the purchase at this point. He wished to purchase an option that would keep the property off the market while he got busy rounding up investors. This method would put some money into my pocket immediately and avoid having to tie up the property by placing it into escrow.

I offered Mr. X a three-month option for $300,000. The sum would be applied in full to the purchase price if he exercised the option before it expired. If he failed to do so and permitted the option to lapse, he would lose the deposit and that would end the deal with no recourse. At the end of the three-month period, he could, if needed, purchase up to three more one-month extensions for $100,000 per month.

Mr. X managed to scrape together the initial $300,000. We retained control of the hotel and were not required to share any of our revenue with him as he took off in search of investors and fresh capital.

After three months had gone by, Mr. X elected to extend the option's term and gave us $100,000 on the first day of each month over the next 90-day period. By the end of six months, Mr. X had given us a deposit of $600,000 in consideration of our agreement to keep the hotel off the market and to sell it to him at the agreed upon price. Mr. X did, from time to time, request that we provide him with documentation, on company letterhead, confirming the terms of our ongoing option agreement. I saw no problem and willingly obliged.

When Mr. X reported, after six months, that he still had not raised sufficient capital to complete the purchase, I agreed to extend the option terms for another six months, but that would be it. If he did not complete the sale after one year, he would be required to walk away with no entitlements and forfeit the $1.2 million he had paid in. I was surprised when he agreed to this second six-month option. Mr. X explained that he was very close and believed that he would be successful in securing the funds to purchase the hotel in very short order.

Mr. X continued making the $100,000 payments on the first of each month and as the one-year deadline approached, a strange thing happened. Mr. X simply disappeared. The option expired and he quietly walked away from his $1.2 million deposit without saying a word. His phone line was disconnected and a visit to his Las Vegas office revealed that it had been recently vacated. Mr. X appeared to have faded into the sunset and I never heard from him again.

While the situation was undoubtedly curious, I certainly had no right to complain. Someone had pulled up in a white Rolls Royce one year before and handed me $1.2 million and all I had to do in exchange was to keep my hotel off the market. Not too tough a job since the hotel was never actually on the market in the first place. Yet, I could not help trying to understand what had compelled this fellow to act as he had done.

I finally figured that Mr. X had miscalculated, gotten himself into a bad deal and was willing to accept the consequences. I had undergone similar painful situations over the course of my career in the real estate business. I had, a few times, misjudged the market and wound up losing my deposit—but never on this scale. His puzzling actions continued to plague me, but it would be several months before I had the occasion to learn some of the truth behind the actions of mysterious Mr. X.

That truth arrived at the doorstep of my home in Newport
early one morning as a few unexpected visitors rang my doorbell
repeatedly. I opened the door and standing there were several
agents from the FBI. Naturally I invited them in although I had no
clue as to why they wished to speak with me. They entered and
quickly explained that they were here as part of an investigation
involving Mr. X. They needed to know if I had been in collusion
with Mr. X as he bilked investors out of their savings. When I
explained my relationship with him and told the story of what
had happened, the FBI agents brought me up to date on Mr. X's
unsavory activities.

Evidently, he had been promising gullible investors a stake in a
prospering hotel-casino involved in "Las Vegas gaming and night
life." He had projected "big profits" to these so-called investors
who were told they were acquiring a major interest in a thriving
Las Vegas establishment. Not surprisingly, I learned, he had offered
this same major interest to a large number of his victims.

Once Mr. X flew the coop, the investors banded together and
managed to impanel a grand jury investigation to bring Mr. X to
justice and retrieve the money he had fraudulently bilked them out
of. As the investigation got underway, the FBI quickly concluded
that I had played no part in defrauding the investors and that
my hands were clean. I did learn that Mr. X had used the printed
material he received from us to fabricate financial statements that
greatly inflated the hotel's operational performance. He would
use these fake reports, along with the papers we provided to
him documenting the terms of the option agreement to convince
investors that he was legitimate.

It became clear that Mr. X was willing to keep the option in
place, even at rate of $100,000 per month, in order to provide
him with the legitimate cover he needed to conduct his scam. If
a potential investor had decided to check out Mr. X's story during

the one-year option period by contacting the hotel, we would have confirmed that Mr. X had paid us and held a legitimate option to purchase the property.

Evidently the $1.2 million he paid us to keep the option in place was a small part of the money he pocketed through his swindling operation. Since it was determined that I had had no knowledge of Mr. X's background and was not involved in his efforts to milk money from naïve investors, I was cleared of all suspicion. I was not asked to return the funds Mr. X had paid me since I had earned the money legitimately and had acted in good faith.

It is my understanding that the Feds finally did catch up with Mr. X and that he served time in a Federal Penitentiary in connection with this particular scam. I have no idea where Mr. X—the slickest con man I've ever encountered—may be today, but somehow I believe he still may be driving that long white Rolls Royce as he plots how to snare his next investors by luring them into the glamorous world of "Las Vegas gaming and night life."

CHAPTER TEN

COLE AUSTIN

Change is the process by which the future invades our lives.

Alvin Toffler

A s we were busy building the Ambassador Inns hotel chain during the mid-1970s, it soon became apparent that our growth was becoming a bit unmanageable. We had erected four hotels and were on our way to building or acquiring eight more. I needed someone to oversee our fast-growing enterprise. With this in mind, I created a general manager position and tried to fill it by promoting from among our existing staff members. When that did not work out well, I decided to bring in an outsider and so placed a "Help Wanted" ad in the classified section of the Los Angeles Times. I received a large number of responses, but only one caught my eye. It was from a young fellow named Cole Austin, who was from out of state. His résumé indicated that he had previously run a chain of hotels and sounded just like the person I needed. His cover letter explained that he wanted to move to Southern California.

I was immediately impressed with Cole during his job interview at my office. He was an engaging and very bright 33-

year old, filled with ambition and the "right stuff." He seemed to
know the hospitality business inside out, and with his charming
and intelligent manner, he cut the figure of what appeared to be a
hardworking young executive. Cole explained that he was married,
the father of three young daughters, and could start work in the
near future. Believing I would not find anyone more qualified than
Cole, I offered him the job on the spot and he accepted.

Cole's job performance turned out to be tremendous. He was
in a completely different league when compared to any of his
predecessors. For the next several years, I could not have been more
pleased with the terrific work Cole performed for our company. He
inspired our crews at each location through his willingness to roll
up his sleeves and work alongside them. He introduced touches
that delighted our guests and kept them coming back. At the same
time, he was very effective in holding down overhead costs and
running our operation at maximum profitability. Then, about three
years into our excellent working relationship, I began to notice
some subtle changes in Cole.

At first, I thought it must have been my imagination. But after
several meetings, I noticed that Cole's hair color was changing. On
some days, Cole's hair was brown, while on others it was blonde.
"Well, so what?" I said to myself. "A lot of men, as they approach
forty, decide to color their graying hair. He probably is just trying
out different shades to see which one looks the best. He's still one
of the best men in the company, whatever his hair color."

I noticed that his complexion was undergoing a change as
well. Some days he appeared wan and pale while at other times his
face was flushed. Although we spoke by phone often, because Cole
traveled on the job, I would only occasionally see him face-to-face.
But, each time we met, Cole looked a little different than he did at
our previous encounter. But, the fact was, he was doing a better
job than ever before, so I kept my observations to myself. The last

thing I wanted to do was embarrass or in any way upset one of the top members of my management team by confronting him with a barrage of intrusive personal questions.

One day, my daughter, Linda, who worked for the hotels and who is an excellent judge of character, approached me and said, "Dad, I was at a party last night for the employees of the hotels. Have you noticed anything odd about Cole lately?"

"Well, yes, a little bit," I admitted, "but nothing I could put my finger on and besides, he's doing a great job for us. Why do you ask?"

Linda responded, "Daddy, I believe Cole has cleavage."

I said, "You must be kidding."

She then said, "No, Dad, I'm not. I was at the company staff party last night and Cole was there, too. He was wearing a shirt that was partially open down the front."

"Go on," I said.

She continued, "I'm not 100% sure. It was pretty dark. But I could swear he had breasts."

"What," I exclaimed. "What are you talking about?"

I wasn't about to approach Cole about this. I couldn't even imagine what I could possibly say to him.

As it turned out, Cole came to me. He called me one day and requested a personal meeting. When we met, Cole informed me that he and his wife were separating. The news saddened me since I truly respected both him and his wife.

Shortly thereafter, I received a phone call from a real estate broker who claimed to have heard that I was interested in selling the balance of our hotel chain. While this was true, I had not yet gone public with this information and did not wish for the news to hit the street for fear it would get back to our employees.

"No, they're not for sale," I responded. "I haven't listed them with anyone. Where did you hear that I wanted to sell?"

He explained that he had run into a blonde woman in a restaurant who had mentioned this fact to him. When I asked the name of the woman, he replied:

"She said her name was Ms. Austin."

"Well, I don't know any Ms. Austin," I said. "But I do know a Mr. Austin."

I was expressing my puzzlement to my wife, Mary Ellen, one evening as we sat down to enjoy dinner at a favorite restaurant a few blocks from my office. Just as we were finishing our appetizers, I looked up to notice a threesome, two men and a woman, enter the restaurant and take seats at the bar. The men were dressed rather nicely as was their female companion, an attractive blonde.

After being served her cocktail from the bartender, the woman slipped off her barstool and slowly walked over to our table and said in a friendly voice, "Hi, Mary Ellen, Hi, Bob." She greeted us as if she had known us for years. I peered closely at her face for several seconds and then issued a puzzled expression to Mary Ellen, who responded with a tiny shrug. The woman looked vaguely familiar, but I couldn't quite place her. It appeared Mary Ellen was equally at a loss. After a few seconds, when she realized that we did not recognize her, she bent closer and said, "Bob, I'm Cole."

Then it hit me all at once. I sat there in complete shock, not saying a word. Here, in front of us, was the man who had worked for me for almost five years as the trusted general manager of my hotel operation. But now he was standing before me as a woman. Cole scooted around the booth to join us. As she did so, I could sense that this moment was a tension-filled one for Cole as well. It had taken a good deal of courage for her to come face to face with her boss. She couldn't know how I would react. It could have meant the end of her career right there on the spot. But it didn't turn out that way.

Mary Ellen and I sat there quietly and simply listened as Cole opened her heart and poured out her whole life story. She had known since childhood that she was a woman trapped in a man's body. Although she had lived as a man, going so far as to marry and raise a family, in her own mind she had always viewed herself as a woman. The changes I had noticed in her hair color, complexion and physique were due to the preliminary hormonal treatments she had received in preparation for her surgery. Cole explained some of the procedures she had undergone and described how the silicone injections had altered the shape of her body giving her a more feminine appearance. Cole's story touched our hearts as she described what she and her family had endured as she struggled with finding her true gender identity. But now, she felt the turmoil and tears were behind her as she had, in some way, found peace in her new life as a woman.

From that moment on, Cole became a woman in my eyes. In looking back, I suspect that many of Cole's co-workers, who saw her on a daily basis, must have known her real story. While I certainly did notice the changes I mentioned earlier, nothing I saw or suspected could have prepared me for the transforming truth that Cole shared with us at the restaurant that evening.

Cole continued working as our general manager, and over the next few months she masterfully engineered the sale of our last three hotels in Las Vegas, Phoenix and Tucson. She sold them all to a San Francisco auto dealer who had cash to invest but knew little about running a hotel business. Part of the sales deal was that Cole would go to work for the car dealer after the purchase and continue to manage the three properties for him. The car dealer had no inkling that his new chief executive had once been a man and, quite rightly, it really didn't matter one bit. It was a great opportunity for Cole. After escrow closed, and in recognition of all the hard work she had expended in closing the deal, I issued Cole a large and well-deserved bonus. She used the money to fulfill one of her highest-flying dreams.

Before coming to work for me, Cole had earned her wings piloting a small single-engine plane she used to get around the hotels she managed. One of the things that Cole loved was aviation. She had fallen in love with the freedom of flight and found it a perfect respite from the stress of operating a motel chain. Not too surprisingly, Cole decided to take the bonus money she had earned and purchase a private plane. She took her check straight to the dealer and laid it down in exchange for a new Piper Saratoga, a six-passenger, high-performance, single-engine aircraft. Cole quickly renewed her SEL (single engine land) pilot's license and was soon winging her way across the scenic skies of Southern California.

Some six weeks after purchasing the plane, Cole and several friends boarded it and took off for Las Vegas where they spent a few fun-filled days. The group headed back to Los Angeles during an overcast, moonless night. They never arrived.

According to F.A.A. investigators who reconstructed the events leading up to the plane crash using radar images and flight reports, Cole had evidently experienced vertigo. A pilot relying upon visual information, rather than instruments, to control the plane can easily become disoriented if there is no point of reference, such as the horizon, within sight. With no moonlight from above and only the darkened desert below, everything looks exactly the same and it becomes difficult to tell up from down. As nearly as it could be determined, Cole's vertigo resulted in great stress being placed upon the plane's superstructure causing it to break up in flight. Everyone onboard perished.

Cole's death was a poignant and an unbearably sad loss for her family and for so many people whose lives she had touched. In addition, her loss was felt not only by our company, where she was an integral and important part of our organization, but now by the

San Francisco auto dealer who found himself the proud owner of three hotels with no one to run them.

In time, the dealer decided not to try and replace Cole, but instead he opted to sell off two of the properties, the Phoenix and Tucson hotels. The sale of these hotels put enough money back into the car dealer's pocket to offset the out-of-pocket down payment he had given to us. For the balance of the purchase price, I had agreed to accept his promissory note secured by the Las Vegas property. Once he decided, after Cole's tragic death, that he didn't want to be in the hotel business anymore, all he had to do was default on the note and go back to San Francisco. And, that's exactly what he did, leaving the Las Vegas Ambassador Inn in my hands. Just when I thought I was out of the hotel business, circumstance had conspired to bring me reluctantly back into the game for a bit longer.

After the many fleeting years that have now gone by since the events described in this chapter, I still often think fondly of Cole. What's interesting is that she inhabits my memory as neither man nor woman, but simply as a good person and one of my finest employees ever. I guess that at the end of the day, it's not your appearance, your orientation, or even your gender that is remembered and retained. What counts, when it comes to shaping a person's legacy, is how well he or she played the game. And, as far as I can recall, nobody played it better than Cole.

CHAPTER ELEVEN

THE ROAD PAVED WITH GOOD INTENTIONS

Honesty may be the best policy, but it's important to remember that, by elimination, dishonesty is the second-best policy.

George Carlin

By the mid-1970s our company had completed dozens of conventional apartment projects. By conventional, I mean that each was constructed as part of a commercial real estate project intended to yield an acceptable return on investment for all concerned. In such deals there typically are three major players: the developer, the builder, and the lender. None of our projects had ever involved the government as a fourth party. But that was about to change.

In 1975, in response to a perceived need on the part of the state for low-cost housing, the California Housing Finance Agency (CalHFA) was established. Its stated mission was to create safe, decent and affordable housing for individuals and families who could not otherwise afford it. The agency was chartered as California's affordable housing bank and charged with making below market-rate loans through the sale of tax-exempt bonds. The bonds are repaid by mortgage loan revenue, not by taxpayer dollars.

The creation of CalHFA triggered something of a housing boom across the state as investors assembled to take advantage of the attractive financing terms being offered. One such investment group approached me with what appeared to be a very worthwhile program. The group wished to erect apartment projects in small-town rural areas where they felt the need was the greatest. They explained that by constructing new apartments aimed at housing disadvantaged rural families, they would be eligible for some very attractive financing terms. These included below-market construction loan rates—as low as three percent (market rates ranged from seven to eight percent at that time), no-down payment requirements, and a forty-year amortization schedule. On top of the economic incentives being offered by the state, there was another factor: the humanitarian factor.

The investor group made a compelling case that if we agreed to provide the construction services, we would be helping people in real need. The apartments we were being asked to build would literally open the door to new opportunities for many of our state's most disadvantaged citizens. I thought back to my own early years of struggle and permitted a wave of compassion to color my thinking. Besides, this venture seemed rather safe. My exposure as the builder was not great since the risks were so low for the developers. Not only did they enjoy a minimal initial investment, they were assured of a constant waiting list of tenants once the apartments were finished. The attractive financing terms allowed the landlord to charge below-market rents for qualified tenants making the units highly desirable and sought-after.

In order to better manage this project, I set up a separate division of my company and dubbed it Mayer Environmental Housing (MEH). MEH's activities were restricted to subsidized housing projects. We would build the units while the investor group would serve as the owner/operators.

Because of the government involvement, I was asked and I agreed to take the job on a "guaranteed fixed price" contract. In other words, while some construction jobs are billed under an open-ended "time and material" basis, in this situation I was required to quote a specific price for each location. Once it was accepted, I was then locked into that price regardless of any changes that may occur during the building process. In other words, if the cost of lumber jumped suddenly, or if we encountered a shortage of plumbing fixtures during the construction period, I would be forced to absorb all financial consequences. By the same token, if we encountered any cost reductions, we would be able to pocket the savings. We normally did not work this way, but this was no normal deal. In hindsight, I can truthfully say that my motives to take on what was clearly a challenging assignment were, for the most part, honorable. I was hoping to turn a respectable profit with a minimum of risk and do some good for our community at the same time. Sadly, the results were a far cry from what I had so idealistically envisioned.

Once the loans were approved and the contracts signed, we began moving dirt in such rustic and remote locations as Beaumont, Perris, Coachella, Banning, Marysvale and Shasta. Each multi-family project consisted of between forty to sixty new units. We tried to hire local skilled and unskilled workers in each community we entered. In this way we were not only helping people in need through the creation of affordable new housing, we were also creating new jobs and benefiting the local economy. I felt quite pleased about our activities during the early days of the venture. But this "warm and fuzzy" feeling was not to last very long.

These remote construction sites were scattered so far from each other, and from our home office, managing them became a very time-consuming affair. It placed a severe burden on our regular staff members who were already busy with all of our conventional projects. I obviously needed a project manager. Someone who would oversee each construction job while serving as an onsite "straw boss" to make sure all materials were properly received, stored, and deployed.

When I explained my plight to the members of the investment group—our project partners—they suggested I contact Ross Spengler (not his real name). "He knows the building trade better than anyone in the state," I was advised. I reviewed Ross's background and, as I was told, it looked very impressive indeed. When we met face to face, I was again taken with his intelligence and believed him when he claimed to know all the "ins and outs" of the construction business. I hired him to serve as our project manager and eventually discovered that by the "ins and outs," he meant money out of my pocket and into his. The man was as dishonest as the night is long.

Ross was a tremendously likable and gregarious person, always forthcoming with a warm smile and a friendly pat on the back. Unfortunately, it often held a knife. You couldn't help but like him. In fact, the sub-contractors he hired for each of our jobs liked him so much that they placed large amounts of cash into his back pocket every month. They could afford to do so because Ross was approving their massively inflated invoices. The love just flowed and flowed. But this rather conventional scam wasn't inventive enough for the very creative Mr. Spengler. He began writing checks to imaginary companies and mailing them to mail-drop lock boxes where he would then pick them up and cash them. Ross was also adept at over-buying building materials and then returning the unused leftovers for a cash refund that never made it past his very sticky fingers. Essentially, Ross performed every trick in the book when it came to cheating and defrauding an absentee employer.

I finally got wind of Ross's shenanigans and, before I had a chance to take any action, he realized that I was on to him. As expected, Ross flew the coop leaving behind a string of unfinished projects in various phases of incompletion. It was a developer's worst nightmare come true.

It would take almost two years of concerted struggle and aggravation to finalize the projects. We obviously couldn't continue using the services of the sub-contractors who had been feeding Ross his kickbacks. So our first challenge was locating new, and hopefully somewhat more honest, contractors who would be willing to take over and complete a job already commenced by another outfit. When we finally were able to locate such tradesmen, we would be forced to pay top dollar since the new contractor understood how desperate we were to get the project completed. At times, the thought of simply folding up our tents and walking away from this quagmire became very tempting. But I had my reputation to think of. I had built an organization upon unquestionable integrity and trust. If the word got out on the street that Bob Mayer had defaulted on a building project, it would be devastating to my future opportunities. I simply had to grin and bear it.

In reflecting about the lessons to be learned from this experience, I concluded that lying at the root of the problem were all the well-intentioned social planners who felt it the proper role of government to redistribute our society's wealth. By sponsoring such give-away programs at taxpayer expense, the CalHFA opened a Golden Gate to every shyster, swindler, and hustler who smelled an easy buck by building homes for the poor. Ross Spengler walked through those gates ready to grab all he could get away with and did so quite smoothly.

Once all the projects were finally completed, I calculated my losses, licked my wounds, and closed up Mayer Environmental Housing for good. I also decided that I was not going to take any further strolls on the road paved with good intentions. It truly was, as I had painfully learned, the highway to hell.

CHAPTER TWELVE

THE STORY OF
BOB THE BANKER

A banker is a fellow who lends you his umbrella when the sun is shining, but wants it back the minute it begins to rain.

Mark Twain

As our construction company continued on its upwards growth spiral during the 1970s, I soon learned that, just like when playing Monopoly, somebody has to play the role of the bank. The success of our business was based almost entirely upon our ability to secure affordable financing for our development projects. In this regard, we had cultivated a tight-knit relationship with Union Bank in Santa Monica. Although they were located some distance from our Downey offices, the bank seemed to be more amenable than any of the local establishments I had talked to. I had a good deal of respect for Union Bank's branch president, Dave Buell, and he, likewise, had a lot of faith in me. Dave had demonstrated that faith by assisting us in securing many prime rate construction loans over the years. Dave was familiar with our track record and was able to assure the loan committee that our company would successfully complete any project we started. One day in 1978, I received an important call from Dave.

"Say, Bob," he burst out after a few pleasantries, "I want to talk to you about a new venture I'm putting together." I didn't think Dave was interested in real estate development, so his comment kind of threw me.

"What sort of venture?" I said.

"It's a new bank," Dave replied. "A group of investors and I are starting up a new bank and I thought you might have an interest in getting involved." The invitation left me puzzled.

"But, Dave," I said, "I don't know beans about banking. I'm a builder. I don't know a LIBOR from a two by four." What I said was true. About all I knew about banking was that if you didn't have enough in the bank, your check would bounce. On the other hand, I always wanted to know what it was like to be on the other side of the table when we went before a loan committee to negotiate the financial terms of our next project. Wouldn't it be great if I were the one granting the approval instead of always being the one asking for it?

I had a lot of confidence in Dave Buell, so after some due deliberation, I told him I would do it and jumped aboard. I was given a seat on the board of the, at this point, unnamed new bank. Our biggest job, initially, was rounding up all our friends and business associates and getting them to commit to opening accounts with us once we opened our doors. Our next step was filing for the government approval process. Dave believed that in order to improve our chances for success we needed a federal charter, rather than a state charter. We wanted to be a "National" bank since, in the minds of many customers, this designation adds a level of perceived security.

It took many long months to obtain the federal charter, but finally in 1979, we opened the Westwood National Bank near the UCLA campus. We selected the name because of the street address, but not long after, we decided that it was not in our best interest to be locked into a specific location. Westwood National was then re-christened and emerged as the more cosmopolitan-sounding Metrobank.

This act proved wise because after a few years we had outgrown our modest digs and needed to relocate. We elected to move our headquarters to the corner of Westwood and Wilshire Boulevard where we occupied the entire ground floor of a modern high-rise office building. The spot was on one of the most highly trafficked intersections in West Los Angeles and our move there benefited Metrobank with a valued high-profile presence.

As I became more and more involved with Metrobank's activities, I did, as a matter of necessity, become increasingly familiar with the basic principles of the banking business. I learned why it was important to build up a bank's "on deposit" assets. We paid out very little in the way of interest on customer savings accounts and nothing at all for checking accounts. It was the money collected from these accounts that we used to first fund our reserves in compliance with federal banking regulations, and second, loan out to individuals and businesses. It was via the spread between what the bank paid out to its depositing customers (between zero and three percent, in those days) and the rate being paid by borrowers (between four and seven percent), that a bank was able to turn a profit. The more checking and savings accounts we were able to attract, the more money we needed to fund our reserves. But the larger the reserves, the more money we were allowed to loan out. And, of course, the more (good) loans we issued, the more money we would make.

I also became familiar with the other side of the ledger. I saw that banks are required to pay all their overhead operating expenses, such as labor, marketing, insurance, etc., out of that sometimes narrow spread. While I was already familiar with such business principals as "economy of scale" from my experience in the construction business (the more doorknobs you bought, the less you paid for each doorknob), in the banking business I began to learn about the value of fixed costs and incremental expenses. For example, there's a certain cost associated with servicing each and every checking account. Each time a new account is opened, such variable expenses go up. At the same time, our rent, marketing, insurance, janitorial and other fixed expenses remain at the same level. As a result, the more new accounts we were able to attract, the higher our overall profit margin.

I began to appreciate what a very thin margin banks really operate under. This revelation underscored the importance of making prudent loans. It helped me to understand why bankers always seemed so conservative and so risk intolerant. One bad loan that goes into default can wipe out the profits generated by thousands of checking accounts. Several bad loans and a bank can soon find itself labeled as "troubled" by the banking regulators as they're forced to report losses to their stockholders. If a bank is unable to then turn things around, they risk losing their charter and going out of business.

I gained a whole new appreciation for why a bank's loan committee must be extremely prudent when approving commercial loans, while at the same time, not being overly cautious and thereby turning away prospective business. It's a real tightrope act and if you lose your (bank) balance, you're dead.

As the banking industry grew at record levels during the 1980s and 1990s, Metrobank soon caught the eye of a number of regional banks that were interested in entering the Los Angeles market. One of the most aggressive was Detroit-based Comerica, that wished to expand their operations to the west coast. They extended a very generous offer and the Board readily accepted it.

Once the deal was finalized, we stockholders were required to exchange our shares in Metrobank for shares of Comerica. Given the value of Comerica stock at the time, this sale represented a terrific return on my initial buy-in investment. But the best was yet to be. Comerica was on a growth path that kept producing value upon value for their stockholders as we watched the value of our holdings climb steadily over the coming years.

Since I wound up with a pretty good size chunk of Comerica stock after the sale, the bank asked me to join the Board of Directors of its California division. The only type of boards I was familiar with were the type you buy at the lumber yard, but nevertheless I agreed to give it try. I recall attending my first Comerica board meeting at the company's headquarters in San Jose. There were about fourteen other members seated around a massive conference table. They introduced themselves and I quickly saw that they were, for the most part, corporate CEOs, big eight accounting firm guys, and banker types.

The main item on the agenda was deciding whether or not to approve the acquisition of another small Southern California bank. After chatting about golfing opportunities, the stock market, and the performance of the San Francisco 49ers, we finally got around to talking about the bank. A fellow got up and gave us a slide presentation that reviewed the target bank's financial picture. Pretty dry stuff. Next, a marketing lady came in and reported about how they were going to improve the bank's performance by putting billboards along the freeway. There was a lot of discord back and forth with board members using terms like "arbitrage," "effective leverage," "basis points," etc. You could say I was "board stiff." After three and a half frustrating hours of this, it was announced that since it was getting late, we should study the matter and come back and discuss it some more at next month's meeting. Very little had been decided. Except for me. I had decided quite clearly that I was not going to attend any more of these board meetings. I turned in my resignation the following day.

When Comerica took over, they insisted that Metrobank founder and president Dave Buell sign a "non-compete" agreement that would keep him from going into the banking business in this region for at least a two-year period. This is standard procedure since had Dave decided to either work for a competing bank, or start a new one, he could easily have taken many of Metrobank's former customers with him and, of course, Comerica did not wish to risk losing any of them.

Almost three years to the day after closing the Comerica deal, I received another call from Dave.

"Bob, you came onboard when we founded Metrobank and I think you'll agree that deal turned out pretty well," he said. I had to agree with him.

"Well, we're doing it again. We're setting up another bank," Dave explained, "only this time it's going to cost you a little more to get in on the ground floor." He then proceeded to give me a quick description of the deal including my investment requirements.

"Well, Bob," he asked finally, "are you in?"

"On one condition," I shot back. "No board meetings!"

It was a deal and we soon were underway again, going through the same regulatory approval procedures and trying to round up new customers. We selected the name Primebank and opened an attractive office in Century City. It was déja vu all over again, only this time around the Monopoly board, I knew a little bit more about the banking business.

I'm happy to say that history repeated itself. Just as Metrobank had done several years earlier, Primebank thrived and soon caught the eye of a bigger fish in the pond. Although its name sounds as though it belongs somewhere around Israel, the East West Bank is actually a major California financial services provider based in Pasadena. In 2000 they decided to expand into Century City as part of a statewide growth spurt. East West came a-courtin' and presented us with a very sweet bouquet of an offer. We just couldn't say "No." Once again we exchanged our Primebank stock for shares of East West Bank and realized a splendid return on our initial investment. Thanks in large part to the talents, hard work and banking savvy of Dave Buell, we had managed to put together a fantastic second act.

Throughout this period, I continued my commitment to my core development business while keeping my banking activities on the second burner. All told, I put in hundreds of hours at various board meetings and at associated committee meetings. In looking back today, I feel it was time well spent. Not only did it result in a handsome financial yield, the experience also yielded less tangible, yet significant, benefits. During those years I went from a guy who didn't know a debenture from a denture to someone who eventually had a pretty good grasp on the inner workings of the financial marketplace.

These days, I'm still on the lookout for attractive real estate financing deals. The fact is that today I am able to fully place myself into the shoes of the lender. I feel that I can completely understand the thinking and motivation of any bank considering the issuance of a construction loan to me. And being armed with that knowledge has proven to be a great asset time after time.

CHAPTER THIRTEEN

THE LONG BEACH PIKE

And the seasons, they go round and round; and the painted ponies
go up and down. We're captive on the carousel of time.

Joni Mitchell

Someone once said "Nostalgia isn't what it used to be," and I agree. That's why I don't often indulge in it. But when I do, it's back to a stretch of Long Beach oceanfront that my mind will sometimes fondly wander. During those last few summers of innocence before Pearl Harbor officially scuttled my youth, I could often be found hitchhiking the fifteen miles from our home in Huntington Park down to the coast and "The Coney Island of California." Known simply as The Pike, it was there that I would rendezvous with my school buddies and assorted pals to enjoy what were undeniably "The Best Years of Our Lives."

The Long Beach Pike was a classic American amusement center opened in 1911 by a German immigrant, Charles I.D. Looff. Looff, a wood craftsman, arrived in New York through Ellis Island as part of the great immigration wave of the 1870s. When an immigration clerk insisted that the young man provide him with a middle name "For your I.D.," Looff simply repeated "I.D.," and that became part of his permanent American name. A few years later, Looff designed

Coney Island's first carousel. He would go on to build forty more classic carousels during his lifetime. The Looff carved horses from that era will fetch over $100,000 today.

Looff built his first California amusement park at the terminal end of the fashionable Red Car electric streetcar line that connected downtown Los Angeles to Long Beach. The Pike was originally a beach and bathhouse resort, featuring Roman pools and a unique attraction known as The Plunge. Under Looff's direction, it soon grew into a full-blown Luna-style amusement park with fun, games, and thrill rides for every age group—and best of all, it didn't cost very much to have a great time. While you had to buy a ticket for some of the rides, there was no general admission fee.

The Pike featured an enormous, gut-wrenching wooden roller coaster called the Cyclone Racer that extended out over the water. But my favorite attractions were the Deep Sea Diving Bell, the Penny Arcade, the Crazy Maze and the Laff-in-the-Dark Funhouse. The latter contained a House of Mirrors where a normal person could appear to be four feet high and five foot wide. I also loved the "Let's Shoot" shooting gallery where I could take aim at moving targets with a .22 rifle, and I never failed to stop in the big Chinese curio store by the east entrance.

At night The Pike was a blizzard of colored lights and motion. Cotton candy and sideshow barkers competed for attention with brass bands and carnie pitchmen. One of my earliest memories at The Pike was paying a penny to peek at a dead body. The body was that of bank robber, Elmer McCurdy, who had been killed by a California posse around 1900 and then stuffed, mummified, and set out for display at sideshows ever since.

The Pike went into a decline during the 1960s and by 1979 had closed its doors. Since I was in the real estate development business I picked up a rumor that the property might be for sale. Until its demise, the park had been operated by Looff's son-in-law and upon his death, ownership had been transferred to Looff's granddaughter, Mary Dwyer.

While I had no interest in owning and re-opening the amusement park itself, my fond memories of the place prompted me to drive to Long Beach and have a look-see. What I found was a magnificent waterfront location and a high-potential development opportunity—if it could be purchased at the right price.

The property consisted of roughly ten acres between Ocean Avenue in Long Beach and the harbor. Naturally, any development would mean the removal of all the former amusement park arcades, abandoned attractions, and ancient bathhouses. Although Long Beach was a good-sized and well-established city, it had experienced very little modernization or commercial redevelopment. The town was populated mostly with 1900 vintage high and mid-rise structures that gave the place a sort of laid-back and sleepy atmosphere. I decided that a major multi-use development—office buildings, hotels, condos, etc.—would be the best thing to come down "The Pike" in a long time.

I contacted Mary Dwyer, who lived in Palm Springs, and confirmed that, yes, they were thinking of selling the property. At our first meeting she struck me as very warm and cordial and I walked away believing that a successful deal could be put together. Naturally we began by discussing the price.

Mary had enlisted a team of lawyers and CPAs to appraise the property and, after wrangling with them for several months, we arrived at a tentative meeting of the minds. I would pay seven million dollars for the property and give the seller an equity position that would entitle them to a piece of the action. If that price sounds a bit low, you should remember that we're not talking about virgin land where construction can begin the day after closing. No, in this case we had hundreds of thousands of dollars of demolition to consider, not to mention the fact that several of the structures were protected under the town's historic preservation provisions and could not be torn down.

We next drafted a purchase agreement and asked Mary to execute it, thereby sealing the deal. But she put me off.

"Let me see what you plan to do with the property, first," she insisted. "We want to make sure we're happy with what's going to happen to The Pike after we've sold it."

While this request seemed a bit unusual, I could understand Mary's attachment to the place and her desire to make sure it wound up in capable hands. We obliged and began to present Mary and her crew of consultants with artist's renderings, detailed floor plans, and even hand-made models of the structures we were planning to erect on the site. I thought I could detect a glimmer in their eyes as we waltzed in and unveiled a massive ten-foot cardboard replica of one of the high-rises we planned to construct. Her crew would always find a few flaws in our plans and decline to sign off on the deal until some obscure detail was corrected.

Since they had a potential slice of the profits, Mary would say: "Just keep proving to us how profitable this project can be." Being naïve, I continued to indulge her and after almost two years of this "Coney Island" cat and mouse game, I found I had spent hundreds of thousands of dollars on architects, consultants, models and the like. This in addition to the hundreds of hours of my time and my staff's time all in a misguided effort to impress the sellers with what outstanding developers we were. The more time, money and energy I had invested into this so-called deal, the more determined I became to make it happen. By the time I realized that I had dug myself into a pretty deep hole, the purchase price had risen from seven million to twenty million. You see, we had done such a cracker-jack job of convincing the seller that this property could be turned into a real California gold mine, that they were no longer willing to let it go for such a paltry sum. By painting such a rosy picture about the future of the site, we had opened the seller's eyes to its real value. Around here, this maneuver is known as shooting yourself in the foot.

I was crushed. At twenty million this project no longer made any sort of financial sense. And even if I had agreed to pay twenty million, I felt certain that they would have decided to raise the price to twenty-five or thirty million. By now it was obvious that these folks had strung me along for much longer than I should have permitted and it was time to cut the string. So I swallowed hard, bit the bullet, and tore up the purchase agreement. I simply walked away from all the dollars, sweat, years, and tears we had invested and chalked it all up to a bitter experience.

Evidently Mary and her associates ran into similar difficulties when they attempted to reach deals with other developers. The property sat idle and undeveloped for twenty years until 2001. Our original plan, back in 1981, called for the construction of about 1,500 mid and hi-rise residential units. The condominium communities that were actually constructed were of a much lower density and in compliance with newly implemented municipal height limits. The property today includes a shopping mall, a parking garage, and sits adjacent to the Long Beach Convention Center and a new Hyatt Hotel. But thanks to historic preservation, traces of the fun-packed Pike of my youth still remain.

The peaked roof of the Gazebo that housed Looff's Lite-A-Line building that once stood at the very center of the park remains intact and is now attached to a new visitor's center. The current developers have done a good job of integrating some of the old and a lot of the new.

I will never know if the Pike redevelopment plan I had put together on paper some thirty years ago would have been successful or not. It may sound like sour grapes, but in some ways, I'm pleased that I was denied the opportunity of putting a new face on the Old Pike. It would have been painful for me to go in and demolish those crumbling temples of my fun-filled youth. I would have done it without hesitation, but it would certainly have resulted in some genuine mixed emotions. Sort of like watching an IRS auditor drive off a cliff in your new Lexus.

Perhaps it was sentiments such as those that I can blame for my naïve behavior at the time. It was an expensive lesson, but one that I've never forgotten. Since then, if a seller is reluctant to put a verbal agreement into writing, then the negotiations are over. Like Samuel Goldwyn, the master of the malapropism, once said: "A verbal contract isn't worth the paper it's written on!"

In looking back, I can still recall the thrill and terror I experienced the first time I worked up enough courage to sit aboard the Cyclone Racer, the Pike's celebrated "killer" roller coaster. But I can honestly say that it pales in comparison to the roller coaster ride I've been on ever since, known as the real estate development game. But despite the fast-paced ups and downs, the delights and the disappointments, after each jolting ride I always find myself back in line and buying another ticket. Why? Because, like I said, the ride is worth the risk.

CHAPTER FOURTEEN

TRAVELS ON THE
HOTPOINT HIGHWAY

A man travels the world over in search of what he needs,
and returns home to find it

George Moore

O f all the various hats I've worn in my business career perhaps the most enjoyable was that of Major Appliance Dealer. This was true for two reasons. One, I only had one customer to deal with—Mayer Construction Company. And two, the travel perks were fantastic.

During our peak building years in the 1960s and 70s, Mayer Construction was putting up two to three thousand apartment units annually. Each one had to be outfitted with a full compliment of major appliances: refrigerators, air conditioners, washers-dryers, stoves and cook tops, garbage disposals, and so on. Because we were acquiring these items in sufficient quantity, we were able to buy directly from the manufacturer. In so doing, we were granted a dealer designation and, in addition to buying at wholesale prices, we were afforded all the associated trappings of being under the dealer umbrella. This included participation in various dealer incentive programs. The most attractive of these incentives was an amazing travel bonus that literally enabled my wife and me to tour the world. We took full advantage of the program and in so doing, enjoyed magnificent vacations in some of the world's most scenic and desirable destinations, often accompanied by friends we were permitted to bring along.

The idea of using vacations as a sales incentive in the appliance business originated with a man named Salvatore Giordano. In the 1950s, Giordano was the president of Fedders, the nation's largest maker of residential room air conditioners. He began by offering any dealer who sold more than 45 air conditioners per year a weeklong, all-expenses-paid vacation to a Florida beach resort. If you sold 90, you got to take along your wife. By 1953, over 500 people had made the trip, so Giordano began offering more lavish overseas junkets for so-called "super sales representatives." By the 1960s the program had grown to the point that over five thousand people per year were being treated to first-class vacations in places like Paris, the Grand Bahamas and Israel.

By the 1960s, when we got involved, the success of the travel junket program was being imitated by almost all of the major appliance manufacturers including Whirlpool, Hotpoint, Westinghouse, GE and Frigidaire. Each company handled the details a bit differently, but for the most part it worked as follows:

In order to qualify, a dealer had to move a certain minimum number of the manufacturer's products over a year's time. A qualified dealer was then presented with a menu of exotic tourist destinations in cities all over the globe. The dealer and his or her spouse were required to pay only a nominal fee of a few hundred dollars. The manufacturer covered all other expenses, including airfare, seven to ten days' lodging, food and entertainment. This, of course, represented an unbelievable bargain. The type of trips being offered would have cost us thousands per person if we had wanted to book them on our own.

If the dealer hit even higher sales targets, he or she could bring along friends or business associates at the same low price per person. Given the massive amounts of inventory we were purchasing each year, we always managed to hit the top sales tier without trouble. Our traveling companions were other appliance dealers and homebuilders from around the country. Every detail of each trip—from sightseeing tours to luggage tags—was exquisitely planned down to the last detail. Plus all the food and beverage you could possibly want. Each vacation was basically the equivalent of a non-stop, 24-hour, seven to ten-day gala party.

To say these incentive junkets were popular among America's appliance dealers would be a grand understatement. They loved them—as did we—and participated in them in ever growing numbers. As a result, these travel incentives served to boost sales for any manufacturer who offered them. Before long these appliance makers were shuttling tens of thousands of people around the globe on a regular basis. How could they accomplish this? How could they keep up with the mounting costs of such a vast program as it rapidly kept expanding? This question puzzled me and I decided to look into the matter. Here's what I found to be a typical situation:

First, all trips were planned during the so-called "off-season" for a particular destination. Participants were offered a ten-day vacation during a specified thirty-day period. The organizer would then contact a major airline and charter the services of several 300-passenger planes over the thirty-day travel window. In order to pull this off, they would assure the airline of full occupancy on twenty flights to and from the destination. That amounted to a guarantee of 6,000 seats to be sold.

For example, a plane would leave Los Angeles carrying 300 passengers, appliance dealers plus friends and spouses, and head for Rome. When it arrived in Rome and deposited its passengers, the plane would then pick up 300 more travelers who had just completed their week-long vacation. The aircraft would fly them back to their originating location, say San Francisco. Managing the logistics of this type of round-robin schedule was no trivial task. It required sophisticated mathematical algorithms so that each plane was never forced to "deadhead" or fly somewhere empty. It was truly an ingenious plan that served to keep airfares down to the absolute minimum.

The organizers made similar arrangements with the top hotels in the host city. They contracted to supply them with 6,000 guests over a thirty-day period. Since the hotels could count on full occupancy in what would normally be a slow season, they agreed to provide deep discounts that again resulted in tremendous cost savings. This same strategy extended to local tour buses, restaurants, and many other vendors who were assured of an ongoing flow of 300 new customers on almost a daily basis. The system delivered benefits to everyone involved. The airlines, the hotels, and the other service providers enjoyed a steady stream of revenue during their normal off-season. The dealers, like us, received fabulous vacations for only a few hundred dollars out-of-pocket. And most of all, the manufacturers benefited from the enthusiasm generated by such trips. While only a few direct pitches were made to us during the journey, dealers returned home pumped up and highly motivated to move even more of the manufacturer's product over the coming year. It was a totally effective sales incentive program that was mysteriously halted in the mid-80s.

I'm not sure, but I suspect that the travel incentive programs were shut down for fear of federal investigation. During this time period, several industries were being examined because of their questionable sales incentive programs. In particular, they were looking into a practice known as SPIFFs. This stood for Sales Performance Incentive Funding Formula and it amounted to a cash bonus paid to a salesperson by a manufacturer in consideration of a successful sales effort. Oftentimes SPIFFs were used to motivate sales people to influence customers into buying out-dated or discontinued merchandise that the manufacturer wished to unload. Or, a sales manager who promoted a particular brand over and above that of a competing brand would receive a SPIFF bonus from the manufacturer of the favored product. The furniture and consumer electronics industries were under particular scrutiny by the government and there was talk that investigators would soon be turning their attention towards the nation's appliance dealers.

Did these travel junkets amount to the same thing as a SPIFF? In my case, I don't feel that they did. Here's why: There really was not a monumental difference between a GE refrigerator and a Frigidaire. Both were priced about the same and offered similar features. So, if I specified one brand over the other in the knowledge that doing so would bring me closer to earning a European vacation, who was harmed in the process? The tenant who ultimately wound up living in the unit received a top-of-the-line refrigerator in any case.

As far as the tax implications go, did we declare the savings we enjoyed as participants on these travel junkets as income and then pay tax on it? The answer is no. Such savings were viewed as a gift from the manufacturer who listed the cost of these travel programs as a legitimate marketing expense. Which is exactly what they were.

Another possible reason that the travel junkets came to a halt was that they became too popular. An incentive designed to motivate someone to buy your product over their competitors' is only effective if you are the only one offering it. Once all the appliance manufacturers began offering identical programs, they lost their effectiveness. What did it matter if I ordered Whirlpool or Westinghouse? I got to go to Tahiti either way. It's possible that manufacturers discovered that the program was not bringing in the desired results any longer and simply moved on to other marketing tactics. In any case, they were great while they lasted. The trips afforded us some of the greatest holiday memories imaginable. We traveled to Paris, Rome, London, Sydney, Hong Kong, Honolulu and Barcelona, to name but a few. The program took me to places and exposed me to sights that I never would have experienced otherwise.

Did all that travel amount to anything more than mere vacation fun? I believe that it did. The trips provided me with a much more global perspective and many of the things I learned turned out to benefit me both personally and in terms of my business career. I already held an architect's license and had always been interested in the style of buildings, but traveling opened up a whole new architectural realm. My first-hand observation and study of Mediterranean architecture during several of our European trips added greatly to my own education. In Southern California, this type of motif is extremely popular in the design of both residential and commercial properties. Thanks to my travels I was able to enhance my understanding and appreciation of this form and that knowledge has served me well countless times over the years.

Because of my exposure to Mediterranean building practices in Europe, our company was one of the forerunners in designing landscaping that incorporated waterfalls, streams, bridges, boulders and waterside walkways into the design of our apartment communities. This type of exotic landscaping became the hallmark of a Mayer project. Although many others have imitated it over time, I can honestly say that the concept originated thanks to our travels in Italy and Spain aboard various appliance manufacturers' junkets. Today I consider it a privilege to have participated in these sojourns on the Hotpoint Highway. Sadly, those days are behind us now, but while they lasted…WOW! What a way to travel!

CHAPTER FIFTEEN

WARNER RANCH AND
THE BATTLE OF THE BEASTS

Los Angeles: Seventy-two suburbs in search of a city.

Dorothy Parker

While not as well known as his younger brother Jack, Harry Warner, the oldest of the four movie mogul siblings, is perhaps best remembered for having remarked, when asked in 1927 about whether or not Warner Bros. Studios would soon be producing talkies: "Who in the hell wants to hear actors talk?"

Besides being somewhat myopic when it came to spotting trends in the motion picture industry, Harry was also an avid lover of horseflesh. Even more than riding horses, he loved betting on them. So much so, in fact, that upon arriving in Hollywood and discovering that Santa Anita, the premier racetrack in Los Angeles, did not welcome him in the manner he expected, Harry and his son-in-law, Mervyn LeRoy, joined with Louis B. Mayer and other studio execs to build a racetrack of their own, and named it Hollywood Park.

In order to keep the track well stocked with fine thoroughbreds, Harry, in 1936, purchased 1,000 acres in what was Girard and now is known as Woodland Hills. He built a mansion on the property's highest point and began using the verdant meadowland, dotted with pepper trees, to breed racing horses.

Several hundred acres of this property, by then known as the Warner Ranch, was sold off in the late 1970s to Kaiser-Aetna—a real estate development joint venture owned by Kaiser Aluminum and Aetna Insurance. Situated in what was then a rural area in an outlying portion of the San Fernando Valley, the land was subdivided by Kaiser-Aetna, who installed the roads, sewers, and other infrastructure components intending to develop the site for both commercial and residential use. Unlike the well-developed eastern section of the valley—just across the Cahuenga Pass from Beverly Hills—the western section remained relatively pristine. Driving along the Hollywood Freeway (Route 101) from the Los Angeles Basin through the mountains towards Santa Barbara, one would see little other than a natural virgin landscape.

It was after having poured millions into obtaining the entitlements, building the roads and installing the utilities, that Kaiser-Aetna ran head-on into an economic recession. As so often is the case, it was the development and construction business that took the first and hardest hit. Unable to obtain attractive financing to complete the project, Kaiser-Aetna decided to place portions of the property up for sale one sub-division at a time. There were, at this point, only a handful of completed buildings on the site, some high-end research and development facilities, and a high-rise Blue Cross office tower.

The good news was that since the entire property had been zoned as commercial, it allowed the land to be utilized for multi-family housing projects without going through the time-consuming and risky rezoning process. Just hire an architect, draw up the plans and start construction. It was a much simpler and quicker process than what is required these days. This fact made the pieces being parceled out very attractive to developers. Especially to residential developers like me.

I first became aware of the Warner Ranch opportunity because I had, for several months, been prospecting the eastern San Fernando Valley for suitable development sites. When I heard that the Warner Ranch in the western valley was being parceled out, I became instantly interested. I was amazed when I visited the area and saw that it had all been fully subdivided and improved by Kaiser-Aetna. While there were some real issues to contend with, this smelled like one terrific opportunity to me.

One drawback was that the western valley was located some fifty miles from our Downey headquarters. This would make it challenging to supervise any project we undertook there. I deliberated long and hard while trying to weigh all the factors involved. Finally, I decided to do it. As things turned out, it was one of my better decisions.

In 1973, we purchased the first parcel and erected one of our signature apartment communities, replete with waterfalls, streams and lakes nestled into the lush landscape. It was an immediate hit and we found ourselves with a waiting list for each of our next rental properties. Every bit as attractive, in our eyes, as the flowing waters that characterized our communities, was the growing income stream generated by a highly positive cash flow.

Our development activities at the Warner Ranch soon caught the eye of investment houses such as Dean Witter and Merrill Lynch who organized limited partnership ventures to raise construction capital for us. Partnership units were sold as tax shelters to private investors who benefited from the advantages such projects provided. Because of component accelerated depreciation, investment tax credits, interest deductions and other favorable items, these projects could be counted on to show a loss on paper during the early years of their life-spans. This fact held true even if the developments were fully leased and generating a positive cash flow. Investors in our projects, in those days of high marginal income tax rates and no distinction between passive and active income, were able to recoup their initial investments in a few years by applying these paper losses against their other income, thereby reducing their overall tax liability.

The unique landscaping and attractive floor plans we employed at our communities set them apart from what other developers were producing for their clients at the time. We also were very careful about the locations we selected, seeking out those that would hold the most appeal to prospective tenants. I always adhered to the old adage about "location, location, and location."

Over the coming years, Mayer Construction built numerous communities in the Warner Ranch area, adding hundreds of housing units to what was fast becoming a highly desirable area. We were turning them around as fast as we could build them and each one had a higher value than the one before. This would have been great news except for one fact. Each time we completed a project, we had to go back to Kaiser-Aetna and negotiate the purchase of a new parcel. Because of the rising property values, driven by all this activity, each parcel we bought cost us more than the one before. In looking back, I now regret that we relied upon conventional brokers and bankers to provide us with the acquisition capital we needed. I am convinced that we would have been even more successful had we partnered with a "deep pockets" venture capital outfit. Such a group would have been able to put together a substantial private placement fund that we could have used to purchase one large parcel at a much more attractive price. This would have allowed us to avoid having to acquire each parcel piecemeal in the dramatically escalating real estate market we were facing. The irony here was profound. It was our construction activity at the Warner Ranch that was driving up the property values and instead of benefiting us, we were suffering by being forced to pay a higher price each time we chose to buy another parcel.

The most extraordinary property we purchased was considered the flagship lot of the Warner Ranch, Harry Warner's former residence. It was a modern, rambling ranch house on a ten-acre spread perched astride the property's highest hilltop. From its front porch you could look out and take in a magnificent vista that encompassed nearly the entire ranch. The home sported half a dozen bedrooms, a private movie theatre and screening room. Walking its halls, you could sense the echoes of the glamorous silver screen stars who were known to have flocked to the ranch for the frequent galas that Warner loved to put on. Back in the studio's glory days, during the 1930s and 40s, the ranch was located far from the urban areas of Los Angeles. Guests adored rubbing shoulders and bending elbows with the likes of Bogart and Hepburn, sheltered by the discrete privacy that the remote Warner Ranch afforded.

We decided to revive a bit of Hollywood tradition ourselves after acquiring the estate. Mayer Construction would host a catered celebration party for our employees, spouses, and friends at the Warner house whenever we would complete a new residential project elsewhere on the Ranch. I recall how the festive spirit of "Hollywood in its Heyday" would always pervade the party atmosphere. It was during one such shindig, amid the ghosts of Garbo and Gable, that I, and several of my associates, sat discussing the future of the Ranch house property that surrounded us.

I explained that while the balance of the Warner Ranch was approved for high-density development, where we now sat—the parcel containing the house itself—was zoned for single family housing only. We would have to get this changed by obtaining a variance if we hoped to erect the condominium community we had envisioned for the site. With its excellent elevation and sweeping vistas, the condos built here would provide each resident with a dramatic view of the scenic western San Fernando Valley. But there was one small hitch: the neighbors. And these were no ordinary neighbors.

Sitting on 425 acres directly adjacent to the Ranch house property was a two-year community college known as the Clarence W. Pierce School of Agriculture. The school would eventually become a more comprehensive institution known as Pierce College, but at this time the school enjoyed an all-male student body and an outstanding reputation in the fields of animal husbandry and life sciences. In fact, the college was the only school in the state that housed a fully functioning farm on its campus.

As anticipated, we were required to appear at a public hearing before the City Council in order to petition for a zoning variance that would allow us to erect our planned condominium community at the Warner Ranch house site. It was there that we came face-to-face with the most unbelievable form of opposition we had ever encountered. Our company was used to dealing with demonstrators at zoning hearings and had often had to endure vocal harassment while pleading our case before various zoning authorities. But never before did the catcalls come from actual cats! Not to mention the bleats, the grunts, the clucks and even a cockle-doodle-do or two!

The good men of Pierce College had turned out in force to protest our planned development. They argued that the erection of a densely populated structure on the site of the old Warner Ranch house would result in irreparable harm befalling the animals they raised and cared for at their nearby student farm. Even though the condos would be located many blocks away from the farm itself, they insisted that the increased noise and traffic the project would bring in its wake would not go down well with the Pierce College goats, chickens and hogs. As I rose to protest these unsupported allegations, I turned to witness the hearing room doors swing open as a contingent of agitated farm animals were herded into the hearing room under the direction of a group of equally agitated college students. Amid the squawks and oinks and the general barnyard brouhaha being generated by these obviously un-housebroken farm animals, it was quite difficult for me to continue making our case. How could I possibly argue against Old Macdonald and Noah's Ark? It was guerrilla theatre (or perhaps "gorilla theatre" would be more accurate), and it proved to be effective.

After the hearing room was cleared and cleaned up, the arguments continued for several more weeks. In the end, the animals carried the day as the Council denied our request for a zoning variance. Repeated attempts on my part likewise ended in failure and so we simply sat on the Ranch house property for several years and eventually sold it as an undeveloped asset when we liquidated our company in 1980. The site was eventually developed by third parties. Over the protestations of the chickens and the goats next door, I presume.

Fortunately, the "Mayer vs. the menagerie" episode was the only major setback we suffered as we went on to successfully develop hundreds of other units on the Warner Ranch parcels we purchased from Kaiser-Aetna.

Today, Warner Ranch, and the other developed nearby ranches, are known collectively as the Warner Center. Over 40,000 people work at the Center and roughly 10,000 people call it home. The headquarters of Health Net, Inc., a Fortune 500 company, is located in the heart of the Warner Center skyline. The Center, essentially completed in the mid-1990s, contains a diverse mix in terms of land usage: many low-rise office buildings, three skyscrapers (the tallest is the 25-story AIG Building), a few hotels, some light industrial, and of course, the residential communities we helped to construct. The area also contains prime retail space such as the Promenade Mall that attracts shoppers from all over who use the area's rapid transit system to get them there. The western-most stop of the Orange Line Transitway, opened in October 2005, is the Warner Center Transit Hub.

Along with the Waterfront Project in Huntington Beach, Warner Center has provided me with my fondest development memories over the years. I'm very proud of what we accomplished at both these locations and I consider them to be the pinnacle properties of my business career.

Chapter Sixteen

Bidding Farewell
to My Business

A business is a lot like a car. The only way it runs by itself is downhill.

Anonymous

The poet T.S. Eliot once observed that the years between age fifty and seventy are the hardest. You are always being asked to do things, yet you're not decrepit enough to say no because of age. In 1980, as I was entering this period of my life, I decided to take stock of my situation and make some decisions about my life's direction. I had worked hard for the past thirty-some years and as a result built a development business that had attracted the attention of many potential suitors. Up until then I had resisted each and every advance, regardless of how attractive the acquisition offers had been. Well, I reckoned, it was time for a change.

I wouldn't call it a mid-life crisis. I didn't grow a ponytail and lounge around in a hot tub, meditating all day long. But I did decide that maybe it would be fun to slow down and relax after so many years of toil. I decided to accept an offer to sell Mayer Construction Company along with all of the company's land holdings. I have to say: my timing could have been better.

Once a meeting of the minds was reached between the buyer and me, it was time for the attorneys and CPAs to step in and finalize, formalize, and document the terms of the sale. This process took months and during those months the U.S. economy went on a gut-wrenching ride to oblivion. The prime lending rate, for example, rose that year from 8% to a high of 19%. Every time the rate went up a tick, the agreed purchase price was reduced. The buyer had secured financing, but in such an environment there was no such thing as a fixed rate of interest. If the seller wished to keep his loan payments constant, the principal would have to go down every time the interest rate went up. By the time the lawyers were ready to conduct the closing, millions of dollars had been removed from the table. What could I do? I knew that if I balked and canceled the sale, there would be no other buyers out there, given the economic outhouse we were now in. The real estate market was especially hard hit and was more or less on "life support" at this point. If I pulled the plug on this deal, it was "Goodbye, Charlie!"

We convened for the final round of negotiations that were to culminate in closing the deal on a Thursday, at my attorney's office. Both sides were well stocked with lawyers and accountants as the meeting got underway at 9 a.m. Over the next fifteen hours the sale was terminated and resuscitated several times as first the buyer and then we threatened to walk out unless certain concessions were met. It was a grueling and bellicose battle that saw neither side give up an inch without a fight.

By midnight, exhaustion and frustration had set in as the final obstacle was finally resolved. We all felt as though we had been through a massive meat grinder, when the seller approached and handed me something that helped greatly to lift my sagging spirits. It was the largest check I had ever seen in my life...and it was made out to me!

I returned home from the hill in the wee hours and fell into bed for a few hours sleep before my first appointment that morning. By Friday afternoon I was dragging and the tension and sleep deprivation began taking their toll. But, instead of going straight to bed, I felt I had to honor a commitment I had made months earlier to attend a Charity Ball at the Century Plaza in Beverly Hills. My company—I should say: my former company—had purchased a table for ten and I had encouraged a number of our key people to accept my invitation to join us at the event. Despite the fact that I was a total basket case, not to mention emotionally and physically drained, I felt I had to be there. Bad decision.

Once in my tux and at the gala, I began to loosen up a bit and savor the relief, now that months of intense bargaining were finally behind me. I tried not to focus on the fact that if I had concluded the sale merely one year earlier, I would be millions of dollars better off. It wasn't easy, but I managed to block this unpleasant line of thinking from my mind. After a few drinks, the process got easier.

There were over 2,000 mingling party guests on hand, decked out in all their philanthropic finery, and I must have greeted and schmoozed with most of them. By the time the main event rolled around—a celebrity auction—I was running on pure adrenaline. Most of the evening was a complete blur, but friends told me later that it looked like I was having one helluva good time.

I do however recall feeling that I had been recently blessed by the biggest payday of my life. "I shouldn't just celebrate," I thought to myself. "I should be generous and share some of my good fortune with those less fortunate." With this altruistic attitude in place, I became very involved, shall we say, in the celebrity auction. You might even say I got a bit carried away.

The next morning, as the haze lifted, I discovered that I had snagged the following items at auction: One of Liberace's rhinestone-studded, full-length fur coats; the privilege of riding in race car being driven by Paul Newman; a speaking part for Mary Ellen in an upcoming movie called "Lethal Weapon," and finally, the biggest item on the auction card: a 1933 vintage Rolls Royce. It was quite a haul.

In order to secure this last prize I had to outbid one of Hollywood's former sex symbols, Connie Stevens. Connie and I went head to head and foolishly drove the price up to $44,000 before she finally withdrew. When I, and a few of my associates, went to pick up the roadster the following day, I was reminded what humorist Oscar Levant once said about the movie capitol: "Strip away all the phony tinsel of Hollywood and you'll find the real tinsel underneath." The car looked like a dream sitting in the auction hall, but it turned into a nightmare the minute we attempted to drive the thing. It could barely limp out of the subterranean garage onto the street level above.

We decided to take the Santa Monica Freeway in order to get the car back to our home quickly. We soon discovered that it was incapable of traveling over 35 mph at full throttle. Angry motorists waved their fists, and other parts of their hands, at us as they sped by at more than twice our speed. As I was driving, I tried my best to hide my face from recognition. I was assisted in this effort by a billowing cloud of blue acrid smoke that poured into the passenger compartment from the engine. The smoke stung our eyes and lungs so badly we had to stop the car along the freeway every few miles to air ourselves out. Finally, our sputtering, choking, turtle-mobile came to a grateful, if not graceful, stop inside the garage in our home.

I gave the vehicle a once over the next day to determine what sort of repairs it would need to get it up and running properly. I planned to take it into the auto shop immediately. What I discovered shocked me. I didn't need a mechanic. I needed an exterminator.

A close-up inspection revealed that in 1933, British-made auto bodies were often built of wood. One look at the woodwork underneath the seat upholstery showed that the wood frame of my prize Rolls had been totally ravaged by termites. I decided to leave the "Silverfish Cloud" parked in the garage permanently. I was afraid that if the Rolls broke down on the street, I'd never be able to find any spare parts for it.

So there it sat for a full year until it came time for us to attend the same charity event at the Century Plaza. Donating the Rolls back to the charity auction seemed like a good idea. It would get the bug-mobile off of my hands and let me take a tax deduction for a charitable gift. Would the auction be able to locate another loose cannon like me this year? Someone willing to shell out $44,000 for this termite colony on wheels? Not too likely, I surmised. I turned it over to the auction officials and offered to let them keep anything over $20,000 that it fetched. They agreed to the deal. I felt that it would bring in $25,000 or $30,000 tops. Both I, and the auction officials, were about to be surprised and delighted.

The bidding on the Rolls reached all the way to $50,000, once again driven ever higher by none other than Connie Stevens and her escort. Boy, she really loved that car and this year she got it. I walked over and congratulated her on her new acquisition.

"You're going to love that Rolls," I told Connie with a grin, "once you get all the bugs out." She just smiled graciously.

I don't know what Connie's experience with the Rolls was like, although I did follow her career with some interest after that. Although her star had faded somewhat, she did enjoy a true reversal of fortune after her appearance in the film "Grease 2." In the 1990s, Connie developed her own line of skin care products and opened the Connie Stevens Garden Sanctuary Day Spa in Los Angeles. Both ventures were enormously successful and launched a second career for Connie as the head of a cosmetics empire.

It appears that Connie Stevens' ownership of the buggy Rolls marked the point in her life when her luck turned around. Likewise, after the car was in my possession I, too entered a new phase of my career that was blessed with success far beyond what I had enjoyed in my prior business. Could it be that a ratty old wreck of a Rolls was actually a good luck charm? I'm not prepared to say, but I do know this much for sure: If I ever attend any more charity auctions, I'll be sure to steer clear of any vintage vehicles—unless they've been fully checked out by an exterminator!

CHAPTER SEVENTEEN

MY DESERT SERENADE

Oh my desert, I come to thee; on a stallion shod with fire;
and the winds are left behind; in the speed of my desire.

Bayard Taylor

The lure of the desert is a difficult thing to explain. The harsh terrain, the blistering summers, and the frigid nights do not normally inspire lust or even affection in man or beast. Yet, to me, there's something celestial about a desert sunset and something impeccably peaceful about an incandescent starlit desert night. Like the haunting ballads of sailors drawn to the sea, I have likewise often been driven to say: "I must go down to the desert again. To the lonely hills and the sky." The simple fact is that I love the desert.

Like many tawdry love affairs, this one began with a motel. It was 1957 and I had owned my construction company for about two years. I received a call from one of my subcontractors—a decent fellow I regularly used to provide me with concrete foundations and footings.

"Bob, I just bought a piece of land out in the desert," he began.

"I understand land's pretty cheap out there in the Coachella Valley," I replied.

"Oh yeah," he said. "I got a pretty good deal and now I want you to help me develop it."

"What do you have in mind?" I asked.

"I've got some plans for a 36-unit motel and I'd like to talk to you about building it."

"Where exactly is the property?" I asked.

"It's on the northern tip of the valley. Right in Palm Springs," he answered.

Although I'd never built anything in the desert before—it gets extremely hot during the summer, I had heard—like everyone else, I had also heard of Palm Springs.

Back before the dozens of "always green" golf courses sprung up there, Palm Springs was, for many years, a safe haven for victims of hay fever, bronchitis, emphysema and asthma. Sufferers would travel there from around the globe to take in the pure air and healthful climate. Palm Springs, at that time, was also making a name for itself as something of a celebrity playground with the likes of Frank Sinatra, Bob Hope, Dean Martin, Perry Como and other luminaries calling it home. Lucille Ball and Desi Arnaz had just finished developing the Thunderbird Heights community in Rancho Mirage that would become home to future president Gerald Ford. The tract had recently lent its name to Ford's new sports car, the Thunderbird, just as Palm Desert's Eldorado Country Club had done with GM's top-of-the-line Cadillac.

The concrete contractor informed me that his lot was located at 350 Chino Canyon Road and he gave me some driving directions. After driving out to have a peek, I submitted a bid for the project and it was quickly accepted. For commercial projects like this one, I would often serve as not only the general contractor but also as the onsite superintendent. In this role it was necessary for me to visit the site once a week to verify that all materials had been properly provided and to oversee the job's progress.

On one of my earliest visits, I headed over to the site to inspect the foundation that was to be poured that day. When I arrived at the site I was in for a shock. There was no foundation anywhere in sight. Not only that, the land had not been cleared and there were no concrete crew workers to be found at all. "Now, this is strange," I thought to myself. Just then I heard the unmistakable rumble of a concrete mixer truck barreling down the road. I turned to see one of the owner's concrete trucks heading away from my location.

I quickly jumped in my car and followed the truck as it turned south on Via Norte and then made a left onto a street called Vista Chino, a major east-west street running through the heart of Palm Springs parallel to Chino Canyon. The cement mixer pulled onto another vacant lot where I could see the ground had been prepped for the pouring of a concrete slab. Once I saw the street address, and saw that it was 350—the same street number as our site—I immediately understood what had happened. Because of the similarity of the street names and their close proximity, the concrete crew had started to build on the right number, but on the wrong street.

All this was just sinking in as I observed the cement mixer begin to churn and the chute open up as it was aimed at the wooden molds that had been constructed to shape the foundation slab. I stood there in horror as I realized they were about to dump twenty tons of concrete onto somebody else's property. I ran towards the mixer with a rolled up set of blueprints in my hand, waving my arms wildly and yelling for them to stop at the top of my lungs. The noise of the mixer made it impossible for anyone to hear me.

"You're in the wrong spot!" I screamed, but the crew chief didn't know who I was and he couldn't make out what I was saying. In desperation, I opened up the plans and pointed dramatically towards the name and address at the bottom of the first page.

"Chino Canyon! Chino Canyon!" I mouthed while pointing to the printed address. I dragged him by the arm down to the corner and pointed to the street sign that clearly read Vista Chino. Aha! I had finally gotten through the fellow's hardhat and he quickly brought the proceedings to a halt.

What if I had arrived an hour later? Or, the following day? I didn't have any set schedule. I'd go down and visit the site whenever I could get away. If I had not shown up exactly when I did, the crew would have poured the slab onto some stranger's property. What a nightmare goof that would have been to try and correct. As it was, we still had to foot the cost of restoring the erroneous lot back to its original condition. I felt as though a guardian angel was looking out for me that day. In fact, I began to feel that way every time I ventured into the desert.

Before the motel job was finished, I was hooked. I began to bring my friends and family out to Palm Springs on weekends and pretty soon the area began to feel like our second home. We would typically stay at the very motel I had built, called "Tuscany Manor," on Chino Canyon. I began to seek out construction projects in the area simply because I wanted an excuse to come out to the desert more often.

The intensity of this love affair had reached a point that by 1973 I felt compelled to purchase a Palm Springs condo where our family could stay during our weekend getaways. We located a lovely place, but were put off by what I considered to be the "way too high" price tag of $33,000. "Hell, I could build one for much less than that," I thought to myself. Of course, building a single unit condo that far from home didn't make much sense, so we took a deep breath and plunked down the money. And that's when the fun really began to kick in.

The following years were rich with memories forged in our Coachella Shangri-La. The kids loved the place and couldn't wait to head down to the condo for some great times. Parties and friendly get-togethers were common, often to celebrate a road trip visit from some faraway friends. Even though I balked at the price when we had first purchased the place, I ultimately wound up selling it at a healthy profit some seven years later. It wasn't that I was such a savvy real estate investor—after all, this was the first property I'd ever bought in the desert. No, it's just that our place, like many others, got swept up in one of the fastest-growing population explosions in the country. With the number of residents in the area increasing so rapidly, housing was always at a premium and, by getting in early, I was able to take advantage of a true sellers' market.

By 1980 we felt that having ready access to golf and tennis facilities would truly enhance our desert experience and so we looked into buying a new condo in a country club community. After some exploration, we wound up settling at The Springs Country Club in Rancho Mirage. It was love at first stroke and to prove the point we wound up living there for the next twelve years.

In 1992 we once again picked up stakes, but we didn't move very far. We were attracted to a new, upgraded community that had been erected across the street from The Springs called Morningside. The same people who built and managed The Springs had opened the new development and it shared its predecessor's high level of architectural excellence and classic ambience. But, Morningside offered new spacious homes sitting right on the golf course with even more attractive amenities.

Becoming part of the desert community fueled my passion for land development. I could see great potential here because of the marvelous climate and the wide availability of raw land. These were wonderful years, filled with a steady flow of exciting and enriching times for our family. But I began to look beyond that aspect and started thinking of the desert as a place of opportunity for my company. Let's face it. I was a land junkie. I had to have sites to develop or I'd simply go nuts. And the desert seemed like the best place to feed my frenzy.

Back home in Orange County during this period, my time was primarily consumed with the Waterfront Project in Huntington Beach. The development was in its infancy and I was, at this time, embroiled in a lawsuit with the City. Actually, there wasn't much for me to do at this point. The team of attorneys who represented me was handling the entire discovery, depositions and other aspects of the litigation. I had a lot of spare time on my hands and soon found myself feeling restless. I was used to a lot of action in the fast-break world of real estate and all the dreary legal wrangling was really grinding me down. I needed a new challenge.

"Why not start another business?" I asked myself. I had recently sold the Mayer Construction Company, the business I had founded back in the 1950s. Included in the sale, along with all the assets of the firm, was its name. The buyer saw the value of the goodwill associated with our name and was keen on keeping it in place. I took this as a testimony to the sterling reputation Mayer Construction had earned over the years. But now I needed to come up with a new name for my new company. I didn't have to look too far. I dubbed the new company The Robert Mayer Corporation and that's still the name it bears today. While not very descriptive of the company's exact operations, it seemed to fill the bill since it was really a "one man operation" at the time. This would be the company that would develop The Waterfront as well as other southland projects, and it also gave me the chance to seek out and acquire new commercial and residential opportunities in the desert area.

The population explosion was raging throughout the Coachella Valley at this point. I felt strong indications that land values were going to skyrocket, especially in areas east of Palm Springs, such as

Palm Desert, Rancho Mirage, Indio and the other communities that found themselves in the path of the surging migration patterns.

This unmatched growth has not slowed down to this day. While the population of Riverside County grew from 80,000 in 1980 to 185,000 in 1990, it stands at over 400,000 today in 2008. And there's no slowdown in sight. Experts predict that the population will rise to 600,000 by the end of the next decade and top 1 million by the middle of the century.

During my semi-retirement period in the early 80s, I was really not interested in constructing buildings other than The Waterfront anymore. Because I was spending all my weekends in the desert, I became enthusiastic about acquiring raw non-entitled land. Before such property could be sold off or developed, it would have to go through a zoning and entitlement process. Eventually, nearly every one of these "desert deals" turned out to be a winner. I did have to wait a bit longer with some of them as the real estate market went through its normal up and down cycles. But eventually I got them re-zoned and succeeded in selling them off to builders who erected homes, condos, office parks and shopping malls on the sites. This entire process shifted the focus of The Robert Mayer Corporation from construction to land development.

On several of the desert properties I would enter into a 50-50 joint venture with a builder allowing me to capitalize on his future success on my site. What was so amazing about such deals is that they were structured exactly like the very first agreements I put together with backers like Johnny Nisser, in the days when I was just getting started. Only this time my role was reversed. Instead of being the builder, I was the land provider. I would receive 100% of the revenue stream produced by the project until I had been paid in full for the land. From that point on, I would receive fifty percent of the profits when the property was sold.

The builders loved this agreement since they received the land from me on spec with only a small cash outlay, and were able to borrow most of the cost of construction from the bank. They had very little in the way of out-of-pocket expense to deal with. I liked the arrangement since I was paid for the land in full before the builder received any portion of the profits. I also became an equal partner with the builder and received the same amount of profit as he did. It was a great deal for everyone concerned as long as the properties were properly developed with capable partners.

That is not to say that such deals were free of risk. On the contrary, there was enormous risk that the finished projects would not sell as quickly as anticipated. That situation would mean I'd have to endure having my land investment tied up for longer than I would have liked. Likewise, if the finished project did not fetch the anticipated price, because of reversals in the real estate market or other factors beyond our control, the builder and I could wind up taking a haircut with little or no profit to split between us.

The truth is that when a project was successful, it was very successful. Just like baseball, one home run could offset several strike outs. This was, once again, the same old risk vs. reward scenario being played out, just as it invariably does in all real estate ventures. I'm pleased to report that we encountered very few strike outs and that only a handful of our deals turned out to be non-profitable. It's all a percentage game, after all. Anyone who claims not to have encountered any failures in the real estate market is either not doing anything in the business or they're not telling the whole truth. No one can predict with 100% certainly what will happen to real estate values down the road, or whether there will be a future demand for their product. As a developer or builder, one attempts to guess right most of the time. As long as you can maintain a positive batting average over time, you'll make it. Those who do not will not survive for long in this high-risk game and will soon be retired to the dugout.

In summary, my love for the desert wound up changing my early retirement plans and set me on a new course as it redefined my company. All of our projects since 1980, when Mayer Construction Company was sold, have been carried out by The Robert Mayer Corporation (TRMC). That includes those in the desert, Los Angeles, Orange County, and other areas of Southern California. Our main headquarters are located in Newport Beach, just five minutes from my home and only a two hour drive to my second home, and my other love, the desert.

Even today, I still enjoy the drive into that rarefied arid atmosphere. You begin to notice the giant wind fans spinning as you approach the huge dinosaur props that were used in the film "Pee Wee's Big Adventure." A short drive down Kirk Douglas Way in Palm Springs leads you to the center of town. If you drive further east into Rancho Mirage, you can have lunch at The River, followed by a stroll through the trendy, hip boutiques that line the streets along El Paseo Drive, in this melting pot called the Coachella Valley. The San Andreas Fault crosses the valley from the Chocolate Mountains in the south along the Little San Bernadino Mountains. It is visible as a strip of greenery set against these otherwise bare summits against a blue sky. It stands as a reminder of our own frailty and the ephemeral nature of all we build. A slight tectonic shift and everything I've ever helped to construct in this area could come crashing down like a toothpick pagoda. However, that possibility has had little impact on the minds and hearts of the residents and visitors living in this beautiful valley.

Some people refer to this region as The Inland Empire and the valley itself is sometimes labeled The Desert Empire. But such imperial designations do not resonate with me. From where I sit, the desert will forever be a seductress, a coquette, a secret lover and that is why I will continue to sing her praises long, long into the night.

CHAPTER EIGHTEEN

ITS GOTTA BE GOLF

*Golf is a game whose aim is to hit a very small ball into a even smaller hole,
with weapons singularly ill-designed for the purpose.*

Winston Churchill

Will Rogers, the great American humorist, used to say that the income tax had made more liars out of people than even golf had done. In both areas, there is somebody always looking over your shoulder to keep you honest. I read once that the word "golf" dates back to the early days when it was a "men only" pastime and that it really is an acronym for: "Gentlemen Only—Ladies Forbidden." If that ever was true, I'm certainly glad it isn't that way today. I would prefer a different acronym. It should stand for the four things I love most about the game: **G**ood times, **O**pen air, **L**aughter and **F**un.

I do have a real passion for the game, but in a lifetime of playing, I have never managed to conquer the courses. My performance on the links has never been stellar. My scores ranged from the mid-90s to the low-100s and if it weren't for the handicap system that allows a mediocre golfer to compete with a top player on an equal footing, I probably would have given up the game years ago.

There is something breathtaking about the architectural splendor of a professionally designed desert golf course. With its dark green fescue fairways and bent-grass greens, its meandering palm trees, exotic fountains and man-made lakes and waterfalls, a Palm Springs golf course is a feast for the senses and a walker's wonderland. A golfer cannot help but be moved by the sight of manicured beds filled with multi-colored flowers that accent the course's borders and walkways. Played against a backdrop of a distant mountain range silhouetted against a deep azure sky, the game takes on a transcendent quality that enriches the soul and revitalizes the spirit.

But beyond the physical delights, what I find most appealing about the pastime is its social dimension. Golf truly is more of an exercise in friendship than in fitness. Bound under the banner of friendly competition, we set off together in our electric golf cart on a quest for that little white ball. As a good golfer, you don't merely compete against other duffers, you also compete against yourself by always trying to improve your game and exceed your personal best. The game requires both consistency and skill. And of the two, consistency is the more difficult to sustain. Your shots will fly long, far, and true on one day and, on the next, you'll have trouble keeping the ball on the fairway. This lack of consistency on my part led to some rather embarrassing moments over the years.

The most extreme case took place early in my golf career on the exclusive and private O'Donnell 9-hole golf course, tucked right up against the San Jacinto Mountain range in Palm Springs. This historic par-35 course was designed by Tom O'Donnell in 1925. It was one of the first courses ever built in the area and today sits majestically in downtown Palm Springs. Although it is restricted to members, sponsored guests are welcomed. I had always dreamed about trying out this short layout course and thanks to a friend who was a member, I would get my chance. My friend had convinced the golf pro to allow me to play the course as a favor to him. I was instructed to come around late in the day when most of the members were gone and I'd be allowed to hit a few balls down some of the course's fairways.

"Should I wait for a foursome," I asked the resident golf pro as soon as I arrived.

"Naw, just go out by yourself, and try it out," he advised.

The O'Donnell course contains some of the narrowest fairways I'd ever come across. Each fairway is laid out parallel to the next one and facing in the opposite direction. If your ball goes astray, there's not much rough and it's easy to land your ball on the adjacent fairway. I went out and did my best to keep my shots straight and true, but I was hitting long and darn if that ball didn't keep winding up in the neighboring fairway where a few golfers were trying to play. To make matters even worse, due to the course layout, those other golfers were always heading directly towards me.

Before I knew it, an angry golf pro came barreling up to me in his supercharged golf cart. He hopped out and began to admonish me: "Listen, pal. You're a wild and dangerous hitter," he shouted. "Would you do me a big favor and get the hell off of my golf course!" I picked up my clubs, placed my tail between my legs, and slithered out of there like a whipped puppy. I had dreamed for years about playing this famous course, and now look. Here I was being thrown off the grounds just because I couldn't keep my drives from hooking and slicing. This truly was one of my life's most embarrassing moments. I left determined to work on straightening out my drives. Over the coming years, I learned how to keep my shots a bit straighter and even entered several of the celebrity tournaments.

One of the many tournaments centered in Palm Springs is the Dinah Shore Women's Golf Tournament. This is a four-day championship event, but during the first two days, professional women golfers are teamed with amateur male golfers like me, along with celebrities from television, movies and the sports world. It's really astounding how coordinated those baseball and football athletes are, even when their main sport is something other than golf. We would compete in mixed foursomes with a woman pro, a celebrity, and two amateurs. I found it absolutely amazing to observe how these petite, thin, world-class champion women could consistently hit their balls straight down the center of the fairway at least 100 yards beyond where my ball would end up. These romps were great fun—and a truly humbling experience.

On the other end of the spectrum, my most thrilling golf experience took place on a long 200-yard par three hole situated over a lake. I could only reach the green with a driver and so I selected "Big Ugly" at the tee. "Big Ugly" was a driver that I had purchased out of desperation after reading some ads in the back of a golfing magazine. Billed as "The Hacker's Lifesaver," I had laid down good money for this unusually shaped monstrosity in the hopes that it would improve my game. Well, it never did. I had decided to retire the darn thing and admit that I had been conned by the slick advertising. As I stood on the tee, cursing "Big Ugly" to the heavens, I came to a decision: "I am sick and tired of this worthless club and if I don't get at least a decent shot somewhere near the green this one last time, I'm going to pitch it right into the lake!"

As I stretched out my backswing and then let go with all my strength, I was rewarded with a very satisfying "Thwack" and I knew that I had given the ball a solid hit. I watched the ball fly over the lake, but I did not see it hit the green. Not all of the green was visible from the tee. "It must have rolled off the back of the green," I said to my foursome partners. When I got to the green and looked around, it was nowhere to be found.

"Found it," exclaimed one of my colleagues as he bent over and plucked something out of the cup. It was my ball. Unbelievable! I gasped as I took in the fact that I had just scored the very first hole-in-one of my life and I had never even seen the ball fall into the cup. You could have knocked me over with a one iron. And, to top it off, I had used my despised "Big Ugly"—a club I had every intention of pitching that day. Needless to say, I hung on to "Big Ugly," mainly for sentimental reasons. It never brought me any more holes-in-one. In fact, it didn't help my game at all after that, but I kept it around merely to remind me how thoroughly happy I had felt on that one-in-a-million day.

The great PGA champion, Jimmy Demaret, once said that golf and sex are about the only two things you can enjoy without being good at them. Well, I don't know about the latter, but I must say he was right about golf. The game has given me countless hours of enjoyment, despite the fact that I am certainly not a great player. But even now, I harbor intentions of improving my game and I'm still looking for my second hole-in-one. A true golfer never gives up hope.

And speaking of hope, permit me to close with an observation that Bob Hope, perhaps Palm Springs' most well-known and beloved golfer, once made:

"If you watch a game, it's fun. If you play at it, it's recreation. But if you work at it, it's gotta be golf!"

CHAPTER NINETEEN

THE WATERFRONT PROJECT

To win without risk is to triumph without glory.

El Cid, 1636

ACQUISITION

The acquisition of a 50-acre oceanfront parcel of land that ultimately became known as "The Waterfront" is a fascinating saga unto itself. My decision to purchase the parcel was the beginning of a journey that has spanned over thirty years. While it has taken much longer than I had ever envisioned, at the same time, it has produced results far more impressive than any I had ever thought possible.

The tale begins one Thursday in 1978 as I was working in my Downey office. I picked up the phone and listened as a real estate broker began droning on about a piece of property in nearby Huntington Beach. Since this broker had previously sent me on a couple of wild goose chases, I was preparing to ignore the call and hang up. But before I could say: "Not interested," the broker explained that because of a bankruptcy proceeding, the property was going to be placed on the auction block the following Tuesday morning. I decided to keep listening. As he went on to describe the location of the oceanfront site, I recalled my experiences as a kid in Huntington Beach, sitting around bonfires on the shore, enjoying marshmallow roasts, and engaging in grunion runs along the scenic coastline. It was those memories that prompted me to go have a look.

The site consisted of 50 acres of land fronting on Pacific Coast Highway and enjoyed a half-mile of ocean frontage from Beach Boulevard running northwest towards the Pier. In terms of improvements, there wasn't much to look at: An old derelict motel, a 239-pad mobile home park, a rundown 9-hole "pitch-and-putt" golf course, an abandoned Texaco gas station, a small beach parking lot, some wetlands and a city-owned beach maintenance yard. Drawing upon the memories of those youthful sweet summer evenings, I was able to somehow look past the current urban decay and visualize how this very well situated piece of property could be successfully redeveloped. This place had true potential, I thought to myself. Without hesitation, I drove down to City Hall in Huntington Beach the next morning to read over the land lease that would control the property. After reviewing the terms, I decided I would definitely attend the auction and attempt to acquire this "dream property."

The land lease had been in effect since 1963 between the City and the original developer who had built the motel, golf course and mobile home park, but who had allowed them to fall into disrepair and had ended up in bankruptcy. Back in 1963, the City had an interest in getting the site developed, and so the lease contained very favorable terms intended to entice a developer to erect those improvements. This "sweet lease" was set to expire in the year 2013.

I would be bidding only on the leasehold interest that entitled the holder to the right to operate the existing businesses. As the purchaser I would receive all rental payments made by the on-site businesses during the remaining thirty-five years of the lease. But, at the expiration of the lease in 2013, the land plus ownership of the existing buildings would revert back to the City. At that point I, or my heirs, would be required to surrender any interests we held at the site back to the City of Huntington Beach.

The rent payable to the City as specified in the original lease was fixed at roughly $97,000 per year and would remain essentially the same except for very slight increases over the balance of the term unless the use of the property changed. That provision would be key to this entire purchase. With this in mind, and since the rent was quite reasonable, I decided to move ahead. I calculated that the worst-case scenario would have me merely running the existing mobile home park, golf course and motel until 2013, and then walking away at the expiration of the lease. At that time I would have enjoyed a modest but reasonable return on my original investment for thirty-five years. With this scenario as my downside, I felt comfortable enough to begin thinking about the possible upside.

As I stood surveying the land, I began to picture populating the site with multi-story office buildings, condominiums, hotels and other commercial projects that could increase the value of the property, both for the City and for myself. If I could come up with viable alternate uses during the term of the lease — uses well beyond the existing assortment of low-rent businesses — then this parcel could yield untold benefits. To accomplish this, of course, would require the cooperation of the City. I felt they might look favorably on redevelopment as long as they were able to participate in that future upside. Once my redevelopment plans were implemented, the City would be collecting much more than the current $97,000 annual rental fee. Instead, they would be collecting millions.

It was my hope that the City would agree to scrap the existing lease and replace it with a much longer-term agreement that would make future redevelopment a realistic possibility. If the City would not renegotiate the lease, the property would remain in its blighted condition for the next thirty-five years and the City would lose the financial benefits that could accrue under a redevelopment plan. I began to get excited as I pondered the possibilities. With such a negotiated agreement in hand, the opportunities for developing this property loomed very large—as did the risks.

Setting aside my dreams and apprehensions, I began to prepare for the auction. According to the auction rules, every bid had to be accompanied by a cashier's check equal to at least ten percent of the increase over the previous bid. In anticipation of Tuesday morning's auction, I went to the bank on Monday and purchased individual cashiers checks in various amounts and each one payable to the bankruptcy court. I did not wish for any of the other bidders to know how many checks I had brought since this would tip them off as to how badly I wanted the property.

On the day of the auction, I stuffed all the inside pockets of my jacket with the cashier's checks. I wasn't sure how many other bidders there would be, but I did feel that most of them would be basing their bids on the income generated by the existing facilities on the site. They would value the property in the standard way, as a multiple of projected cash flow. I was hoping that I might be the only bidder willing to pay enough money to purchase the leasehold interest based not upon what it would produce today, but upon what it could produce tomorrow. Would I be the only bidder who viewed the property in its run-down condition and be willing to gamble that it really had the potential for redevelopment? I certainly hoped so.

As the bidding got underway, I countered each bid with one just a bit higher. Each time my bid increased, I had another cashier's check ready to cover the 10% down payment requirement. I quietly pulled out a check from my pocket, already made out in the correct amount, and handed it to the judge. The other bidders, seeing the price rise above their cut-off threshold, began dropping out of the bidding one by one. It was clear that none of the bidders based their bids upon anything more than the property's current cash flow. As things turned out, I became the successful bidder and ended up with the rights to acquire the leasehold estate, which included a claim on whatever income it produced until the year 2013.

What happened next was so bizarre and unexpected that it left me absolutely unprepared for the shock. After the auction, the City decided to file suit against me. They argued that I had not complied with the regulations governing the auction. If the sale could be rescinded, the City would inherit my position since they were the legal owners of the land itself.

I spent the next three years tangled in litigation with the City of Huntington Beach. During this time, I continued to operate the existing business uses on the property. Since I did not know if I would win or lose the lawsuit, I was reluctant to spend the kind of money it would take to bring the property up to the standards I had hoped for. That money would be wasted if the City were to be successful in winning this lawsuit. Also, during this period, I was not in a position to approach the City with my redevelopment plans since we were now opposing litigants in an unpleasant court case. My grand plan had been placed on hold.

The case went all the way to the U.S. Court of Appeals, Ninth Circuit. In the final outcome, the court determined that the auction of the leasehold interest had been conducted properly and legally and that I did not violate any of the auction's protocols in acquiring the rights. In other words, I won the case. I was finally awarded the clear right to lease the property until 2013—a right I thought I had paid for in full some three years earlier.

When Steve Bone joined me in 1985, the lawsuit was behind us, so we began to formulate, on paper, the ideas we had been considering for the long-term development of the site. Our objective was to illustrate to the City that in order to accomplish our goal, it would be necessary for us to be granted a much longer lease term than we currently held. The amount of capital required for the building projects we drafted demanded that our company enjoy revenue rights for many years beyond the current lease term in order to realize a realistic return on our investments. By granting us those long-term rights, the City would be benefiting itself, we argued, in numerous important ways.

First of all, the annual rental revenue would be increased to a much higher level, bringing needed revenue into the City's coffers. And, secondly, the development of new hotels, office parks, and condo communities would lead to an overall economic renaissance for a town that had heretofore been known primarily as a surfer's hangout. Convincing the leaders of the City of Huntington Beach of the wisdom of this course became a protracted struggle that eventually and happily ended in enormous success in 1987 when the City agreed to enter into a new lease agreement with us.

As things currently stand, each commercial improvement on the property carries its own 99-year lease with the clock starting on the day construction is completed. For example, the Hilton hotel, completed seventeen years ago, has 82 years remaining on its lease. At the end of those leases, the property and its improvements will revert back to the City.

Huntington Beach has been richly rewarded for its willingness to extend the terms of our lease. Instead of a flat annual rental fee, the City now holds an equity position and is paid based upon the performance of each component. They also enjoy new revenue from sales and property taxes. The urban renewal we sparked has vastly transformed the image of Huntington Beach to that of an upscale resort community. The renaissance I described early on has now begun to take shape and Huntington Beach is fast becoming a vital business conference destination as well as a sought-after retirement community. What appeared to be a huge risk so many years ago—the development of my storied boyhood playground—has today resulted in a true win-win situation for us, the developers, and for the City.

The property today, known simply as The Waterfront, was one of the last remaining large parcels of oceanfront land in Southern California to be developed. It is finally nearing completion as the final piece of the vision falls into place.

The next few sections of this chapter describe the actual development of each of The Waterfront's phases. When compared to any of my other endeavors over the years, it is the project that carried the greatest likelihood of failure. Yet, it turned out to be the most successful one of all and was unquestionably worth the risk.

The Hilton Waterfront
Beach Resort

Since the legal agreement had been reached with the City of Huntington Beach and the court case was firmly behind us, we could finally start the decision making process that would guide the actual development of the first new structure to occupy our freshly-acquired property. Should it be a residential project, a commercial project, or some other type of structure that could take advantage of the site's half-mile oceanfront location? Since there were no height limits in place at the time, our first thoughts were "Why not build a high-rise project and benefit from the numerous ocean views that it would afford?"

But, in the mid-eighties, Huntington Beach was a Surf City with crowds of youthful board riders and bikini-clad girls roaming its fabulous golden beach. It was a little premature for a sophisticated 20 to 30-story multi-use project, containing hotels, offices and retail, as one might find in New York City or dotting the length of Miami Beach. It was simply too early in the redevelopment cycle of the City at that time. We also feared that it would be difficult, if not impossible, to convince a lender that Huntington Beach was the magnificent location we believed it someday could be. And without the faith and financial support of a lender, nothing would ever get off the ground.

The original plan consisted of four hotels on the front twenty-five acres along the ocean and a residential component of 875 smaller units on the rear twenty-five acres north of the hotels. Development of these hotels and homes served as the lynchpin of our proposal to the City. As values rose, we reduced the number of homes to 184 and the hotels from four to three. Over the next several years, Steve and I decided that, although risky, a mid-rise 12-story hotel might be the best use for the first phase of development along the ocean. So we put together the plans for the erection of a new Hilton hotel and got down to work.

During the redevelopment process, we encountered a series of very difficult challenges. They came at us one right after the other.

We first had to contend with the existing uses still located on the site. This included the abandoned gas station, the small motel, the miniature golf course, the 239-coach mobile home community, the beach parking lot, the wetlands and the beach maintenance yard. The coaches had been occupied for many years by tenants who, while paying only a nominal rent, had been enjoying a prime beachfront location. We saw no problem with tearing down the rundown motel, leveling the abandoned gas station, and ripping out the rundown golf course, but eliminating the fully occupied mobile home park was a different story entirely. In order to eliminate it, the park first had to be vacated. We could induce tenants to move, but in doing so we needed to comply with City ordinances that called for us to provide relocation fees.

We decided to offer the tenants a relocation plan that turned out to be so generous that we had to actually hold a lottery to see which residents would be lucky enough to first receive our relocation jackpot. A limited number of residents were moved to a new mobile home park built for them adjacent to the City's central park and the rest received many times more than what their coaches were worth. Fortunately for us, our need for the entire mobile park portion was not immediate and this fact allowed us some breathing room. We were able to offer the relocation plan to one group at a time spread over a period of several years during construction of the various phases of the project.

On top of these relocation issues, we were now facing a general recession. The financial markets in 1988 and 1989 were favorable and allowed for adequate construction financing for the 300-room Hilton hotel we were erecting. But all that changed by 1990, just as the building was finally nearing completion. Typically at the closing of a construction phase, a permanent loan is established and its proceeds used to pay off the construction note and any outstanding interim bridge loans. For this to happen, however, there must be a lender willing to issue the permanent financing. No such lender could be located. We found ourselves, instead, facing a sharp downturn in the construction industry and a real tightening of the money supply as the economy slipped into a recession. Many long nights of midnight negotiations allowed us enough time for things to loosen up a bit.

We eventually located a permanent lender in 1995 who, after being assured of some very generous terms, agreed to pay off the outstanding debts incurred by the project. So there we were. Keeping the wolf from the door with one hand while shuffling mobile park dwellers with the other. It was a stressful time, but finally things appeared to be progressing according to plan. But, just as we overcame this hurdle, we found another one standing in the shadows.

We were beginning to think that our ship had finally come in, when, in reality, we were still very much at sea.

On February 7, 1990, less than a year after the Exxon Valdez created the worst oil tanker spill in history, dumping more than 11 million gallons onto the shores of Alaska, the steam oil tanker American Trader followed suit while anchored off the shore of Huntington Beach. The ship was within sight of our newly completed hotel, perched along the horizon and appearing to be lazily moored at anchor. Actually it was parked in water that was much too shallow. It had just received 400,000 gallons of Alaska North Slope crude oil from a larger vessel, the Keystone Canyon in Long Beach, and was now unloading its cargo into the underwater pipelines that would channel the black gold back to the Golden West terminal, not far from Huntington Beach. Suddenly a barrage of ocean swells pummeled the Trader, causing it to collide with its own anchor, thereby punching two holes in the starboard cargo tank. As a result, nearly a half-million gallons of oil were spilled into the Pacific, affecting sixty square miles of ocean and contaminating fourteen miles of recreational beaches—including the beach in front of the Hilton. Wildlife, birds, and marine life were severely impacted as the oil spill reached Bosa Chica, one of Southern California's largest nature preserves. This accident prompted the California Legislature to enact the Oil Spill Prevention and Response Act and is today considered one of the worst oil spills ever to hit California. It took several years before the impact of that disaster was no longer being felt by the Hilton, and it would take another fifteen years of litigation before a settlement was reached with our insurance company regarding the damages we suffered due to that unforeseen disaster.

None of these challenges were easy to overcome. They tested our will on a daily basis. There were many difficult moments during and after the completion of our first hotel at The Waterfront. But, the Hilton did survive and eventually began to thrive. It performed so well, that we began to visualize another, even more magnificent, hotel facility on another portion of the site.

Hyatt Regency
Resort and Spa

A fter a number of years of operating the Hilton Waterfront Beach Resort, we embarked upon the planning of a second hotel for the complex. We had originally imagined an urban resort similar to what you might find at an exotic tropical destination, but ours would be in the middle of a heavily populated area along the Orange County coast.

Instead of building twelve stories, as we had done with the Hilton, the new hotel was to be only four stories high, yet still contain an impressive 517 guest rooms located above a 1,000-car subterranean parking structure. The hotel complex would be spread out over fifteen acres and feature the type of luxurious ambience you might find at a Caribbean or Hawaiian Rock Resort. This was going to be something totally new for Southern California and Hyatt Regency was going to help us create it.

We initiated negotiations with the Pritzker family and the Hyatt organization to fashion a workable joint business venture. It was agreed that Hyatt and the Pritzkers would provide some capital beyond what our company had already invested and would manage the completed hotel. We would contribute the land and the expertise to oversee the construction phase. It was a great partnership that benefited both parties.

The architectural firm of Wimberly Allison Tong & Goo (WATG) is one of the most respected designers of resort hotels in the world. They did an outstanding job in designing the Hilton, so we again commissioned them to do the plans for our new project.

Two years, and thousands of critical decisions later, the Huntington Beach Hyatt Regency Resort and Spa at The Waterfront was completed and opened its doors amid fanfare and flourish and, thankfully, began generating a positive cash flow immediately.

The Resort sports a distinctive lighthouse bridge that crosses Pacific Coast Highway and connects the hotel to the beach. The Hyatt today stands along the Southern California coastline as one of the nation's most outstanding examples of Andalusian architecture—the type indigenous to the picturesque southern region of Spain. The Hyatt is not only a stunning sight to behold, but like the Hilton Waterfront only a block away, it has also proven to be a financial success.

THE WATERFRONT
RESIDENTIAL COMMUNITIES
SEA COVE AND SEA COLONY

During the negotiations with the City of Huntington Beach for the development of The Waterfront complex, we were never entirely comfortable with the fact that the entire 50-acre property was under a lease that could make future development difficult—especially residential development. To us, it seemed that the logical plan for the rear twenty-five acres should call for housing, rather than commercial, construction. But, on leased land?

Building and selling residential units on leased lots was risky. There had been several prior projects over the years in Orange County that had tried this and suffered serious problems due to the fact that the homeowners did not actually own the land under their homes. In addition to their mortgage payments, homeowners were therefore required to make monthly payments to a separate entity that was supposed to aggregate the money and forward it on to the owner of the land. This multi-step process often led to problems.

Since our twenty-five acres were located just north of our two hotels, we realized that most of the homes would have little or no ocean view. However, residents would enjoy a close proximity to the beach, a mere five to six hundred feet, and this fact was a tremendously important selling point.

After many more months of negotiation with the City, and a good share of legal wrangling, we completed an agreement that allowed us to obtain clear ownership of this 25-acre portion of the site. The deal called for us to pay the City an initial purchase price for the land and granted them a share of our profits as we developed a community composed of 184 condominium units. We planned to build and market the homes in several different floor plan configurations, and the City received a percentage on each unit that was sold.

Because our company was no longer in the actual home construction business, we formed a joint venture with two separate well-known builders who would then physically build the units. They each believed they had a product that could be easily developed over the following two years. Our timing could not have been better. We entered the market just as property values began to climb in 2003 and managed to sell our last home before things began going the other way in late 2007. The homes sold at competitive yet realistic prices that succeeded in attracting buyers, yet allowed for a reasonable return for the builders, for the City, and for our company.

In summary, during the 1990s, we completed construction of the 300-room Hilton Waterfront Beach Resort along the ocean and continued planning out the balance of the 50-acre site. During the late 90s and early 2000s, we completed the 517-room Hyatt Regency on its fifteen-acre site, and constructed and sold 184 residential units located on the northerly portion of the property. The last remaining commercial portion of The Waterfront is a three-and-one-half-acre parcel located between the Hyatt and the Hilton. The final phase of this portion of the project is still in the planning stages. We will, in all likelihood, soon break ground at this site for the creation of another hotel with completion projected about 24 months later.

A wag once said that when all is said and done, more has usually been said than done. That certainly is not the case with the Waterfront Project. If anything, it has delivered to the City of Huntington Beach much more than was promised and will continue doing so for decades to come. The Waterfront has turned into the life's work of my later years and I could not be more pleased with the outcome. Once completed, the development of this particular piece of my boyhood nostalgia will have taken over thirty years. This is amazing when you consider that the Great Pyramid of Giza took only twenty years to construct. Of course, they didn't have a Coastal Commission to deal with back then.

Chapter Twenty

The Steve Bone Story

---

*We are continually faced by great opportunities
brilliantly disguised as insoluble problems.*

Lee Iacocca

One of the hottest buzzwords of 1985—aside from Reaganomics, Aerobics, and Break Dancing—was "timeshare." This is a concept that was surging in popularity thanks to companies like RCI (Resort Condominium International) who offered buyers low-priced vacation homes that they could opt to occupy no more than two weeks out of each year. Participation in a timeshare program also entitled the condo owner the right to schedule a two-week stay at any of any of the other vacation homes in the network. The buyer was not merely buying a home in a fixed location, but in addition signing up for the opportunity to stay in different homes in premier destinations all around the world. Not surprisingly, Timeshare Fever swept through Las Vegas where we operated the Ambassador Inn Hotel. Naturally, I began to investigate the possibilities of cashing in on this craze by converting our hotel into a timeshare project.

At first blush, the numbers looked enticing. I could sell off the equity on a room-by-room basis while still collecting a healthy management fee. If the units sold out, I would enjoy a return many times greater than my cost basis in the hotel. I had already conducted some due diligence by researching the Las Vegas market as I looked further into the feasibility of this idea.

I was making the rounds, checking out some of the other comparable properties that had undergone a timeshare conversion, when I was introduced to Steve Bone. Steve was a Columbia law-school-educated lawyer from North Carolina who was living in Las Vegas temporarily. He had been brought in as a consultant by one of the city's major real estate developers to advise him about converting some of their hotels to timeshare properties. The two were discussing the possibility of Steve moving permanently to Las Vegas where the developer would be his client.

I asked Steve if he would be available to look at my situation and offer some recommendations and he kindly agreed. After some discussion and analysis, Steve and I concluded that the Ambassador Inn was not really well suited for timeshare use. Based upon research, I concluded my investigation and decided not to move ahead with any conversion plans.

During our discussions, I happened to mention to Steve that I also owned the property rights to a 50-acre oceanfront property in Southern California. I gave him a bit of the background and shared my feelings that the spot was ripe for redevelopment. I told Steve about the litigation with the City of Huntington Beach that had tied up any progress at the site for the past three years.

"If we can secure the City and Coastal Commission entitlements," I shared with him, "we'd be wide open to build a commercial project like a hotel or even something residential." Steve seemed genuinely interested and so he said "Yes" when I asked if wished to take a look at an aerial photo of the property. The large format image clearly showed the rooftops of all of the existing improvements on the site. Steve could see the small motel, the abandoned gas station, the nine-hole "Pitch & Putt" miniature golf course, and all the others. The photo did not really reveal the rundown disrepair into which these businesses had fallen. It did show the property's most attractive feature, however—its stunning half-mile of Pacific Ocean beach frontage.

After taking this all in, and after listening to me share my future vision of this property, Steve agreed that the spot held great potential and accepted my invitation to come to Huntington Beach and look at the property first hand.

A few days later, as I stood on the beach waiting for Steve to arrive, I visually surveyed the site for the hundredth time and once again used my imagination to construct a beautiful beachfront skyline in my mind's eye. Now that the lawsuit was behind us, the envisioned hotels and high rises appeared in much sharper focus. The day was bright and balmy as I greeted Steve with a handshake and a welcoming grin.

"Well, this is it, Steve," I said as I gestured broadly. "What do you think?"

"It looks wonderful, Bob," he replied. "I really believe that if all of the obstacles can be overcome the property has real potential."

I'm not sure, as I look back, if Steve knew at that moment how dramatically this meeting would change his life. He was on a course that was supposed to take him from his home in Charlotte to Las Vegas. Once he was established there, his wife, Patricia and their children were planning to follow him and relocate the family to Nevada. It now appeared, as we stood with our feet in the sand, that another destination just might be possible.

I explained to Steve that I wanted him to consider foregoing his current plans and join me in Southern California as part of our organization. I did not have to explain the obvious. The opportunity I was presenting to him was a far cry from the comfortable consultancy position he had been contemplating in Las Vegas. But

Steve also fully realized that by throwing in with me, he had a much greater upside than any "billable time" work he was looking at in Las Vegas. At the same time, it had a much more dangerous downside. What if we didn't get the necessary permits? What if we couldn't attract the necessary financing? What if….? I could see these concerns crossing his mind, but I do believe he saw, as I did, the great potential of this property.

As we parted ways, Steve agreed to give my offer the serious consideration a major decision of this type deserved. After discussions with his client in Las Vegas, his wife, and others, Steve made the tough decision. He decided to accept the risks and join our organization. Steve made it clear on day one that he was in for the long haul.

Even with Steve's help, it was going to be a long, hard struggle. It would take several years for the entitlement process to make it clear for what uses the land would be approved. Next came rounding up the financing and locating strategic partners and then several more years of construction before any real monetary results could be realized. A long haul it certainly was to be.

After only a few months, I could see that Steve was now as enthused about the project as I had always been. Once this fact became clear to me, I sat down with Steve and offered him an equity position in the project. Steve was more than pleased. We shook hands and from that day forward, Steve jumped in to what was to become the Waterfront Project with both feet.

Steve understood the importance of really being a part of the City in which we would be involved over the next few years. As a result he became involved in the civic and cultural life of Huntington Beach. Steve today is considered one of the city's prominent citizens. He is the founder of the Visitors and Convention Bureau, was the president of the local Chamber of Commerce, founder of the Orange County Film Commission and Tourism Council, and chairman of the Orange County Business Council.

It's now been over twenty years since Steve and I took that fateful walk on the beach and I am proud and pleased to say that I am impressed with the work he and his crack staff perform day after day. It is a testimony to Steve and his team: Shawn Millbern, Riley Robinson, Larry Brose and Larry Kleinschmidt.

Today, as the Waterfront Project nears its final stage of completion, it has produced success beyond any imagined by either of us back there on that beach. Part of the credit belongs to a man who was able to share my vision of the future's promise. His name is Steve Bone.

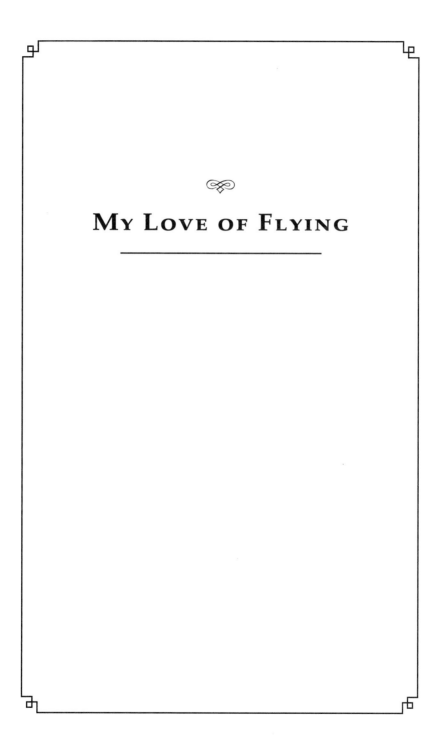

MY LOVE OF FLYING

CHAPTER TWENTY-ONE

LOVE IS IN THE AIR

I like flying at the right altitude because it gets you where you're going, fast.
But having the right attitude will get you to where you're going even faster.

Donald Trump

I fell in love with aviation at the kitchen table when I was just nine years old. As I would carefully piece together my prized aircraft models late into the night, I developed a strong passion for all things avionic. In those days modeling involved a bit more than merely gluing together mass produced pieces of injection-molded plastic. When you opened a model kit, out poured what looked like small pieces of scrap lumber. The challenge was following the blueprint-style instructions and thereby transforming that heap of balsa wood into something that would, in my young imagination, actually glide gracefully through the air.

I recall building a 1/16-scale replica of a Curtis Sparrowhawk biplane. By the time I finished shaping the struts and fashioning the 19-inch wingspan, I felt that I had gained a fundamental understanding of aerodynamics. The power source for my earliest balsa-wood and tissue paper creations was rubber. A simple twisted rubber band attached to a mini-propeller would push the plane skyward—for a little while.

A little later I graduated to gasoline powered engines. One of the first I recall was a Brown Junior Buccaneer that I finally succeeded in getting airborne after several unsuccessful takeoffs. I was amazed at how long it would stay aloft on just a tablespoon of gasoline. I built many different models over the years, including a Army Fighter that sported a 32-inch wingspan and was the star of my collection.

I eventually graduated up to radio-controlled models at age fourteen. This move represented the culmination of my years devoted to model aircraft construction and experimentation. This cherished boyhood experience planted a seed that would soon grow into my lifelong love of all things fast and high.

During the Second World War, it was this same love that drove me to enlist into the Army Air Force as soon as I turned eighteen. I yearned to be a pilot and to do my part in the Pacific Theatre. I studied hard and succeeded in passing all of the qualifying exams...except for one. The physical. No amount of study would result in increasing my stature by one inch, which is what I needed in order to meet the minimum height requirement. I was dejected, but not deterred.

I soon began gunnery training as a "ring gunner" assigned to a B-29 bomber. I had never even seen a B-29, much less flown in one, but I soon learned that a ring gunner is officially known as a Central-Fire-Control or C.F.C. gunner. I controlled the machine gun in the top ring of the turret above the right and left waist positions in what were called the side blisters. My .50 caliber weapon was able to revolve a full 360 degrees. The trick was to avoid shooting off parts of your own plane as you spun around. The automated safety system normally took care of this, but I could not help but worry that if that system malfunctioned I might end up ripping off chunks of my own tail assembly. Fortunately, the system worked as advertised, so I'm still here to describe my anxieties at the time.

After a year and a half of training, our crew was finally ready to see combat. As we waited for our orders to ship out, we received word about the "rain of ruin" that the United States had inflicted upon Japan at Hiroshima and Nagasaki. The war was over and we were young and just dumb enough to feel cheated by being denied our opportunity to see some real action. But wartime forces a young man to mature very quickly. So before long we all realized just how lucky we really had been to have avoided the fate of so many of our lost comrades who went down into the Pacific in a hail of anti-aircraft shells and enemy bullets.

The frustration was still fresh immediately after the war as I sought to satisfy my blue yonder yearnings by taking private flying lessons. I received my first pilot's license at age 21 in 1947, but it would be a full year before I actually owned an airplane…or at least a piece of one. By this time I was married. My brother-in-law, Jamie and I, along with Eddie, a third friend, managed to scrape together enough cash to purchase a ten-year old, well-used Piper Cub for the sky-high sum of $600. That plane became our baby and we spent our weekends and holidays for the next year re-covering the entire plane, re-upholstering seats, polishing the hardware and otherwise transforming the Cub into what looked like a brand new aircraft. While we normally did our pleasure flying together, the three of us worked out a rotation schedule to determine who would actually serve as the pilot. We were all very safety conscious and avoided unnecessary risks, but sometimes our impatience to get airborne got the better of us.

The Cub, like most pre-war aircraft, did not have an automatic starting system to fire up the engine. The start-up procedure was just like you may have seen in the old movies: one person would stand at the front of the plane and sharply pull down the propeller while a second person sat in the cockpit and shouted "Contact!" while releasing the hand brake and adjusting the throttle. Eddie,

Jamie, and I had been cautioned many times during our training to "never, ever try to start the engine unless someone is sitting inside the cockpit!"

One sunny Sunday, Eddie arrived a bit before us at the airfield where our Cub was parked. Finding himself alone and with no one to "prop" the plane to life, Eddie decided to go it solo. He wedged chocks under the front wheels and secured the hand brake before proceeding to give the propeller a spin. His plan was to "prop-start" the engine and then quickly pull the chocks, run over to the side of the plane and hop into the cockpit before the engine had had a chance to build up any real power. Needless to say, things did not go as planned.

As soon as Eddie propped the engine to life, the propeller began swiftly rotating causing the aircraft to start moving forward, albeit slowly at first. Eddie reported that he was staring straight into the rotating propeller and it was "coming right at my face!"

Eddie hopped quickly out of the way and tried to reach the cockpit through the door on the side of the plane, but the wing struts blocked his path. He had to run out around the edge of the wing in order to reach the door. Before he was able to do so, he watched in horror as the plane begin to taxi down the runway, heading away from him with NO ONE on board! With no guidance, the plane lurched erratically down the tarmac, slowly building up speed. Eddie could only stand there gape-mouthed wondering if the plane would actually lift off on its own. Obviously this was a situation that had not been covered in flight school, or in any of our training publications.

After meandering about 75 feet down the runway, our beloved Cub—still on the ground—smashed nose first into another parked aircraft. That slowed her down, but she didn't stop. Our plane kept plowing forward into the body of the other plane, cutting a slice out of the metal cowling every time the wooden propeller went around. Eventually the prop hit something hard and shattered causing the engine to finally quit. The two mangled planes were sitting in a twisted smoldering embrace as Jamie and I arrived on the scene.

"I tried to start her and take her up by myself," explained a mournful Eddie.

"They told us never to do that," I replied.

"Well, they were right," he said as we rushed over to assess the damage. Although we repaired both planes, our little Cub was never quite the same after that. It took a few years to get over the pain, but all three of us were eventually able to laugh at the incident and to realize how lucky we really were that there was no serious damage or injury as a result. Jamie and I teased Eddie about this exploit mercilessly for years, going so far as to buy him a copy of "Aviation for Dummies" on his birthday.

Over the next few years, I purchased several single-engine aircraft, each one a little faster, and a little more sophisticated than its predecessor. Those were wonderful years of lifting off, landing, and learning. I absorbed a great deal about climate patterns and how to avoid flying in rough weather. Most aircraft mishaps, I learned, were caused by pilots not understanding the weather hazards they faced. Understanding cloud systems, storm fronts, pressure drops, and so on, was particularly important before I received my instrument rating clearance. Once I obtained that license, I was no longer at the mercy of the weatherman. I could use my instruments to go above a storm system, for example, and reach my destination safely even if the weather was not all that cooperative.

I've owned a series of planes over the years and have developed sort of a mental Scrapbook of the Sky filled with airborne memories. Each plane has its own story—some a bit wild, others somewhat mellow—but all exciting. Here are a few mental snapshots:

- The heart-stopping experience of losing an engine while flying over downtown Phoenix. This was particularly terrifying since I was piloting a single-engine plane. A carburetor malfunction had killed the engine and I suddenly found myself at the helm of a glider. Thanks to my training, I did not panic but stuck to the rulebook and managed to limp into nearby Phoenix International airport on a wing, a prayer, and lots of adrenaline.

- Flying through a mile-high cloudbank over Santa Barbara looking for a hole that would lead me to a patch of clear sky. I was not instrument rated at this time and could not ascend high enough to travel over the thick clouds. I also was in a non-pressurized cabin, so I probably would not have been able to reach an adequate altitude in any case. Fortunately I did not experience vertigo after losing sight of the ground and I was finally able to find the hole and sail through it to a safe landing.

- Deciding to fly to Catalina Island to sample some of their famous Buffalo Burgers at the Runway Café. The café is located in the center of the island at an elevation of 1,602 feet. It's accurately billed as "The Airport In The Sky." The airport's 3,250-foot runway is just a bit longer than one found on a typical aircraft carrier. With the difference being that if you overshoot your landing here, instead of winding up in the drink, your plane falls off a steep cliff situated right at the end of the runway. The runway itself was constructed in 1946 by the Army Corps of Engineers who blasted off the tops of two of the Island's mountains. As you come in for an approach, you are forced to maneuver around dangerous craggy cliffs that are often shrouded in fog due to low cloud cover. After several return visits, I eventually became adept at landing on Catalina, but that first time is gurraranteed to be an unforgettable knee-knocker for any pilot. I still haven't figured how they get those buffalo up to the top of the cliff, however.

- Flying into Palm Springs for a night landing in the desert in my Cessna 310 and discovering that the nose gear landing light was malfunctioning. I could not determine if the nose wheel was up or down. Normally the nose wheel indicator functions in tandem with the main landing gear wheels, but at this point the light was showing "Up," while the main wheel light showed "Down." I aborted my landing and climbed up well over the airport, avoiding the nearby mountains in the dark. Once I was cruising at the higher altitude, I reached down and grabbed the emergency hand crank in order to lower the nose wheel. Even after doing so, I could not be 100% certain that the nose wheel was down and locked into place. If it was down, but not locked, the nose wheel landing assembly would fold upon touching down, possibly causing a crash or a dangerous fire.

  I was in constant radio contact with the tower throughout this episode and the controller there instructed me to make some low passes so they could train their search lights on my nose wheel and visually determine its status. After making several passes, the controller said he could see the wheel was down, but he could not be sure if it was properly secured in place or not. Looking down at the airfield I could see the ominous rows of fire trucks lining up along the edge of the runway. We had done all we could possibly do and now it was simply a matter of luck and pluck. I could not remain aloft indefinitely and so I gulped hard and began to bring the plane in for a landing. The main wheels hit the ground first and then, a few seconds later, the nose wheel touched down with an exquisite solid "thunk." I had held the plane in a nose high attitude as long as I could to lose as much air speed as possible before touching down. If the gear did fold up, the slower I was moving, the better. I started breathing again and said words of thanks. The wheel was locked in tight and we did not need the fire trucks. I did, however, need a little time to calm down after that one.

After flying single-engine aircraft for many years, I began to hunger for more speed and comfort. I stepped up to a four place, non-pressured twin-engine aircraft, then to a six place Piper Aztec, a Cessna 310, and, finally, a pressurized, high-powered eight place Cessna 421, the largest plane I have flown. I always considered it, but I just never quite graduated to "kerosene burners," also known as jet aircraft.

After over 50 years of life among the clouds, I had become truly proficient at doing everything I needed to do in order to keep my "instrument rating" current. Eventually, however, I acknowledged that trees do not grow to the sky and all chapters must sooner or later come to a close. It was time to let the younger generation do the actual flying. I decided it was just as wonderful to charter a plane, as it is to fly one, and that's how I've been scratching my itch for altitude in recent years. I had accomplished everything in flying I had ever set out to do. In looking back over that high and mighty expanse of my life, I feel lucky indeed to be able to sit here, safe and sound, and able to share my collection of mile-high memories with you.

The common expression goes: "There are old pilots and there are bold pilots, but there are no old bold pilots." Although I enjoyed my share of thrills over the years, I was never a serious risk taker or in any way "bold" when it came to personal safety.

The funny part is that I don't feel like an old pilot either. I suspect it's because flying keeps a person feeling young. Whether it's a radio-controlled plane in the park, a military plane on a mission, a pleasure flight, or a chartered business trip, there's something undeniably liberating and invigorating about leaving the ground behind. That's why I intend to keep flying high for as long as I can.

After reading about some of my "close call" experiences, you may rightly wonder why anyone would love flying as much as I do. My answer can be summed up this way: "You either love it or you hate it!" There's not much in between. After the tension of the moment had passed, I would often think: "That wasn't really so bad, and it probably won't happen again."

It's probably true when pilots say: "Flying can be 95% boredom and 5% sheer terror." Maybe that's really what brings us back for more: the speed, the action, and the lure of that 5% kick.

CHAPTER TWENTY-TWO

ZERO GEE WHIZ

That's one small step for man; one giant leap for mankind.

Neil Armstrong

A s any visitor will attest, Las Vegas is an extremely easy place to have the weight of your wallet reduced down to zero in no time at all. But since October of 2004, thanks to the efforts of an enterprising space enthusiast named Peter Diamandis and his Zero-G Company, adventuresome visitors may now experience the unique thrill of making their entire bodies weightless as well.

I have often wondered, while watching TV coverage of space shuttle flights, what life must be like for astronauts operating in a zero-G environment. How does it feel to float gracefully suspended in mid-air? How do you do simple things like sign your name, or comb your hair? Well, thanks to the thoughtfulness of my grandson, Bob III, and the generosity of his good friend, Noah, my curiosity about such things was about to be satisfied.

In early 2008, Noah and Bob III booked passage for me aboard the G-Force One, a modified Boeing 727-200 aircraft operated by Zero-G. The departure point was the Signature Air Terminal at McCarran International Airport in Las Vegas. The destination was out of this world!

Zero-G offers normal citizens the opportunity to experience weightlessness using the same method that has been employed by NASA over the past 45 years in the training of its astronaut crews. Once airborne at 24,000 feet, the plane embarks on a precision series of parabolic ups and downs that will take it up as high as 32,000 feet at the peak.

All of this was explained to me and the other thirty-four hardy passengers during an intense video pre-flight briefing session on the morning of our flight. The video contained all the safety instructions and explained the reasons for the do's and don'ts that we were required to observe while in the air. Once that step was completed, we were issued special jumpsuits and then shown into the aircraft. The interior of the plane is mostly empty and features walls and ceilings covered with thick foam safety padding. We were escorted to the 40 standard airline seats situated towards the rear of the padded playground and asked to strap ourselves in. Within a short while after our smooth take-off, we climbed to our cruising altitude of 24,000 feet and flew out to our designated maneuvering area.

The flight attendants instructed us to move into the open area of the cabin as the plane began the first ascent in its parabolic flight path. The entire flight lasts about one-and-a-half hours including the flight to and from the assigned area, and consists of 15 two-to-three minute segments. When the plane reaches the top of each parabolic curve at 32,000 feet, there is a 30-second rollover period before it begins its steep descent. It is during this 30-second interim that passengers are thrown into freefall and experience the very liberating sensation of being unbound from the mortal coils of Earth.

As the G-Force One began the first of its fifteen steep ascents, we felt our body weight steadily increase as we were pressed inexorably against the spongy floor. Our training had prepared us for the fact that we would ease into this experience step-by-step through three degrees of weightlessness. This all became clear once we reached the apex of the first parabola. We were—as if by magic—lifted a bit from the floor and found that our body weight had been dramatically reduced to a third. For example, a 150-pound man now felt as if he only weighed 50 pounds. "Who needs Weight Watchers?" I wondered aloud as I observed the gleeful faces of my fellow "tourist-onauts."

One-armed push-ups became ridiculously easy as we all experienced a taste of "The Man of Steel"-style super-strength. This giddy feeling was short-lived, however. After thirty seconds, the plane began its swift and steep descent back down to the 24,000-foot level. During the trip back down, passengers slowly began regaining their normal body weight until, at the bottom of the parabola, everything was back to normal. These transitions each felt as if they were happening in slow motion.

The second ascent was billed as a "Trip to the Moon." This time when we reached the parabolic peak, we found that we weighed in at only one sixth of our regular body weight. Just as he might experience on the surface of the Moon, a 150-pound man now felt as if he weighed a mere 25 pounds. We now found we could bounce around the cabin easily, in the manner of graceful ballerinas—shoving off smoothly from the sides and then coming gently to rest, like a floating feather, back on the floor of the cabin. If they had piped in some classical waltz music at this point—The Blue Danube from 2001; A Space Odyssey, for example—it would have been perfect. But, as before, after thirty seconds of high stepping pirouettes it was back down towards Mother Earth and our old friend, Mr. Gravity.

As humans, having lived on the surface of the Earth for our entire lives, we take the presence of the planet's gravitational pull for granted. Only when a person is freed from this bond—albeit briefly and partially—does one become aware of its existence. Certainly weightlessness may be simulated in everyday life via such activities as scuba and ski diving, but these pale in comparison to the real McCoy. And now we were prepared to fully experience true Zero-G on this, our third ascent, as well as during each of the next twelve trips to the top.

Once we reached the parabolic summit for the third time, that 150-pound man found himself weighing absolutely nothing. I floated around the cabin feeling like a helium-filled human-sized balloon. Thirty seconds of this delightful buoyancy does not sound like a long time, but it really is sufficient to perform a number of physical maneuvers that leave you well acquainted with the wonders of weightlessness. I found that I had full use of my arms and my legs, but familiar concepts like "up and down" no longer held any meaning. Mid-air somersaults and spinning like a top on your body's central axis were favored activities among my co-passengers. Given the number of people and the total space available, becoming somewhat intimate while bumping into other free-floating fun-seekers was inevitable.

The crew had provided us with a supply of bottled water and countless M&M candies to play with and try to consume. The water, of course, came out in spherical globs and floated luxuriously by our faces. The M&Ms spread everywhere, giving the cabin a festive, confetti-filled appearance. Many of us tried to suck or snap at the floating goodies, but without much success. Of course as the plane began its eventual descent, the candies began to pick up weight and eventually floated serenely to the floor—as did we. You didn't want to be under a water-globule during this part of the flight, however.

By the end of the 45-minute experience, passengers had been weightless for a total of about eight full minutes. More than enough to create a memory that will last each of them a lifetime. Some might assume that after about the thirteenth or fourteenth time around, the novelty would have begun to wear thin and some of this weightless wonderfulness might have started to diminish. Not so. I found the entire experience entirely enthralling and totally mind-boggling throughout.

I came away with an understanding of why astronauts love space flight so much. The freedom from gravity's bondage is something that appeals to a very fundamental core of the human psyche. I believe that it is ingrained in our DNA and universal among the human race. If you've ever had dreams in which you find yourself able to fly through the air, you will understand my point. At the apex of parabola number fifteen, I felt like Superman, comfortably whizzing through space.

Since returning home and sharing my experiences with others, I have been asked about how weightlessness affected me physically. The answer is: Most passengers, including me, do feel a little tired upon returning to full gravity conditions. But the side effects were minimal and disappeared quickly. They in no way diminished the overall joy I felt during this true once-in-a-lifetime experience, but I now do understand why astronauts need a short transition period to regain their normal equilibrium after extended periods in space.

Some participants, I noticed, found their time in zero-G-land to be a soothing, almost Zen-like, experience. While others, like me, found it to be the world's most extreme roller coaster ride—minus the coaster.

Proprietor Diamandis claims his purpose in offering this one-of-a-kind thrill ride to the public has been "to make weightlessness available to the broader general public; getting it out of the realm of just the space enthusiast and allowing the public to more directly participate in space." Since its founding, the company has offered rides, emanating from both Las Vegas and the Kennedy

Space Center in Florida, to educators, television and movie producers, government researchers and corporate executives. For about $135,000, a company may charter the entire plane for an unforgettable sky-high management retreat. Several science fiction films, such as 2007's *Sunshine* and Tom Hanks' *Apollo 13* movie, include footage that was shot onboard the G-Force One.

One of the plane's most celebrated passengers was the noted physicist, Professor Stephen Hawking. Confined to his wheelchair for over forty years due to the crippling effects of ALS (Lou Gehrig's Disease), Hawking, a strong advocate of space exploration, was able to float and spin around the cabin without any difficulty. He described the experience afterwards as life altering and completely delightful.

Without question, my flight aboard the Zero Force One, which occurred just days before my 82nd birthday, was the most unique and "out of body" experience of my entire life. I recommend it to any free spirited person with a taste for adventure and a healthy curiosity. I'm truly looking forward to my next journey into the "Wowee!" world of weightlessness.

CHAPTER TWENTY-THREE

GOAT'S POINT GETAWAY

Security is an illusion.
Life is either a daring adventure or it is nothing at all.

Helen Keller

The native people of the Baja California Sur are often known as "Los Cachanillas," after the wild aromatic plant that grows there. They have dubbed the Sur's Pacific shore as the Cruel Coast—particularly when it comes to gringos. A fair number of Americans have met their misfortune among the cachanillas—both the aromatic and the less-than-aromatic variety. Jayne Mansfield was both married and divorced in Baja, and the cremated remains of Erle Stanley Gardner (creator of Perry Mason) were scattered over Baja.

I, too, encountered some Mexican misfortune back in the 1970s while on a getaway junket with three of my "compadres." We had all four agreed to meet at the fishing village of Punta Chivata or "Goat's Point," a scenic spot about twenty miles off the coastal highway, between the towns of Santa Rosalia and Mulegé. Since I didn't care to spend a day bumping over the unpaved pock-marked roads along the coast, I chose to fly down to Punta Chivata in my plane and then wait for the other three to arrive by car.

The village boasts a 4,000-foot graded dirt airstrip, although modern niceties, such as radar, Avgas (aviation fuel), and running water, were unavailable. The airstrip overlooks the sparkling Sea of Cortez, into which Punta Chivata proudly juts. This section of the Sea is said to contain the remains of several wrecked airplanes whose pilots made less than successful landing attempts on the primitive airstrip. The scuba diving tourists often explore these wrecks and travel just up the coast to another bay favored by vacationers, intriguingly known as Caleta Muertos or Dead Man's Cove. It's enough to give any pilot the Willies! With all this in mind, I carefully brought my plane in on a steady approach so as to avoid becoming next year's tourist attraction.

As I inspected the fuselage upon landing, amid all the desert dirt and sagebrush, I realized that I had some time to kill before the rest of the crew arrived. I thought of heading over to the small tienda next to the weather-beaten Hotel Posada de las Flores and then thought better of it. I'd be safer staying hungry and waiting until the others arrived with the grub instead of risking a dose of refried reflux at the local tacoteria.

Many people have heard of the Hotel Punta Chivato, and it is indeed a luxurious four star resort. Unfortunately, it's located in the relatively larger town of Santa Rosalia and not in tiny Punta Chivato itself. Our little village was known as an outpost for the adventurous traveler and offered a magnificent menu of outdoor sports activities. From diving and snorkeling off of Shell Beach to whale watching and numerous dorado fishing tournaments, Punta Chivato meant fun in the sun for bold voyagers like us who had discovered its many charms.

After completing the inspection of my plane, I stood beside her, admiring the powdery sand, the swaying palm trees, and the lush mangroves along the breathtaking beachfront. I had just pulled out some reading material to pass the time and when I looked up

I spotted a group of young Mexican boys heading right towards me. These kids were used to seeing the small single-engine aircraft that typically landed here, but my twin-engine, six-place model was something these six to eight-year olds had never laid eyes on before. I smiled and indicated it was okay for them to have a look. A few of the youngsters could speak a bit of English:

"Ola, Señor," said the tallest one, brandishing a broad grin. "We go up? Si?" He gesticulated with his hands indicating all of the kids while pointing skyward and then imitated an airplane with his two arms extended while he made a whooshing sound.

"You guys want to go for a ride?" I said with a knowing smile and then tried out some of my broken Spanish: "Muchachos van para arriba?"

At that they all broke out with enthusiastic shouts and whoops. "Si, si, señor! Arriba! Arriba, por favor!" They pleaded and prodded until I began to think "Why not? This might bring some fun into these kids' lives."

I looked about to see if there was a parent or any adult around for me to ask, but there was no one in sight. The boys, while not exactly street urchins, seemed to be pretty much on their own. I don't know if the tropical sun had refried my brain or if I temporarily lost my grip, but I opened the cabin door and invited the five excited kids on board.

"Just one short trip around the field and then we come back down, comprende?" I advised.

"Si, si, señor. Muchas gracias," they all repeated dutifully. I showed each junior airman how to fasten his seat belt and got ready for a quickie trip in the sky above the airstrip. After take-off, the kids were all glued to the windows and I could hear a constant stream of "Ooohs," "Aaahs," and "Carambas" emanating from their wide open mouths. None had ever flown in an airplane before and it was clear they were having a blast. It did my heart good to see them enjoying something I loved so dearly. "Who knows? This experience might even inspire one or two of the boys to become pilots," I thought to myself.

It was a short, uneventful trip around the landing pattern, and as I made my approach, I noticed nothing unusual on the airstrip—although I definitely should have. What I overlooked was a deep pothole in the runway surface that was lined up exactly with my left landing gear. If I had touched down a mere 12 inches to the right or to the left, I would have easily missed it. But that's not the way it went down. Literally.

As my left wheel hit the pothole, the wheel sunk in and became trapped as the plane continued to push ahead. As a result, the entire landing assembly collapsed under the engine. This action caused the left wing to dip down and hit the ground as the still spinning propeller dug into the dusty surface until it suddenly ground to a halt.

Inside, the boys and I felt a sharp thump as the plane lurched and hit the deep chuckhole. I never saw that hole, but I did observe the left wing dipping down and watched as the propeller abruptly came to a stop. I immediately shut down the right engine and applied the brakes with all my strength. Even so, I could not bring the plane to a smooth stop and only managed to slow down the left hand slide we were now experiencing.

Mercifully, we skidded to an upright stop a few moments later. Thank goodness all the kids were merely shaken, but otherwise fine. I could not say the same for my collapsed ego that now lay deflated and shattered, just like my crippled airplane. I had, at this point in my career, logged thousands of flying hours without so much as a scratch. I was a seasoned pilot, with years of experience, and should have easily managed to avoid a simple obstacle like a runway pothole. I had never had a flying accident before and, I'm proud to say, I've never had one since. Yet, here I was, carrying a

Cachanilla kindergarten and this is the moment that the Curse of the Cruel Coast decides to rear its ugly head. I was incredibly mad at myself. And, as I was soon to find out, I was not the only one.

The kids were all smiling and in great spirits as they tumbled out of the crippled plane. But the crowd that gathered was anything but. The mishap had stirred up a huge cloud of dust and the noise of the grating propeller easily reached the ears of Punta Chivato's citizens—including the boys' justifiably outraged parents. As I peered out from the cockpit, it seemed like the entire village had gathered at the airstrip and were now surrounding my plane. They did not look pleased as they glared in at me and I did not blame them one bit.

How would I have felt if some stranger from across the border had shanghai-ed my little kids, flown them around without my permission, and then ended up in a crash landing? As I looked from face to somber face, I began to wonder if hanging or the firing squad was the preferred method of execution in these parts.

Once the kids ran into the loving embrace of their parents, and everyone saw that they were unharmed, the tension seemed to let up a bit. Soon the local gendarmes arrived and the townsfolk began relating all at once what had happened in a cacophony of Spanish curses and a lot of fingers pointed at me and towards the sky. I felt that I was headed straight for the jailhouse—if I was lucky! But then a funny thing happened.

The kids began to defend me before the police and before their parents. I couldn't understand their conversations, but I could tell from their body language that the youngsters were relating what a terrific time they had just had to their parents. Little by little, the crowd grew mellower and the hostile tension began to subside. Evidently the kids were able to make their parents understand that I was a good guy and that the kids themselves had pleaded with me for a ride in the big "aeroplano." The parents and the police finally concluded that no harm had been done and that the muchachos had, in fact, enjoyed the time of their lives.

Once the commotion had subsided, I had to figure what to do with my heavily damaged airplane. Amazingly, some of the very town folks, whom just a ten minutes before I had feared would have me jailed, were now assisting me in moving my plane off the airstrip and securing it nearby. The plane would sit on the ground for weeks while I conducted the complex process of flying in mechanics and new parts to carry out the extensive repair work. I was even able to employ some of the locals to provide security for the plane while it awaited repair. What wonderful, forgiving people these were.

Just as the last piece of airplane debris was carted away, here came my buddies, joyfully oblivious to the misfortune that had just befallen me. As their car pulled up alongside my disabled sky pony, they hopped out and surveyed the damage.

"Wowee, Bob," one exclaimed in genuine shock. "What happened to your plane?"

"Would you believe me if I said I was coming in for a landing after conducting a guided tour for a bunch of six-year olds and my left wheel fell into a deep chuckhole as I was landing?"

"Quit kidding, Bob," they retorted. "Tell us what really happened?"

They finally believed me after hearing the whole story and agreed that the cruel coast of the Baja Sur can be very tough indeed for flying gringos like me. But the hardest blow of all was the cruel ribbing I had to endure from my buddies about this incident for many, many years to come.

CHAPTER TWENTY-FOUR

PASSING THE HAT

---

*Part of the secret of success in life is to eat what you like
and let the food fight it out inside.*

Mark Twain

There are times when Dame Fortune sneaks up behind you and, for no apparent reason, takes you into a big loving embrace. Well, that's exactly how I felt back in 1985—lucky as I could be—after I decided not to join three of my buddies on an ill-fated flight to Loreto, a scenic little fishing village nestled along the Gulf of California. After they had returned home, I invited over one of the plane's passengers, my good friend Tom, who was soon seated in my den as he recounted the details of their mile-high misadventure. Before long I was laughing so hard I couldn't breathe.

Even though I was not onboard—and thank goodness for that—I nevertheless decided to include Tom's story in this collection since it's one of the funniest tales ever told. Actually, I was originally planning to join this jolly group, and if not for some pressing business at home, I would certainly have been on that flight. Had I done so, I would have soon encountered a different type of pressing business to deal with. But let's start at the beginning.

Tom was not an experienced flyer and this was his first trip south of the border. His two buddies had encouraged the soft-spoken CPA to join them for some fun-filled fishing along the Baja coast. Once onboard, and after a few drinks, his nervousness subsided and he didn't blink an eye as the four place aircraft came in for a landing on one of those small, dirt airstrips that dot the Baja peninsula. The men piled out as the plane's pilot explained they would be on the ground for about 30 minutes. They were invited to use the time to re-fuel themselves as he re-fueled the plane.

Tom was quite taken with the colorful surroundings of the quaint Mexican village adjacent to the airstrip and he joined the others inside a small cantina for some tacos and more drinks. Inside he found a typical selection of locally made tourist souvenirs. Tom tried on a huge felt sombrero that was decorated with the image of a burro and a cactus. Although the massive piece of headwear made Tom look like the Speedy Gonzales cartoon character, his friends raved about the chapeau and, with their encouragement, he decided to purchase it.

His two compatriots were glad that Tom was loosening up a bit as they sat munching on their tacos and throwing back the tequila shots. As the trio re-boarded, Tom had to remove his new sombrero in order to get in through the cabin door.

"My kids are going to love this hat," he commented as he set it carefully in the storage area behind the seats.

With both the passengers and the gas tank refilled, the pilot took off and headed southward into the perfectly clear blue sky. After about an hour, Tom heard something strange coming from down below. It was his stomach. In another moment, the rumbling spread to his abdomen and was now accompanied by some uneasy feelings of queasiness.

"Excuse me," he asked his seatmate, "but do you feel alright?"

One look at his buddy's green complexion gave Tom his answer. The pilot, sensing there was a problem, looked around to see that all of the Three Amigos were suffering some sort of intestinal distress.

"It must have been the tacos," moaned Tom while clutching his bloated belly. He came to this conclusion because the pilot had evidently had the good sense not to eat at the ptomaine cantina and he looked to be just fine. After a minute or two, Tom felt like his bowels were turning into hot water as he, and the others, began to experience the impelling symptoms of that cursed condition known alternately as "Montezuma's Revenge," the "Aztec Two Step," or "Turista Tummy."

Any person who has ever been so afflicted while firmly planted on the ground will understand the great sense of urgency that this condition brings on. However, when you're 5,000 feet up in the air, in a cramped cabin, with no landing strip for miles, you suddenly realize that you have no place to hide and no place to run. The men all felt that disaster was about to erupt within minutes. Tom's anxiety spiked even higher when he was informed that their single-engine aircraft was not equipped with any sort of toilet facilities.

"Have you got some kind of bucket or ice chest up there?" one of the besieged passengers managed to beg the pilot between belches. The answer, sadly, was "No."

"We're going to need...ulp... something in a hurry," said the other, and then they both turned directly to look at Tom.

"Oh, no," he thought. Tom looked back and forth between the two greenish faces and then shook his head warily.

"No. C'mon guys," he got out as he felt a dire sinking feeling in the pit of his very upset stomach. "No. Not that. Not my new sombrero!"

"Give it to me, Tom," growled his seat partner. "Now!"

If this wasn't a matter of life or death, then it was certainly the closest thing to it. Realizing this, Tom reluctantly handed over his new prized sombrero to be used as the men's necessary receptacle. I'll spare you the details.

Minutes later, after their internal discomfort had subsided somewhat, the men were forced to face an important and intriguing new question. What to do with this foul fedora. Tom, not being overly familiar with the design of small aircraft, made the following suggestion:

"Look, I'm never going to use that hat again. Let's just dump it out the window and forget about it." It was a bad idea, but they went for it.

Now, I don't suspect that anyone has ever tried to shove a large sombrero full of...uh, well, full of anything...out the window of a small plane traveling at 160 mph, but, if you can imagine such a thing, then you've probably figured out the rest of the story.

My three friends tried their level best to squeeze that big enchilada out through the tiny window opening, but as soon as it was protruding out but a few inches, the contents were quickly blown back by the strong propeller wash. What happened to it? That's right. The "It" hit the fan and ended up all over the inside of the plane and its passengers.

The flight of the Ex-Lax Express continued on to Loreto where the sombrero was given a proper burial at sea and the pilot was able to enlist some poor locals to help him clean up his besmirched Beechcraft.

Once back in the States, the plane had to be completely reupholstered, fumigated and sanitized before being placed back into service. Tom never learned if the owner's insurance policy covered the sombrero loss or not, but it did help out with the cost of the clean up, he told me.

"That's quite a story," I said after I wiped the tears of laughter from my eyes. "I'm sure glad that I decided not to come along."

"Yeah, you really missed one wild ride," Tom said with a sorrowful sigh. "It gave the term 'sh*t-faced on tequila' a whole new meaning!"

MEMORABLE MOMENTS

CHAPTER TWENTY-FIVE

THE WINDS OF HEAVEN

The only thing wrong with immortality is that it tends to go on forever.

Herb Caen

When it comes to embracing immortality, the Eskimos are the world's greatest. According to ancient tradition, when an Eskimo warrior dies his remains are fed to a hungry polar bear that is then summarily slaughtered. The meat of the beast is quickly cooked and eaten by the tribe members in a time-honored consummate ritual. By ingesting the flesh, the warrior's essence is thought to somehow be passed on to the tribe. My late friend, Jim, would have loved the Eskimos. I was expounding on all this to my wife, Mary Ellen, as we wound our way down Highway 1 through Corona Del Mar from the San Joaquin Hills to attend our friend, Jim's, funeral.

Jim was a member of our "Sky High" club based out of Orange County back in the mid-nineties. Like the rest of us, Jim shared a passion for flying, golf and the good life that still defines Southern California. But his deepest affection was reserved for the rugged, craggy Laguna Beach coastline that the Mexicans call "El Barranca." Jim had perched his grand and gracious home high above the crashing surf that constantly pummeled the black rocks below. A sweeping veranda extended along the ocean side of the house and it was here—at the time of day when the sun melted languidly down into the Pacific—that we were to convene and bid Jim a grand and final adios.

Mary Ellen and I both gave Jim's widow a hug at the front door and offered our condolences. We were directed to the deck where I expressed the obligatory "Wow!" response to the dramatic ocean view and then began pecking discreetly at the guacamole dip and other proffered refreshments.

"Leave it to Jim to go out with bang," commented one of the 75 or so other well wishers circling the crudités. He was impressed with the bagpipers, in full-kilted regalia, bleating out the mournful strains of "Amazing Grace" and "Danny Boy."

"I didn't know Jim was Scottish," I said.

"I don't think he was," offered another guest, "I think he just liked single malt Scotch."

Now that sounded like a good idea. I quietly questioned the bartender as I dropped a bill into his tip cup: "When's the main event?"

"The helicopter should be here right at sunset," was the reply. Helicopter? I should have expected as much.

That was the thing about Jim. He was a dynamic, witty fireball who always had a sparkle in his eye and a trick or two up his sleeve. During the illness that finally took his life, Jim had made his last wishes as clear as a new Ferrari's windshield. He wanted no casket. No funeral home. No overblown eulogies. It was to be cremation and dispersion to the winds of heaven that blew by his beloved beachside home in the company of friends and family. That was to be Jim's windswept swan song.

Just as the sun dipped down, the helicopter rose up, its pounding rotors positioning it level with the balcony—about 100 feet above the pounding surf below. As I glanced about, I could see that everyone had adopted a somber persona for the upcoming ritual, but the undercurrent of excitement was nonetheless electric. Jim, who had by now been converted into an urnful of ashes, was being held snugly by the helicopter pilot who, right on cue, carefully opened the cockpit door just as the bagpipers reached a dramatic crescendo.

The crowd rushed to the railing to get a better view of Jim's final fling, while the pilot carefully maneuvered the porcelain urn and extended it at arm's length. He next removed the small lid and tipped the vessel over ever so slowly, allowing the contents to spill out into the air. I'm sure, I thought, that this is just what Jim must have envisioned his last request would be—this moment where his ashes would lazily float from the urn down towards the shore, the sea, and the points beyond. But, that's not quite the way the fates and the winds would have it on this day.

His ashes fell out in a clump and then were immediately scattered by the backwash of the helicopter blades and an unexpected updraft arising from the surf below. Instead of being carried out to sea, Jim's ashes created a temporary dust storm that headed straight for us. In two shakes and a blink, Jim was everywhere. There was Jim in my hair and Jim on my face. There was Jim in the punchbowl and Jim in the guacamole dip. The front rail group got a good dose of Jim all over their clothing, not to mention in their lungs. I'm sure Jim found his way into the plants, the purses and perhaps into some of those new cell phones we had all started toting around. I even spotted some of Jim being puffed out of one of the bagpipes!

After recovering from the shock, and as we surveyed each other's ashen faces, the humor of the situation began to hit us one by one. Even Jim's widow shook her head and sent a smile up towards the heavens.

"Do you think Jim planned it this way?" suggested one dust-covered friend.

Someone else recalled that one of Jim's favorite songs was "If I Had To Do It All Over Again, Babe, I'd Do It All Over You."

The rest of us patted Jim from our clothing, wiped Jim from our faces on some freshly provided linens, and proceeded with the service as planned, while the bagpipers managed another mournful melody, now somewhat muffled by Jim's molecules stuck deep among the pipes.

Afterwards, as we all gazed out thoughtfully at the darkening sea and enjoyed some of Jim's single malt, I shared my polar bear story with some of the other "Sky High" guys.

"Jim would have loved going out that way," observed one close friend after learning about the Eskimo rite, "but I think he would have really gotten a chuckle out of the way it went down today."

"It was almost like he was controlling the wind flow from on high," stated another, and we all agreed that this observation called for a toast to "Jim's memory and to the capricious Winds of Heaven."

In the days that followed, as I washed Jim from my hair and had my clothes "de-Jimmed" at the dry cleaners, I wondered if his spirit, his essence, his whatever, would stay with me a bit longer thanks to the "dusting on the deck" I had received. Somehow, I felt that it would. And maybe that was the whole idea in the first place.

Chapter Twenty-Six

Where's the Fire?

One of the tests of leadership is the ability to recognize a problem
before it becomes an emergency.

Arnold Glasgow

The great Swedish filmmaker, Ingmar Bergman, once compared growing old to climbing up a mountain. The higher you climb, the more tired and worn out you become. But at the same time, your view of the world keeps growing wider and wider. I've always appreciated the second part of that observation as my horizons have definitely grown wider over the years. But until I hit age 75, I never gave much thought to the first part.

I had always enjoyed an active, vigorous life that to some degree, I believed, was the product of living in healthy Southern California. In fact, I've always felt younger than the age on my driver's license. If I were to suddenly contract amnesia and not be able to remember my true age, I would guess it to be around 45 or 50. That's just the way I regard myself. I always believed that "old" was at least a good fifteen or twenty years beyond whatever age I happened to be at the time. I never really thought too much about my own death, but then something happened on my way to work one day that would put me firmly in touch with my own mortality.

I had felt sluggish for some reason all morning and by the time I reached the highway, heading towards our Newport Beach office, I was really dragging. I also started to experience some odd tight and tingly feelings in my upper chest. It wasn't painful, just sort of unusual. When I began to also feel a bit light headed, I decided to stop in at the fire station near our home and have a chat with the paramedics.

I got out of my car and entered the fire station, but couldn't spot anyone within sight. I checked the garage and the fire truck was still there, but no firemen and no paramedics anywhere on the premises.

"They're not out fighting a fire," I thought to myself. Strange, so I decided to move on.

I got back into my car and continued on to work. As I approached my office, I began to feel worse. I did not think I felt bad enough to warrant a trip to the emergency room, but I definitely wanted to learn what was going on. I remembered that there was another fire station not too far from my office so I headed over that way.

I parked my car and walked into the firehouse. This time there were several firefighters on hand. I approached one and introduced myself.

"What's the trouble, sir?" he asked politely.

"I'm not sure," I answered and noticed that I was out of breath after just that short walk from the car. "My chest feels tight and knotted up and I'm starting to feel a little woozy."

"Why don't you sit down?" he suggested and I took two shaky steps over to the chair he was pointing to. I never made it.

I woke up shocked to see several of the firemen hooking me up to various instruments and monitors. I couldn't say anything because they had placed an oxygen mask over my mouth and nose. I looked around and saw that they had placed me on a low gurney while I evidently had been unconscious. I fought back the panic that was welling in my gut and followed the advice I was being offered:

"Just breathe deeply and try to relax, Mr. Mayer," said a young paramedic. I guessed that he had been through my pockets and found my wallet.

After checking my blood pressure and other vitals, they popped me into the back of a waiting ambulance and we took off for Hoag Hospital. Once inside the speeding vehicle, I was informed that I was having some sort of cardiac distress. The gentleman delivering this news was not dressed like a paramedic. He understood the quizzical gaze I shot him and responded:

"Today's your lucky day, Mr. Mayer," he said with a smile— obviously trying to raise my spirits and calm me down. "I'm Dr. Hurst and I'm a cardiologist at Hoag Hospital. As part of my C.E. training—that's continuing education—I'm required to spend eight days of each year riding with emergency vehicles in the field. Today is one of my days. You just happened to wander into a fire station with its own resident heart doctor today. You're a real lucky guy."

Once we arrived at the E.R., I was given further tests and both my family and my office were contacted. Dr. Hurst came in and gave me the news.

"We did a cardiac catheterization and found some pretty extensive blockage," he advised. "We thought about putting in a stent or two, but the blockage is just too widespread. We're going to have to go in and do a bypass to improve the blood flow to your heart."

"Did I have a heart attack, Doc?" I asked.

"Not quite, but you were on your way. If you and I hadn't of met up at the fire station when we did, then things would have gone downhill pretty quickly."

I underwent open-heart surgery the following day and when I had regained consciousness I was told that they had performed a six-way cardiac bypass. Or to put it into contractor terminology, they had re-plumbed all the pipes servicing my main pump. I felt immediately invigorated and full of renewed energy after having been given a "new lease on life." But this was not one of those "net-net-net" leases. There were some strings attached. I understood that if I wanted to continue feeling great I would have to make sure I didn't allow my arteries to get clogged up again with gunk or plaque. I immediately switched to a low cholesterol diet and began taking medication to control the lipids in my bloodstream.

After an experience like that, a person tends to become appreciative of many things that were previously taken for granted. I certainly feel that way and I also feel compelled to share the lessons I learned with as many people as I can. And that includes you, dear reader. If you take nothing else of value from this book, I urge you to heed the following advice:

If you find yourself feeling unusually tired and out of sorts, resist the normal tendency to simply push it aside and ignore your symptoms in the hopes that they will pass and you'll soon feel better. Call 911 immediately and get some professional help to learn what is causing your problem. Like it says on the gym shoes: Just do it!

I count myself as very lucky to have come through it all as well as I did. I certainly must have had someone looking out for me that day. Guiding me into one of the only fire stations in Orange County that had a cardiologist on duty was nothing short of a miracle. As a result, I've been able to keep climbing that mountain a bit longer and, from where I'm standing, the view just keeps getting better all the time.

CHAPTER TWENTY-SEVEN

THE CLÉNET COLLECTION

No other man-made device since the shields and lances of the ancient knights fulfills a man's ego like an automobile.

Sir William Roote

The late seventies are best remembered as a time of leisure suits, CB radios, and disco music. It was also a time when a few independent entrepreneurs sought to loosen the stranglehold that the Big Three Detroit automakers held on the American auto market. Since the failure of the Tucker back in the early 1950s, no one had dared to offer drivers a non-Motown made car. But with the rise of a few free thinking renegades like John DeLorean and others, all that was about to change.

It was during this period that I first laid eyes on the most exquisite looking automobile I had ever seen. It was called a Clénet (pron: Clay-nay) Roadster and it was lust at first sight. The two-passenger classic speedster, with its long elegant lines, and its rich 1930s-era styling, was created by Clénet Coachworks, a company, I later learned, that was housed in an airplane hangar at the Santa Barbara municipal airport. An extraordinary French born auto engineer, Alain Clénet, founded the firm and his story is a fascinating one.

The son of France's most successful Ford dealer, Alain grew up with an engineering and design background. He apprenticed in Detroit, designing vehicles for all of the major automakers and also worked in France creating bulldozers and other types of heavy machinery. He soon came to the conclusion that these venues were not the right environment for his aesthetic sensibilities. Detroit cars were merely extensions of their makers' marketing strategies, he complained, and had nothing to do with the type of innovative design Alain cherished. After leaving the auto industry in the early 1970s, the 33-year-old Frenchman, for a while, considered producing new housing designs, and investigated a revolutionary foam-based building material. But this did not pan out.

In late 1974, Clénet decided he "needed something with wheels." Leaving his homeland behind because, as he put it, "I had a profound distaste for socialism," the cheerful capitalist set up shop in Southern California with a concept for a custom auto venture that was both old and, at the same time, quite new. In the true tradition of classic, style-conscious "body-only" designers like Dietrich and Body by Fisher, Clénet planned to place his ultra-stylish fiberglass auto bodies atop stock Detroit chassis and power trains, such as Ford's Lincoln Continental with its massive power plant. The concept worked brilliantly.

In 1976, the first Series I Clénet Roadsters rolled out of the hangar and into my heart. I was smitten by the car's sleek, clean lines and its gleaming paint finish with a gloss so polished it almost glowed in the dark. The matching leather upholstery and lamb's wool carpeting gave the car a look that was both Old World and ultra-modern at the same time. Clénet designed his cars with the collector in mind. Each one was built to order and then numbered like fine art lithographs. Prospective buyers like me were advised that unlike a stock Detroit car, a Clénet would appreciate, rather than depreciate, over time.

In 1977, I finally broke down and placed my order with Clénet for a two-seat convertible coupe with an extended front-end engine compartment. The hood was so long it felt as though you were driving it from the back seat. The car boasted huge supercharger chrome exhaust pipes emerging from under the hood and running down the entire length of the vehicle on both sides. It garnered stares of amazement everywhere I drove it.

My first car was labeled Series I, Car No. 23 of 250, but actually it was the 21st car Clénet produced since there was no Car No. 1 nor Car No. 2 ever made. By the time he had produced 200 cars, Clénet had implemented a number of technical improvements, such as power steering, a tilt steering wheel, and a three-speed automatic transmission. Clénet had added numerous luxury touches as well, such as a solid walnut dashboard, Italian crystal ashtrays, cut glass vent windows, Danish teakwood accents, hand-rubbed acrylic lacquer paint, and an optional padded hardtop and a swanky luggage trunk. Attracted by these new features, I sold my No. 23 and, in 1979, placed my order for Car No. 222 of Series I. It arrived loaded with the latest niceties and coated in a blindingly bright "fire engine red" finish.

Clénet Coachworks continued producing flamboyant 1930s-style vehicles after the first series was concluded with Car No. 250. The Series I Roadsters were next followed by the Series II Cabriolet models, and then the Series III Asha, named after Clénet's daughter. These later models, built on Ford and Mercury Cougar chassis, were often larger and could accommodate four passengers. I purchased a third Clénet, a Series II No. 23 model, and kept it for about five years. The later cars were not as successful as the Series I because they did not have the dramatic styling appeal of the earlier models. In total, just over 480 Clénet's were produced before the company closed in 1986, forced under by high interest rates that put the brakes on many of America's custom car makers. It was, as they say, the end of an era.

Alain Clénet went on to form an engineering company he also dubbed Asha. Asha, the company, produced a Geodesic locking differential, such as the GM Quadra-TRAC, that was used in both racing and street vehicles. Clénet became the controlling stockholder of the McLaren Automotive Group when it acquired Asha, a post he held until resigning in 1998. Recently Clénet and his son, Kelly, founded Ergomotion, a company that designs and distributes articulated hospital beds made in China. These days Alain Clénet restricts his horsepower to the four-legged variety, raising show horses on his farm in the Santa Ynez valley. But his legacy and his contributions to the automotive world are still cherished by collector groups, known as Clénet Clusters, all around the world.

Many auto aficionados consider the Clénet Series I to arguably be the most beautiful automobile ever built. I certainly felt that way during all the years that I was the proud owner of Car No. 222. I kept that "little red roadster" sealed in my garage and only drove it on very special occasions. When I finally sold the aging beauty at a Palm Springs auto auction in 2007, it had only 11,000 miles on the odometer and looked just as stunning as the day I first drove it twenty-eight years earlier.

Was the promise of the Clénet turning into a "Collector's Dream" fulfilled? That depends. Financially, I probably would have done better investing in Apple Computer stock. But it's more than mere financial gain that warms the heart of any collector. There's the knowledge that I was the custodian of an artistic masterpiece for nearly 30 years. Of course it wasn't a Rembrandt or a Stradivarius, but just looking at its long elegant design always caused my heart to soar. I am confident that, thanks to groups like the Clénet Clusters, whoever is now Car No. 222's custodian will likewise care for it and preserve its classic beauty for future generations to enjoy.

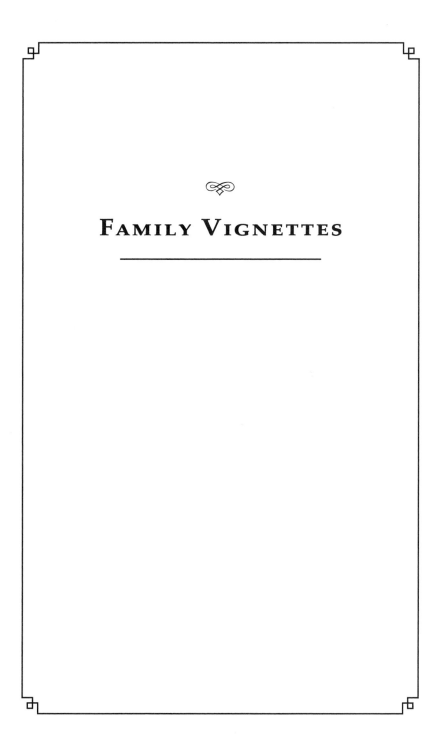

FAMILY VIGNETTES

CHAPTER TWENTY-EIGHT

THE STORY OF
BERT AND BETTY MAYER

The voice of parents are the voices of gods,
for to their children they are heaven's lieutenants.

William Shakespeare

In her "Little House On The Prairie" books, Laura Ingalls Wilder wrote about the "big city" to which her characters would often travel in order to obtain supplies. That big city was Mankato, Minnesota, a picturesque town described by Sinclair Lewis as "New England reborn." It was here that my father was born in 1901 and where he spent the first fourteen years of his long life. Mankato sits at the junction of the Minnesota and Blue Earth rivers and is known for its lakes, bluffs, natural prairies and breathtaking landscapes. It had become a bustling turn-of-the-century town by the time my father came along.

Bertram Joseph Mayer was the eldest of seven children born to my grandparents, Lorenz and Anna Mayer, both first generation descendants of German and Austrian immigrants. It was here in Mankato that Bert's father, Lorenz, along with my Dad's two uncles, Louis and Conrad, collectively known as "The Mayer Brothers," made a name for themselves.

When my father, Bert, was fourteen years old, Grandpa Lorenz decided to move his wife, Grandma Anna, and their children 350 miles due east to the small town of Kaukauna, Wisconsin, not far from Green Bay. The city had just approved the construction of five new hydroelectric plants, an act that would soon earn it the nickname of "Electric City." Grandpa Lorenz worked closely with the designers of the massive municipal project, providing essential components for the huge turbine engines.

My father was greatly influenced during his formative years by the hard-working and inventive atmosphere created by his ingenious father and uncles. This was the era of Tom Swift, Horatio Alger and the Wright Brothers. A golden time at the dawning of a new century filled with new dreams and aspirations. And the inventive and enterprising Mayer Brothers embodied this spirit fully. But there was another powerful influence on my father during this time: the Catholic Church.

In Kaukauna, the family had become well-established members of the parish and my father, Bert, had served as an altar boy during many church services. Reaching his late teens, Bert felt a calling to join the priesthood and went so far as to enroll at a seminary for a short while. However, the aspiring novitiate later decided to instead complete his engineering studies at the University of Wisconsin in Madison. As fate would have it, while Bert attended college, something happened that would divert the young man's path away from the completion of his college studies. He met, and fell in love with my future mother, Benerita Pizzo.

Betty, as my mother was affectionately known throughout her life, was born in Madison in 1904. Like my father, she too was the product of a sprawling immigrant family. Her parents, Ferdinando and Juanina Pizzo, had emigrated to the U.S. from Sicily, after which Ferdinando "Americanized" his first name to Fred. Grandpa Fred did not come directly to America from his homeland. He was a free spirit who traveled the world before arriving at the New York harbor in 1882. Fred worked at odd jobs and eventually landed in New Orleans where he met and married Juanina. The couple later moved to Chicago where Fred worked in a small repair shop. His English skills were proficient enough that he was often called upon to translate Italian legal documents. This side job would occasionally take him to the courthouses in Springfield and to the Wisconsin state capitol, Madison. Eventually, the couple settled in Madison where Fred worked in a knife-sharpening shop and as a translator. Over the course of their forty-four year marriage, Fred and Juanina had seventeen children, of which ten survived, including my mother, Betty.

After a short courtship, Bert and Betty were wed in Detroit in 1923, and moved back to Madison after their wedding. Shortly after the ceremony, Betty's parents, Fred and Juanina, left Wisconsin and moved to Los Angeles because of Juanina's health. Bert and Betty remained behind in Madison where my father found work with the State Highway Engineering Department. It was during this period that I was born, followed two years later by the birth of my sister, Dolores.

In 1937, when I was eleven years old, my parents made the decision to leave Madison in order to get away from its blustery and frigid winters. They settled in Huntington Park, California, not far from my mother's parents. Like her own mother, Betty's health was suffering due to the harsh climate that existed in Madison. Betty and Juanina's bloodlines stretched back to the sunny regions of eastern Sicily. They never felt at home in the Nordic climes of Wisconsin.

With no employment for Bert in hand, and only the most tenuous of family connections available to find any, our small family arrived in 1937 in Huntington Park, a sleepy, but very sunny community about six and a half miles southeast of downtown

Los Angeles. Boasting a year-round comfortable temperature, Huntington Park was the perfect place for our family to defrost. During the pre-war years, my father worked at a series of odd jobs to supplement his sporadic engineering work. These were years of financial struggle for our family and one image stands out clearly in my memory from this difficult period.

My parents had managed to scrape together $2,500 to purchase a small and flimsy bungalow. The place was a true "fixer-upper" and my father got to work doing just that. I recall watching Dad attempt to paint the ceiling of the home in utter frustration as rivulets of paint ran down both his arms. His depression was obvious as he wondered aloud if he had made the right decision in moving the family to the west coast. Dad was a brilliant engineer, but not much of a household handyman, I'm afraid. His frustration was compounded by his ongoing need to find permanent employment. Only then would he feel secure that our family had been properly relocated in California.

I vividly recall my own difficult period of relocation adjustment that I had to undergo as an eleven-year old moving into a new state, a new school, and a new circle of schoolmates. I arrived at school on the first day of sixth grade dressed in my regular school outfit; a plaid shirt and a pair of plus-four trousers or "knickerbockers," more commonly known as "knickers." These were pants that extended to just below the knee where they were gathered atop over-the-calf woolen stockings. Knickers were popularized by early golfers and are still favored by traditionalists out on the links today. Back in Wisconsin during the 1930s, knickers were as widespread among schoolboys as denim jeans are today—but not in California where long pants were the prevailing fashion. I was immediately singled out for mockery by my new classmates and earned the humiliating nickname of "Knickers." The group's leader, a pudgy schoolyard bully, named Gordon, targeted me.

"Hey, Knickers!" he'd taunt, "Where's your golf bag, Caddy?"

After three days of this, I had had enough. I made up my mind that if the teasing didn't stop, I was going to make it stop. During recess, Gordon and his crew again confronted me.

"Where ya going, Knickers?" he shouted at me from across the playground. I approached him head-on and proclaimed firmly: "Don't call me that!"

"What are you going to do about it, hunh, Knickers?" he sang out.

I lunged and caught him around the knees, bringing him to the ground. I'm not sure which of us won the ensuing tussle, but I do know that no one called me names again after that. Although I had successfully defended my honor, I nevertheless decided to play it safe and requested that my parents buy me some long pants.

Since that fistfight, I have never again been required to resort to physical violence in order to resolve a problem. But it's comforting to recall how I took a step closer to manhood in that California schoolyard and that I was not afraid to stand up for myself when the situation required it. Although I never heard him admit it, I felt that my dad was proud of me when he learned about the knickers incident. His guidance and highly developed sense of right and wrong served me well as I grew into adulthood in California.

During World War II, when I was a teenager, Dad found employment with an engineering company that assigned him to work on a project in nearby San Pedro Harbor. He was required to construct floating concrete dry docks used by the shipyards. While concrete blocks would normally sink, thanks to my father's ingenious design, the superstructure contained enough trapped airspace to keep the docks afloat.

After World War II, Dad found his niche with an Alhambra engineering firm, C.F. Braun. Founded by Carl Braun in 1922 in suburban San Gabriel Valley, the technology firm was a world leader in the manufacture of heat exchange units, gas processing equipment, and cooling towers. Dad was helpful in finding me a job at C.F. Braun shortly after Marcie and I were married in 1947. I worked there for a couple of years until I met Claude Howard and began my career in the construction industry. Dad remained with Braun until he retired.

Like many women caught up in the home front war effort, my mother, Betty, went to work during World War II in order to "do her part." She landed a clerical job at the Rabun Bronze Foundry, a company that manufactured grave memorials. In addition to her work at Rabun and the job of raising a family, my mother devoted every Sunday, from 1942 through 1945, to sitting at a desk outside of our church selling war bonds to the exiting parishioners. This was strictly volunteer work and she received no compensation other than the fulfillment of her patriotic commitment plus some valuable sales experience. It was this second benefit that served her well when, after the war, she decided to continue working. Mother took the necessary classes and eventually obtained her license as a real estate broker. She was soon actively selling residential properties throughout Southern California.

When it came to personalities, my parents complimented each other perfectly. Dad was rather easy-going, laid-back, and far more of a thinker than a talker. He reminded a lot of people of Gary Cooper. My mother, on the other hand, was more like Gina Lolabridgida—fiery, hot-tempered, and deeply passionate. She was a hustler and a "go-getter," both professionally and during her off-duty hours. She never saw a house she couldn't sell and never met a challenge she couldn't overcome—except for her heart condition that eventually led to her death.

I was fortunate to enjoy close ties with both of my grandmothers, Anna and Juanina. Although they were from far different ethnic and cultural backgrounds, I viewed them both as strong, sturdy women whose primary role in life was to serve as the cornerstone of their sprawling, and sometimes brawling, families. My mother, on the other hand, seemed quite different. Unlike the women of her prior generation—who were primarily traditional custodians and caregivers for their many children—my mother had a more independent streak. She completed high school, studied for a career, and became that most rare of commodities in the 1950s—a working mother. The effect on me of seeing both my parents go off to work each day was profound. It stiffened my work ethic and made me regard hard work and sacrifice as part of the natural order of things.

An appreciation for the value of hard work was not the only trait I inherited from my parents. They demonstrated their devotion and love for their children and for each other in everything they did. Bert and Betty were wonderful parents and I credit them with whatever success in life I may have achieved. I feel I inherited my relaxed and tolerant approach to life from my dad and my tendency towards tenacity and perseverance from my mother. As all good parents should be, they were my first mentors during the years that shaped the man I was to become.

My parents' marriage lasted for sixty-eight years until my mother passed away at the age of eighty-seven in 1991. Dad died of complications of old age in 1996. He was ninety-five years old.

They say that the best inheritance parents can give a child is a few minutes of their time each day. I am fortunate in that I was the beneficiary of a truly rich inheritance in this regard. It was given to me by two wonderful people, my parents, whose memory will endure as a blessing forever.

Chapter Twenty-Nine

Why I Quit Smoking When I Was Five Years Old

If what I have to say in these pages does not reflect the mellowing of age,
that's only because I've never found that life and memories respond
to time the way that tobacco does.

Caleb Carr

It's funny how the smallest stimulus to one of your senses will sometimes throw open the floodgates of memory. For example, just a whiff of lima beans will take me back to my Army days. Or tasting a Coney-style hot dog will send me off to my teenage summers at the Long Beach Pike. But the trigger that will transport me the furthest back in time involves my sense of hearing. Just a brief listen to the clanking of glass bottles and the clip-clopping of horses' hooves on pavement, and I'm back to my pre-school years, seated alongside my dapper Uncle Joe on his milk wagon as he made his early morning rounds.

One of Madison's many milkmen, my Mother's brother, Joe, lived with our family during the earliest period of my life. I remember him quite vividly as a young dashing figure, even though I was only five years old at the time. Starched in a crisp white uniform that included a peaked cap and a black bowtie, Uncle Joe would climb aboard his horse-drawn milk wagon every morning, except Sunday, at 3:30 am. I would normally be fast asleep when he left the house, but one autumn day, Uncle Joe decided to give in to my pleas and awakened me to join him on his route.

I can still recall how we first made our way through the dark city streets to the dairy in order to pick up his cargo. The steep, rain-slicked avenues of working-class Madison were eerily empty and dead silent. With only the steady clip clopping of Joe's faithful horse, Matilda, echoing through the darkness, we next made stop after stop all along Joe's proscribed milk route. Old Matilda did not have to be guided. She knew every stop from memory and could even back up the rig along a steep curb without a hitch. As Uncle Joe ran each customer's milk bottles up to their doorstep, Matilda and I would wait patiently till he climbed back on board the wagon, ready to head down the road to the next stop.

The wagon was not refrigerated. When the weather was warm, Uncle Joe would pick up blocks of ice at the dairy that would keep his load chilled all morning. While today this type of home delivery is considered a nostalgic vestige of America's past, in the late 1920s, over 70 percent of all milk sold in the U.S. was distributed door-to-door by an army of uniformed milkmen. Everyone understood the meaning of the Broadway show tune lyric that commented on the lateness of the hour by saying: "Good-night, baby. The milkman's on his way." I doubt that too many people under age fifty would understand that line today.

In the era before home refrigerators, most working people considered owning an icebox to be a luxury. We had one, but I remember visiting other homes and noticing that the quart glass milk bottles were often kept in a galvanized tub of cool water, usually located outdoors on the back porch. I also remember how the un-homogenized milk would form a layer of cream on top expanding the contents of the bottle. Uncle Joe delivered milk in special cream-top bottles that would provide a two to three inch space for the cream to rise, making it easy to spoon it off before consuming the bottle's contents.

Uncle Joe was a marvelous raconteur and I was his best audience. He explained how more and more milkmen were moving away from horse-drawn wagons to the new Divco milk trucks in order to save time.

"I'm not in that big of a rush," Joe explained with a smile. "And besides, hay and oats are still a lot cheaper than gasoline." He appeared to be the smartest person in the whole world in my young eyes. Not only that, Uncle Joe was simply the most charming person I knew and I idolized him completely. He was a handsome, well-dressed, and unmarried man in his early twenties and clearly enjoyed his life to the fullest. His kindness and affection towards me created a strong bond between us at a time when both my parents were leading very active lives. By the time Joe had completed his morning rounds his workday was over. That left the entire rest of the day for doing what he enjoyed best: chasing girls, dancing, and plain having fun. Smoking several packs of cigarettes each day was also among his litany of vices.

Uncle Joe was a Luckies man. With their green wrapper (the package was changed to white in 1942 when "Lucky Strike green went to war") and distinctive circular logo, Lucky Strike was America's top-selling brand of cigarettes. Every schoolboy within earshot of a radio knew their famous slogan: L.S.M.F.T. or Lucky Strikes Mean Fine Tobacco.

Since I wanted to do everything "just like Uncle Joe," I decided that I was going to smoke Luckies, too. So, one morning, while Joe was out making his appointed rounds, I quietly snuck into his room and foraged through his drawers until I found a pack of his cigarettes and a book of matches. Concealing both in my pants pocket, I next looked around for an ashtray. That wasn't hard to find since they were scattered throughout the house. Now, for the big challenge. Where do I go to light up? Outside was out of the question. It was freezing cold out there. Looking around I spotted the perfect spot to hide while I carried out my childhood crime: under the big dining room table. The table was covered with a huge tablecloth that hung all the way to the floor. I had often imagined this space as my secret tent when playing Cowboys and Indians and other games of imagination. I was certain no one could see me under there, so I lifted up one side and crawled into my hideaway, ready to take my first puffs.

Figuring out how to unwrap the cellophane wrapper and then forcing out just one cigarette from the package was a bit of a challenge, but I managed it eventually. I placed one end of the Lucky to my lips, just as I had seen Joe do countless times before, and then fiddled free a match and struck it. I knew the cigarette-lighting protocol from having watched Joe so many times. I gracefully cupped both hands around the tip of the Lucky, touching it to the flame while inhaling mightily. I deftly blew the smoke out of the side of my mouth, extinguishing the match at the same time. It was a perfect impersonation of Uncle Joe, who undoubtedly had borrowed the maneuver from Humphrey Bogart. Even though the term was not in vogue in those days, at that moment, I felt about as "cool" as any five-year-old could have possibly felt.

After a few more puffs, the area under the dining room table could no longer contain the billowing grey smoke clouds I was creating. In a few minutes, the entire dining room became hazy and filled with blue cigarette smoke. Sniffing something out of the ordinary for this hour of the day, my mother walked in and immediately tried to determine what had caused the room to fill with smoke. Fortunately, she did not panic and did not call the fire department. Instead, she calmly picked up a corner of the tablecloth and quickly realized there was no fire danger. She also realized that her young son needed a good lesson about the evils of smoking. In her infinite wisdom and saintly patience, Mother did not scold me. In fact, she seemed to be supportive. This threw me since I was expecting her to be quite upset.

"Are you having a good time with that cigarette down there, Bobby?" she asked in an apparently sweet voice. I did not respond. "Well, it looks to me like you are. Why don't you go ahead and finish it?"

What was going on? Instead of berating me for smoking one of Uncle Joe's Luckies, my mother was encouraging me to finish it. I shrugged and went on puffing as told and, when the cigarette had burned down to where I could no longer hold it in my fingers, I stubbed it out in the ashtray just as I had seen Uncle Joe do a million times before. Mother grabbed the Luckies and pulled another cigarette halfway out of the pack. She offered it to me.

"Here, son," she said earnestly, "smoke another one. You seem to have enjoyed the first one, so why not have another? Only this time, suck the smoke all the way into your lungs." She demonstrated as I pulled the next cigarette from the pack. I lit up again, in the same off-hand Bogart manner, and, as Mother had instructed, I pulled a big load of nicotine-laden tobacco smoke directly into my innocent lungs. This, indeed, had the desired effect.

I coughed and wheezed as my eyes began to tear. I turned in red-faced anguish to my mother.

"Go on, Bobby," she implored. "You've started it. Now you've got to finish it."

I again did as I was told and by the time I had finished the second cigarette, I felt nauseous, light-headed, green to the gills, and anything but "cool."

I gave up smoking that day almost eight decades ago and, as a result of my mother's "tough love," I have never smoked again to this day. Not in the Army, despite serious pressure to be "one of the guys." Not in Las Vegas casinos and not in the barroom or the bedroom. In fact, I am still affected by the smell of cigarette or cigar smoke. Just a single whiff will send me back to that fateful day under the dining room table where a little boy tried to emulate his favorite uncle and ran into a very powerful force: his Mother's love.

After the smoking incident, I still adored Uncle Joe, but I remained puzzled about what he found so attractive about those awful "smokes." Chasing girls made perfect sense to me, but his love of Luckies remained a mystery from that point forward. Uncle Joe, unfortunately, was not very lucky. He died at an early age and I was never sure about which of his vices did him in at the end. Was it the wine, the women, the song, or those thousands of Lucky Strike cigarettes he voraciously consumed? I can't be sure, but I do remember Uncle Joe fondly every time I'm reminded of an old-fashioned milkman and whenever I hear that old Merle Travis song: "Smoke, Smoke, Smoke That Cigarette:"

Tell St. Peter at the Pearly Gate
That I just hate to make him wait,
But I just gotta have another cigarette.

CHAPTER THIRTY

MEMORIES OF MARCIE

Elusive butterfly. She may only live one day,
Oh! But what a happy day it is!

Portuguese Children's Song

"You need to get out and meet people!" Dolores admonished me. "The war's over, you're almost twenty-one, and there's a whole world out there waiting." My sister was right. It was 1946 and I was freshly mustered from the Army Air Force and just becoming used to civilian life. As a teenager I had never been much of a "lady's man." I'd never even attended any of our high school proms. Once I'd joined the service at age eighteen, my military and flight training occupied almost all of my waking hours. If I received a weekend pass, instead of chasing girls with the other fellows from my outfit, I'd usually head out for some sightseeing to explore the area in which I found myself stationed.

Since my discharge I'd been working at the engineering company where my father was employed and where he had helped me secure an entry-level job. Dolores was right; it was time. So when she suggested that I meet one of her co-workers from her job at a Bank of America branch, I consented.

"Marcie just moved here from San Francisco and is living with her sister," Dolores informed me. "She's really sweet and very cute. I know that you two would make a swell couple." I didn't need the build-up. Dolores made the arrangements for a rendezvous at a local café where Marcie and I met each other for the first time a few days later. I'm not sure what sort of impression I made on her, but I was certainly attracted to this petite and bright-faced beauty right there on the spot. Her walnut-colored eyes matched her shoulder-length hair and her smile simply radiated. Marcie and I began dating and I soon discovered that she was an exuberant, fun-loving free spirit with a fiery temper. Qualities that I enjoyed. Not many months later, in early 1947, Marcie and I became husband and wife.

The courtship was such a whirlwind, I really did not learn a great deal about the background of my 19-year old bride until after the honeymoon. Her proud immigrant heritage paralleled that of my own family and accounted for the many values that she and I shared and upon which we would build our marriage. The path that brought Marcie into my life is another fascinating example of the American Dream in action.

Marceline Ann Correa was born in Oakland and spent her earliest years outside of Berkeley. It was here that her father, André, a young Portuguese fisherman, had settled during the early 1920s after arriving in America by way of the Azores in 1918. André's departure from his homeland was part of a mass exodus that followed the fall of the Portuguese monarchy in 1910 and the subsequent anti-Catholic government that followed in its wake. Many young men like André joined the flood of immigrants in order to flee the mandatory military service that was instituted during World War I.

André somehow managed to obtain passage as a crewmember aboard a vessel that would soon become one of the world's foremost luxury ocean liners, the S.S. Paris. Originally commissioned in 1913, the ship was designed with emigrating Europeans like André in mind. But after World War I, the vessel was re-furbished and enlarged by the Red Star Line. When it set sail again in 1923, the Paris was the largest vessel ever built in France. The level of luxury aboard the new Paris was astonishing. From the grand Art Deco ballroom to the mammoth staterooms equipped with private telephones and unique gold-trimmed "square" portholes, the Paris was truly a floating palace. She saw service throughout the decade, until finally a fire in Le Havre devastated the ship in 1929.

Aboard the pre-luxury Paris, André passed through the Port of Jucaro in Cuba before arriving at Ellis Island in New York Harbor. A freewheeling nineteen-year-old adventurer, André navigated across the "ocean of land" that made up his new homeland. His travels eventually brought him to the Portuguese farming community of Milpitas, California. He settled in a nearby area of Oakland dubbed "Jingletown." The area got its name from the predominantly poor Portuguese immigrants, who would walk the streets with the few coins they received as payment for cotton picking, jingling in their pockets.

André was not the typical Portuguese immigrant, however. Instead of finding work, as other young Portuguese men had done, in the whaling industry or as a laborer in the agricultural communities around the central San Joaquin Valley, André purchased and operated a small Texaco gas station on the eastern side of the San Francisco Bay. It was there that he met his future wife, Sarah, a feisty, independent Portuguese woman who already had several children of her own. André and Sarah had only one child together, a fire-eyed daughter they named Marceline—a name that means "warlike."

We set up house above the garage in one of the rental properties my parents owned in Huntington Park. Not long after, when my parents bought a small apartment building there, Marcie and I moved to Lynwood and worked as the on-site managers. Eventually, we purchased our first real home in Whittier and, a few years later, moved to Downey. We lived in various homes in Downey for the duration of our twenty-year marriage and it is this community that stands, in our family's collective memory, as our actual hometown.

The town of Downey was established in 1873 from the raw land of Los Nietos township in southeast Los Angeles County. It was named for California Civil War Governor John G. Downey and began its growth as a farming stop along the Southern Pacific Railroad line connecting Los Angeles and San Diego. In the 1940s Downey moved away from its agrarian heritage as the nation's top producer of castor beans and began its real growth as the home of many of the country's foremost defense contractors. An era came to end when a major facility, North American Rockwell, a company that had, for over seventy years, produced many of the components used in the nation's aircraft industry and the NASA space program, closed its doors in 1999. But in the mid 1950s, Rockwell, along with many similar companies, was undergoing a huge expansion burst.

Driven by the aerospace industry, our years in Downey were characterized by nearly uncontrolled economic growth. The intersection of Lakewood Boulevard and Firestone Boulevard, in the town's central business district, was soon labeled as one of the busiest intersections in Southern California. In the 1970s a Downey brother and sister team, billed as "The Carpenters," shot to fame as a top musical entertainment act. The surf music phenomenon of the 1960s had put Downey on the map when tiny Downey Records had an international smash hit with "Pipeline," an instrumental by a local group called the Chantays. The title had nothing to do with transporting oil, but rather referred to the hollow space in a crashing wave favored by serious surfing fanatics.

As another type of wave—a wave of new home construction—swept over Downey, driven by the influx of arriving residents drawn to the area by the defense and aeronautics industries, we saw our business mushroom from a small "mom and pop" operation into the largest developer of multifamily residential housing in Southern California. In addition to taking care of our three young children during those years, Marcie worked by my side building our business and taking care of all the essential back office duties. She maintained the books, sent out the statements, paid the bills, and generally made it possible for me to remain in the field, putting together deals and attracting new business.

Over the course of our marriage, Marcie and I were blessed with three wonderful children, Linda, Bob Jr. (RJ), and Michael, who all spent their teenage years in Downey. I recall Marcie as the first of what would later be known as a "soccer mom," although the game favored by the kids at that time was Little League baseball. As our business made such things possible, we purchased a series of "grown-up toys" that succeeded in delighting the kids. A succession of cars, private planes, and pleasure boats gave our family the freedom to travel and build up a lasting reservoir of unbeatable memories.

One of our favorite travel destinations in those days was a resort in the Palm Springs desert known as the Desert Air Hotel. This cozy and somewhat isolated facility was surrounded by hundreds of date palm trees that provided an ambience of rural privacy. The facility offered all the amenities imaginable and guests could enjoy the balmy desert breeze by the pool or out on the golf course. A wonderful feature was a private grass airstrip that allowed guests to taxi their planes right up to the door of their rooms.

Although we usually traveled to the Desert Air with our kids, on one occasion, in early 1967, Marcie and I planned a little "grown-up getaway" time for some sorely needed relaxation. During our

absence, we brought in a very capable baby-sitter to keep an eye
on RJ and Michael.

We arrived at the Desert Air on Sunday and parked our plane
on the nearby grass airstrip. Since I needed to be back in the office on
Thursday morning, our plan was to fly back home late Wednesday
evening. When Wednesday arrived, those balmy desert breezes
had grown more turbulent as an unexpected desert storm blew
into the region. Since by this time I had obtained my instrument
rated pilot's license, poor weather conditions were no longer much
of a threat. Despite this, Marcie simply hated to fly in any type
of bad weather. So on Wednesday morning, we quickly revised
our plans and decided that I would fly back through the storm
early the following morning, while Marcie would rent a car that
afternoon at the resort and drive home by herself. Marcie preferred
doing her desert driving during the cooler evening hours, but for
some reason, her departure was delayed and she did not begin
her journey until late Wednesday night. She never made it past
Colton.

In the wee hours of Thursday morning, our closest friends in
Downey, John and Rosalie Nisser, received an urgent phone call
from the San Bernadino County Sheriff's Department. They had
tried to reach me but since I was not in town, they were referred
to the Nissers. The police informed our friends that there had been
an accident in Colton involving Marcie. Her car had left the road,
flipped over, and landed upside-down after dropping twenty feet
onto the roadway below. Marcie was killed instantly.

The police suspected that she might have fallen asleep just
prior to having reached the overpass. John and Rosalie knew
how to contact me in the desert, but did not wish to convey such
horrific news over the telephone. They also felt it was important
that I not be alone when learning of the tragedy. They got into their
car immediately and drove two hours to the Desert Air where they

awakened me and broke the bad news. The three of us then traveled the sixty miles to Colton in order to identify Marcie's body. The shock of Marcie's loss was without question the worst experience of my life. One moment Marcie was alive and the next moment she was gone forever like some elusive butterfly.

A funeral service was held at our church in Downey and Marcie was buried at the Calvary Cemetery in Los Angeles. Not surprisingly, given Marcie's community involvement in Downey, hundreds of people turned out to pay their respects and say their farewells. It was a magnificent tribute to the memory of a truly wonderful woman.

The impact upon our children of so suddenly losing their mother was something that would take years to assess. Our oldest, Linda, was twenty at the time and was more or less on her own. The two boys, RJ and Mike were fourteen and twelve respectively, and I was grateful for Linda's assistance in helping me and the boys get through those very dark days following Marcie's untimely death.

It took some time, but I eventually began the business of putting my life back together. At age forty-one, I found myself a widower with three children and a thriving business. Fortunately, I did not succumb to despair and, as a form of self-therapy, poured myself into my work. I would remain a widower and bachelor father for almost five years before fortune and circumstance would allow me to overcome the sorrow brought on by Marcie's death and take my life in an entirely new direction.

CHAPTER THIRTY-ONE

ALL MY CHILDREN

Who of us is mature enough for offspring before the offspring arrive?
The value of marriage is not that adults produce children
but that children produce adults.

Peter de Vries

This imaginary headline could well have announced the birth of our first child, Linda, in late 1947: "New mother and baby girl doing fine. Dad in fair condition." At the time, Marcie and I were living in a tiny apartment at my parents' home in Huntington Park, California. The main house, where Mom and Dad lived, was closer to the street and situated near the front of the lot while the garage, with its two upstairs apartments, sat towards the rear. We had been living in one of those cozy units since our marriage earlier that year. As Marcie, nine months pregnant, emerged from the bathroom, she gave me a little smile that said "Now's the time." We had discussed what to do, so Marcie calmly gathered her overnight bag as I escorted her down the stairs to inform my parents that they were about to become grandparents.

"Are you two ready to go to the hospital?" Dad asked, but I never had a chance to respond. The next thing I remember is staring up directly at the light fixture that hung from the ceiling of my parents' living room. I was shocked to realize that I was lying flat on my back. I had evidently passed out from the excitement and fortunately landed on my parents' deep pile carpeting. After determining that I was okay, my Mother helped me up and held back her laughter long enough to say:

"Bob, you froze up and fell over like a house of cards. It was straight out of a Charlie Chaplin movie!" I was glad that the carpeting had cushioned my fall and helped me avoid a concussion as I hit the deck. Marcie was taking all this in stride, but the anxiety and anticipation of becoming a first-time Dad was enough to flatten me. The experience was particularly embarrassing because I liked to cultivate an image as "Mr. Cool and Sophisticated" in those days. This episode, while serving to deflate that particular self-image, was the source of much merriment at my expense over the ensuring years every time our family would retell the story of Linda's birth. While the chiding stung, even Mr. Blasé had to eventually admit that it was a hilarious and unforgettable moment.

After this minor setback, we piled into the family car and drove to St. Francis Hospital in Lynwood. Linda was born soon thereafter, weighing in at a respectable eight pounds three ounces. She was the most beautiful little baby in the world and instantly became our family's pearl, surrounded by the nurturing protective shell of parents and grandparents.

We brought Linda back to our little one-bedroom upstairs garret as Marcie and I were officially inducted into the "hood" — parenthood, that is. We continued to live above my parents' garage for a few more years. In 1949 Dad and Mom bought a six-plex apartment building in Lynwood from Claude Howard who owned the Howard Construction Company. Part of the sales agreement was that Claude would extend a job offer to the buyer's son — that being me. So, with little two-year old Linda in tow, Marcie and I left my father's house and moved to Lynwood to manage this new property for my parents.

The following year a delightful young couple bought the triplex apartment building right next door to ours. John and Rosalie Nisser soon became not only our next-door neighbors but also our closest friends. Marcie and Rosalie became as buddy-buddy as Lucy and Ethel and they even had a few madcap adventures. Over the next few years our two families meshed into one as we planned picnics and vacations together and spent every holiday and special occasion in each other's company. Those were heady days; filled with hard work and the bright promise of a better tomorrow. Until the Nissers began having their own children, Linda was our common daughter and was blessed with two fathers and two mothers. We may not have been an entire village, but we were certainly bigger than your average family.

Shortly after Linda turned six, I purchased a small lot on Cookacre Street in Compton and put up a duplex apartment. This is where our expanding family would reside for the next few years. We had only just moved in when along came Bob, Jr. (known as RJ). Linda was delighted when we brought her new baby brother home to the Cookacre apartment.

Little Bobby appeared perfectly healthy at that point, but after a few days at home we discovered that there was a serious problem. He was unable to hold down any food. After each feeding of either milk or formula, Bobby would immediately throw up everything he had consumed. The poor child was hungry, but was not getting any nourishment. When he was ten days old, Bobby was taken back to St. Francis Hospital where he was diagnosed as suffering from a congenital condition known as "pyloric stenosis." The pyloris is a valve at the base of the stomach that controls the flow of nourishment into the small intestine. In about one percent of all births, the muscle tissue surrounding the pyloris will expand causing the valve to close off, thereby trapping the stomach contents. Further feeding results in vomiting and, if the opening is totally obstructed, no food may be digested.

Bobby immediately underwent surgery to correct the problem. Dr. Paul Kouri, a highly capable surgeon, who has remained a family friend to this day, performed the surgery. It was a fright-filled and harrowing ordeal for our young family, but ultimately Bobby recovered fully and was never bothered by the problem again.

After having lived in apartments for the first eight years of our marriage, Marcie and I bought our first real home in Whittier in 1955. We paid $9,700 for a nearly new three-bedroom, two-bath ranch style house in a charming neighborhood. As with our two prior homes, this one, too, was blessed with the arrival of the stork as our second son, Michael was born in September of that year.

It was in Whittier that I decided to leave the Howard Construction Company and set up shop on my own, operating out of our garage. After a few years of this, we moved into the first of the three houses we would call home in Downey. In Downey I was able to move my business out of our home and into a legitimate office. Downey also served as the foundation for our children's formative years. This is where they attended elementary and high school, where they played sports, and otherwise grew up. In essence, the "Downey Years" represented the time we all grew up and grew together as a family.

Unfortunately, those wonderful years would end with tragedy in 1967 when Marcie lost her life suddenly in an auto accident. As a result, all of our lives took off in a different direction. Over the coming years, we relied upon friends and family for moral support. None was more vital than the kindness extended to us by our dear friends, John and Rosalie Nisser. For my children, the Nisser's home became an extension of our own. While no one could possibly fill the void in our children's lives that was created by Marcie's untimely death, the Nissers did all they could to somehow diminish the pain of her absence.

I recall how I threw myself into my work during those difficult years. While I did not yield to despair or fall victim to depression, I nevertheless could not overcome a feeling of guilt. While staying busy running my growing business, I felt I was neglecting my responsibilities as a parent. Instead of acting as both a mother and a father to my kids—especially the two younger boys—I found myself acting like neither. I compensated for these feelings by showering RJ and Mike with the flashy and expensive adult toys they loved: hot rod cars, high-powered inboard speedboats, a luxurious cabin cruiser, and several types of aircraft. If one of the boys smashed up his car, I'd pay to have it repaired or just get him a new one.

In retrospect, I sincerely regret my actions during those years. In hindsight, it is clear that I was trying to make up for my absence in the boys' lives. While the kids truly loved the high-octane playthings, I obviously could have handled things a bit better. If I had it to do all over again, I would figure out a way to cut down on my job duties and upgrade the quantity and the quality of the time I spent with my children as they were growing up. Of course, the past cannot be undone, but we can learn from mistakes and pass the wisdom gained on to others. That's why I feel everyone should remember that no man on his deathbed ever said: "I wish I had spent more time at the office."

Despite my shortcomings as a single dad, I can honestly say that I am extremely proud of "All My Children." All three of my kids have worked, at some point and in various capacities, in our family business. They grew into adulthood, parenthood, and grandparenthood with flying colors and they have woven those colors into a never-ending tapestry of cherished memories and blessings. I have come to realize how hard working and resilient they are and how devoted they are to their own wonderful families. Even more rewarding is the high quality of character and integrity

I observe among my children and their families. In summary, I feel nothing but optimism as I work to prepare for their future that will transcend my own lifetime. This is a person's only true shot at immortality: building a legacy of love that arises straight from the heart. This legacy is rooted in the passion of my life's work and will continue to grow, I am convinced, across the generations yet to come. What more could any man, or father, ask for?

LINDA

During the year immediately following my wife, Marcie's, death in 1967, our twenty-year-old daughter, Linda, became something of a surrogate mother for her two younger brothers. She was a big help in looking after the "Three Boys," as she referred to RJ, Mike, and me, and helped us get through those tough times. She put aside her studies in Las Vegas to assume her new role. She did the shopping, the cooking, and took care of some of the domestic drudgery. Linda even worked part-time in our Downey office. Somehow, while serving as our family's stable rudder, she managed to find time to marry and later give birth to my first grandchild, Marceline Ann, named in loving memory of her grandmother. Little Marci brought a renewed sunshine into all of our lives at a time we really needed it. It would be years before I could actually call Marci by her name and for a long time I referred to her simply as "the baby" or "my granddaughter."

Not long after Little Marci's birth, Linda became a single working mother. For four years she worked at J&M Sales, as a "Girl Friday," before moving up to outside sales. Then in 1977, Linda was hired to work out of our Ambassador Inn's corporate offices as the "White Glove Lady." Her job assignment was to carry out surprise inspections at each of the chain's twelve hotels several times each year. She would simply appear in the lobby unannounced and begin going through her checklist. Linda carried out her duties with characteristic diligence and if she found something that didn't meet the company's standards or simply didn't smell right, it would get reported.

She tells the story of one such visit the day she arrived unexpectedly at the Phoenix Ambassador Inn. She came upon a guest room door at 6 p.m. with a "Do Not Disturb" card dangling from its doorknob.

"How long has that been on the door?" she asked the head of housekeeping, who was accompanying Linda during the inspection.

"It's been there since the night before last," she was told. "We've knocked on the door lots of times, but he doesn't answer."

"Well something smells funny to me. Open it up," Linda instructed.

"We've tried that," said the housekeeping manager. "He's thrown the deadbolt and we can't get in with the master key."

"Well then call maintenance and go around outside and break in through the window." They did just that and soon the room door was opened and Linda went in. The stench was overpowering and there on the bed was the cause: the dead body of an apparent suicide victim. Linda learned that the hotel business was full of surprises—and not all of them pleasant.

During the 1970s, my mother, Betty, and I both encouraged Linda to study for her real estate license. To her credit, Linda heeded our advice and succeeded in becoming a successful residential real estate broker. She faced some very challenging times when, soon after she got into the business, the U.S. economy started suffering from "stagflation" as home mortgage rates rose as high as 19%. This more or less killed the residential real estate business. Through her tenacity and toughness, Linda hung in there and, as the market recovered, she was soon turning houses quickly as the home real estate boom started to pick up speed. In talking to her about that period of her life, Linda explains that she was driven by her need to be a good provider for her daughter.

"Dad, in those days I had just two goals," she told me years later. "One, I dedicated myself to getting Marci through school and seeing that she graduated. The second goal was my dream of living at the beach." Both goals were realized at the same time. As soon as Marci graduated from high school, Linda packed up and moved surfside to Ocean Boulevard in Long Beach.

One evening in 1989, Linda had been invited to a Halloween Fairy Tale Ball and was fashioned in a stunning Little Red Riding Hood costume. Instead of goodies for Grandma, however, Linda's basket was filled with Alka-Seltzer and Tums in preparation for the post-Halloween hangovers that the party guests were sure to experience the next morning. As Linda was handing out some of the goodies in her basket, she was spotted by a Prince Charming named Mike Howit. The party was filled with people, so Linda was only marginally aware of Mike's presence, but Mike was immediately smitten with Little Red. It would take Mike four months to work up the courage to ask her out, however.

At the time they met, Mike was a supervisor at the Ports of Los Angeles and Long Beach where he oversaw the loading and unloading of vast amounts of cargo on behalf of the Pacific Maritime Association. Michael had lived most of his life on the colorful San Pedro peninsula among the wharves and piers of Los Angeles Harbor. In 1969 Mike was drafted into the Army and received training as a medic before being shipped out to Vietnam. He saw heavy combat and found himself caught in a vicious crossfire while attempting to attend to his injured comrades. He sustained a massive head trauma and endured hundreds of shrapnel fragments all over his body before being Med-Evac-ed to a Saigon hospital. Mike came home totally paralyzed on his left side. His doctors advised him that he would never be able to walk again. Thus began a grueling process that saw Mike struggle bravely as he underwent endless physical therapy sessions and as he moved in and out of a series of VA hospitals. After several long years, Mike beat the odds. He eventually was able to return to work at his beloved San Pedro Harbor.

Linda and Mike were married in Lake Tahoe in August of 1992. At the time, Michael had two teenagers, Kimberly and Matthew, and together with a now grown Marci, they formed a family of five.

In addition to having her hands full with her real estate career and her family duties, Linda began working as a Red Cross volunteer and spent many hours as a disaster relief worker. Her Red Cross rescue work would take her from the worst of the Sacramento floods to the disastrous New Mexico fires. She often worked as a liaison officer between local municipal relief agencies, the police department, emergency crews, and various fire departments. Her Red Cross relief efforts have made a real difference in the lives of many distressed and displaced people caught up in a life-threatening disaster. Linda also worked in our company's philanthropic division as a coordinator of our charitable efforts. This began as a part-time endeavor and soon grew to a full-time assignment. She continues to keep a hand in some form of worthwhile volunteer activity to this day.

Sharing her affection with the ocean and the docks with Mike, today Linda and Mike live on a scenic hillside overlooking most of Long Beach, the Pacific, and the harbor they both love. After sixteen years of marriage, Linda and Mike have seven grandchildren.

※

Bob, Jr. (RJ)

One of the benefits of owning your own business is that you are able to provide employment for members of your family. Both of my sons, RJ and Mike, worked part-time throughout their high school years on one or another of the various construction projects being carried out by my company. The jobs were menial and often involved hard outdoor labor.

Primarily, RJ and Mike got the jobs that no one else was anxious to perform, such as cleaning up the site at the end of the day. The experience was a valuable one, I believe, since it gave them both a true taste of the physical demands associated with the manual labor side of the construction business. I feel that those experiences were great learning lessons for the boys. In later life, when they were, at times, faced with other challenging work environments, they could console themselves with "This may be difficult, but at least it's easier than working at a construction site."

Demonstrating that he had no fears of tackling jobs that involved getting his hands dirty, RJ, after graduating from high school, worked as a truck driver for a radiator manufacturing outfit in Los Angeles. In very short order, he was moved off the street into the company's sales office, and while working there, RJ met his first wife, Nancy. This union produced two children, Samantha and Bob III.

In 1974, around RJ's twenty-first birthday, he joined our company as a construction superintendent on one of our apartment projects in Orange County. After completing the job, he came into our office and worked in the purchasing and land acquisition department for the next several years.

RJ did an outstanding job but there was an itch that still needed scratching. Ever since childhood, RJ had cultivated one driving passion: He wanted, more than anything else, to become a police officer, so he decided to go for it. He enrolled at the Rio Hondo Police Academy, the regional training center for Los Angeles County located in Whittier. After graduation in 1976, RJ joined the South Gate Police Department. He went through the ranks and fulfilled various assignments, everything from "walking a beat" to dangerous auto pursuits. Eventually RJ was promoted to detective in the department's narcotic division and worked on street level intervention.

Then in 1988 the department switched to a new 12-hour-per-day, three-day-per-week work schedule. This move freed up enough of RJ's time so that he could rejoin the family construction business on a part-time basis. Many officers, in those days, held down second, and sometimes third jobs in order to supplement their city compensation.

In 1992, RJ was offered a unique assignment to work with the Los Angeles office of the California State Bureau of Narcotic Enforcement as an investigator. Through intensive training, RJ became a recognized expert in the field of organized crime, money laundering and asset seizure. His strong work ethic and aggressive personality permitted him to lead his team in making some of the largest seizures of cash and narcotics in Southern California history.

From that time on, until 1996, when he retired with a 20-year history of police work in South Gate, he was able to devote a portion of each week to working with us and used this time to familiarize himself with all aspects of the company. RJ got to know our various departments intimately such as land acquisition, construction, property management and all the other facets of our operation. This provided him with the background he needed to rejoin the company upon leaving the force, but this time it would be on a full-time basis.

Today, RJ currently serves as Vice-Chairman and is the company's President of Real Estate Development. RJ's son, Bob III, has followed in his Dad's footsteps and has, over the past several years, worked at various positions both in the office and out in the field. Bob III is currently serving as Vice President responsible for land acquisition.

Around 1986, while RJ was a South Gate police officer, he overheard a friend talking about Rhonda Stout, whom he had known years ago while in high school. She had been his childhood sweetheart in Downey but because their lives took a different direction, they had each married someone else, and had lost touch with one another. He was told that Rhonda had been a widow for almost five years and had two children, Stacy and Ryan. The friend simply mentioned to RJ that Rhonda had been asking about him. As a trained investigator, it was not long before RJ was able to locate Rhonda and call her up on the phone. Things clicked and their romance was soon rekindled.

Before the year ended, RJ and Rhonda were married on a yacht in the Newport Beach Harbor. RJ and his two children, Samantha and Bob III, joined Rhonda and her two children, Stacy and Ryan, to form a blended family of six. Today, after twenty-one years of marriage, RJ and Rhonda have six grandchildren.

MICHAEL

I believed entertainer Danny Kaye when he said: "Children are the greatest natural resource any country can have." As they grew up in Downey, all my children were ample evidence of the truth of that observation. They each shaped their own destinies by whatever interested them the most in life. And Michael was certainly no exception.

From an early age, Mike enjoyed a rare type of discipline that allowed him to pick himself up and start all over again if he didn't succeed the first time around. A good example was when Mike dropped out of high school during his senior year. He quickly realized what a serious mistake he had made, so he enrolled in an evening G.E.D. program while he continued working during the day. It was not easy, but Mike persevered and obtained his diploma. Throughout his life, Mike always managed to finish whatever he started.

During the late 1970s, while Mike was working at a variety of different jobs, he met Carol. They lived together for a short time in Simi Valley and it was during this period, in 1980, that Mike's only child, Amanda, was born. Mike and Carol later separated.

Mike decided to return to school for more vocational training, this time studying electronics. He graduated with a degree in 1984, and he soon found work with Graham Magnetics, a Texas-based manufacturer of computer tape media and testing equipment. Mike worked as a service technician out of the company's California branch and initially covered a territory that included the southwest portion of the U.S. His territory grew as he advanced with the company and before long he was responsible for the entire western half of the country. Shortly after that promotion Mike met a colleague named Mary who was from Texas and who covered her home state as well as Oklahoma, Louisiana and Arkansas.

Mary was a single mother with two children, Deen, age 11 and Dawna, age 15. She and Mike started dating even though their homes were some 1,400 miles apart. They maintained a long-distance courtship until, in 1991, Mike asked Mary to become his wife. Mary agreed and in early 1992, Mary and her son, Deen, moved to California. Dawna, in her senior year in high school, opted to stay in Texas to finish her studies. In April of the same year, Mike and Mary were wed at the Hilton Waterfront in Huntington Beach.

Shortly after the wedding, there was a downsizing at Graham Magnetics as the nation shifted away from magnetic to optical media. Mike and Mary both left their respective jobs with Graham and, in 1993, they decided to start their own company. Mayer Enterprises provided technical support for mainframe computers and provided magnetic tape certification for large corporate data centers. As it gained its momentum, Mayer Enterprises branched out to service and repair personal computers as well. At this point Mary found another job but continued to work in the electronics field part-time. By 1997, their business was humming and Mary returned to take over the primary responsibility of running Mayer Enterprises while Mike returned to school.

"Dad, I've always been interested in investments and trading," he told me sincerely. We discussed the pros and cons of a career in this high-risk field and I gave Mike my full encouragement. He enrolled at Momentum Trading, located directly across the street from the University of California's Irvine campus and, at the time, the largest electronic day trading facility in the nation. Mike learned the ropes and was soon carrying out small-scale trades every day while Mary continued to run Mayer Enterprises. The bursting of the tech bubble in 2001 was a setback for Mike and led to some rather hard times for day traders all over. Thankfully, Mayer Enterprises was doing well and the company managed to carry them through this difficult period.

It was not long afterwards that I decided to branch out from my core business and purchased a security company called CamWatch. That organization provided video surveillance of construction job sites to help stem the theft losses that oftentimes plague them. Since this was a side business for me, I wanted someone trustworthy from the family to become involved in this operation. Mike filled the bill perfectly and I requested that he join us to help out. He agreed and did a crackerjack job. He was the first one to arrive onsite in the mornings and the last one to leave every day. His responsibilities took him to various construction sites throughout Southern California and Nevada.

Eventually, we sold the company and Mike went back to equities trading. He has enjoyed success in recent years and his investment earnings today represent a major portion of their family's income. I regularly turn to Mike whenever I'm looking for some growth in my own investment portfolio.

Mike and Mary's family has experienced growth as well. Mike's daughter, Amanda, is the mother of three: Hailey, Donnie, and Jaythen. Mary's daughter Dawna, in recent years, provided Mary with her first two grandchildren: Tallon and Sage. Both of

Mary's children, Dawna and Deen, entered the military upon reaching adulthood and both were called to duty in the Middle East. Deen has seen action in both Iraq and Afghanistan. Mike and Mary now have five grandchildren.

CHAPTER THIRTY-TWO

THE CATALINA STEAMER

A wet sheet and a flowing sea, a wind that follows fast.
And fills the white and rustling sail and bends the gallant mast.

Allan Cunningham

There's an Indian saying that goes: "You can't cross the sea merely by standing and staring at the water." I've always believed this to be true and that's why I've never been one to remain on the shore or on the sidelines. This attitude accounts for my passion for flying my own airplanes and in 1966, it was what led me to stop "staring at the water" and purchase my first boat. She was a trim twin-engine cabin cruiser that we christened the S.S. Naughtiness. Taking her out to sea from Los Angeles Harbor for her maiden voyage was a major event for my wife, Marcie, for our three young children, and, most of all for me: Captain Bob.

The problem was that I knew next to nothing about skippering a boat. If there had been a book called "Yachting for Dummies" in those days, I would have rushed out and bought it. I did take a brief course called "Yachting Protocols" and read through the standard "Rules of the Sea" manual, so I felt I was rather well prepared in the fine art of seamanship when the family and I shoved off for the first time and set course for scenic Catalina Island. I was about to learn that what a person might read in books does not fully cover what may happen in the real world once you find yourself out on the open sea.

Catalina Island, sometimes called Santa Catalina, is a rocky pleasure spot some 22 miles southwest of Los Angeles. The island is 22 miles long and is home to Southern California's first golf course, built in 1892. One of the well-known figures who frequented that course was Chicago chewing gum magnate, William Wrigley, who owned most of Catalina and, for thirty years, brought his baseball team, the Chicago Cubs, to the island for spring training. In 1936 a good-looking sportscaster from radio station WHO in Des Moines, Iowa, arrived on Catalina to cover the Cubs' spring training session. Finishing his assignment, the reporter decided to stick around Los Angeles and try out for a Hollywood screen test. He did well and was offered an acting role by the Warner Bros. film studio. His name was Ronald Reagan.

It was a brilliant cloudless day as we backed out of our berth and headed towards Catalina. Just as we pulled away, we caught sight of the well-known "Great White Steamer" about one mile ahead of us, as it was leaving its dock in Long Beach. It was on its daily trip across the channel and traveling at around ten to twelve knots. Of course our boat was much faster with a cruising speed of 25 to 28 knots, and so it did not take us long to catch up with the big beauty. As we approached the Steamer, I told my kids a little about the ship's background.

Mr. Wrigley had built the 300-foot Steamer in 1924 at the unheard of cost of one million dollars. He wanted a way to elegantly transport well-to-do passengers from Los Angeles to his Casino resort in Catalina's Avalon Bay. The Steamer did just that for nearly fifty years. During the World War II years, the ship was commissioned as the U.S.S. Catalina and did her part by transporting a total of nearly one million soldiers overseas;

more than any other transport vessel throughout the war. Despite being named an historic landmark after her retirement in 1975, the Steamer met an ignominious end. A Beverly Hills real estate developer purchased her in 1977 as a Valentine's Day gift for his wife. She quickly lost interest and abandoned the boat in the harbor of Ensenada, Mexico, where she was left to decay and eventually sink (the boat, not the wife).

But all of that misery was yet to come. On this lovely mid-sixties day, the Steamer cut an impressive figure as it plowed across the channel waters. As we approached her from the rear, I decided I'd like to sail past her starboard side and wave to all the passengers on board. Performing this maneuver involved crossing the ship's wake, however. From a distance, this did not seem like much of a big deal, but as we neared the ship I realized that the Steamer was really churning up the water and creating a pair of five to six foot waves in its wake. In my very limited experience, crossing behind a large vessel in a small craft like ours was not something that was in my repertoire. I thought back to what I had read on the subject and recalled that I should cut my engines and then try to hit the wake at a forty-five degree angle traveling at no more than 15 or 20 knots. I found that slowing down a fast moving boat is not quite the same as putting on the brakes in a car. It takes awhile to actually reduce speed, so we were still moving at a pretty fast clip as we hit the wake of the steamer. I went by the book and tried to follow the instructions to the letter. Even so, our little dinghy was picked up like so much flotsam and tossed high into the air. The only part of our boat that remained in contact with the water was the propeller. The rest of the hull was riding on the crest of the huge wave like a surfboard. Everyone hung on for dear life as time stood still and the fate of our family crew hung in the balance.

Finally, we were slammed down on the far side of the wave with such force that I felt sure we would be smashed to splintered smithereens. But, after checking to make sure that we hadn't lost anyone, I was surprised to see that the boat was still in one piece. The only damage sustained was to the china, and the pots and pans that had not been properly stowed in the galley.

Of all the stupid things I've ever done in my life, this little stunt ranks near the top of the list. I don't think I've ever experienced more fear than during those airborne moments behind the Catalina Steamer. Not knowing if our boat was about to be sucked into the giant ship's churning engines or tossed into the open sea was harrowing to say the least. But what truly made the moment so terrifying was that I was not only placing myself in peril, but I had also brought my entire family along for the ride. I had placed the people I loved most dearly directly into harm's way. While my kids were oblivious to the danger and thought the ride was great fun, Marcie and I almost decided to sell the boat right then and there. I'm not sure we would have found too many buyers given what she had just been through. After inspecting our boat afterwards, I was amazed to see how little damage it had actually sustained.

Fortunately, I was able to learn from the entire experience. I learned, for example, how much shock a well-built vessel like ours was able to absorb. More importantly, I learned to never again attempt anything quite so foolhardy that might result in placing my loved ones in jeopardy.

Over the ensuing years, my experience was enriched as we enjoyed the best of times sailing around scenic Catalina Island. Fishing junkets that saw us play host to eight or ten subcontractors or business associates were a popular activity that blended enterprise with entertainment. The channel waters and Avalon Bay had not yet become as depleted as they are today and the fishing was simply fantastic. Thirty to forty pound white giant sea bass, and other exotic marine species, were common catches and always resulted in a sumptuous seafood buffet to top off a great day of sunshine, sailing, and smiles.

Of course, coming back into dock, sunburned and windblown, after eight to ten hours at sea—voyages that often included the consumption of healthy quantities of cold beer—could become a bit challenging. Positioning our extra-wide boat into a rather narrow slip required a good deal of control. I guess you could call it "berth" control. And if there was a stiff breeze blowing as we tried to park her, things could get a little hairy.

I recall one episode that could be filed in the "take a long walk off a short pier" department. One of our novice crew members volunteered when I requested that someone jump ashore with a mooring rope and tie us off. The valiant fellow took a running start as he leapt across the five-foot gap separating the boat deck from the pier. Unfortunately he was holding on to a three-foot rope at the time. He froze in mid-air and landed right in the drink, much to the besotted amusement of the rest of our jolly crew.

As much as our family loved these sea-faring adventures, there invariably came one moment that was always a let down. As our guests would bid farewell and teeter off to their cars leaving a trail of "thank you's" and "see you soon's" in their wake, it was our desultory duty to carry out the lengthy clean-up procedures. The boat had to be hosed down, the saltwater spray wiped off, the leftover food and beverages put away, and so on and so on. It was up to us to make sure that everything onboard was left "ship shape," and those chores sometime took hours to complete.

Eventually, as the kids grew older, some of the charm of the boating experience began to wear thin. We grew a bit weary of operating a floating hospitality center and after the nautical novelty had more or less worn off, we decided to sell the boat.

I suppose I proved the old adage correct. The one that is embroidered onto throw pillows that are often used to decorate the interior of countless cabin cruisers and that reads:

"The happiest two days in a boat owner's life are the day he buys the boat and the day he sells it."

Yes, those were probably the two happiest days, but I'm pleased to say that we enjoyed countless wonderful days filled with excitement and fun in between those two.

CHAPTER THIRTY-THREE

MEMORIES OF MARY ELLEN

By taking a second wife he pays the highest compliment to the first,
by showing that she made him so happy as a married man,
that he wishes to be so a second time.

Samuel Johnson

"That should about do it," said Al as he closed the file on our latest development project. "What do you say we grab some lunch?" Al Fink was both brilliant and gregarious—qualities I valued in an attorney. In addition, Al was a successful, dapper man about town who looked considerably younger than his years. I would invariably look forward to my visits to Al's office in West Los Angeles since he always had a great way of combining business with pleasure. It was now some four years since the accidental death of my first wife, Marcie. As was our custom, Al and I started chatting about our social lives as we headed off to lunch.

"Dating anyone special?" Al asked.

"Work's got me pretty tied up," I replied honestly. "I've met a few women in Downey and I've been dating off and on," I added. Actually, what social life I did manage to make time for consisted mostly of weekend getaways with my fishing and golfing buddies.

"I met a very attractive girl who I think would be just terrific for you," Al announced. "She works over at Union Bank." Both Al and I enjoyed banking relationships at Union Bank, but since Mayer Construction was headquartered some 30 miles away in Downey, I rarely set foot in the place since nearly all of our business transactions were conducted through the mail.

"I appreciate the matchmaking, Al," I responded, "but I'm down in Downey and I really don't feel like driving that far just to meet someone new." My protestations had no effect on Al, the love broker. He kept extolling the praises of "Mary Ellen" to the point that I finally agreed to call her just to get him to change the subject.

"When will you give her a call, Bob," Al persisted.

"I don't know," I said. "When I get home."

"Why don't you just call her up when we get back to my office, okay?" Al insisted.

"Sure, Al," I said. "Now let's go eat."

As soon as we walked back into Al's office after lunch, he picked up his phone, dialed Union Bank and asked for Mary Ellen. He then stuck the phone into my hand.

"Uh, hi," I said. "This is Bob. Al Fink is my attorney and he asked me to call you because he, uh, thinks you and I should meet."

"Oh, I see," said a sweet-sounding voice on the line. "You're calling me at the advice of counsel." There was a little twinkle in her voice.

"Yeah, that's right" I went on, going along with the gag. "So I really would like to meet you someday. Maybe the next time I stop by the bank."

"Well, if you're a friend of Al's, you are no doubt someone I'd be very happy to meet." I was struck by her bubbly personality over the phone. I told Al that she sounded great and that I would definitely call her back. But I never did.

Almost a year passed, and I again found myself in Al's office when something triggered his memory. "Did you ever call that girl back at the bank," he asked. "You remember. The one you called from my office." I had really meant to, but I had gotten busy and forgotten all about it.

"I won't lie to you, Al," I admitted. "I told you I'd call her back and I never did. But how's this? I'll call her again right now, on your phone, and if she's there at the bank, I'll drop by and say hello immediately." Al nodded.

"I'm sorry, sir," intoned a nasal voice after I got through to Union Bank. "Mary Ellen no longer works here. She now works as an account representative at Home Savings & Loan." Not to be deterred, I asked for the number and dialed it. Once she was on the line, I re-introduced myself to her.

"Hello, Mary Ellen," I said. "This is Al Fink's friend, Bob. I don't know if you remember me but I phoned you from his office about a year ago." I could hear her thinking for a few beats.

"Oh, wait," she exclaimed. "Yes, I remember you. But weren't you supposed to call me back?" Uh-oh, I thought. I've blown it. But, yet there was something in her voice that told me she wasn't really all that upset with me. I decided to press on.

"You're absolutely right," I blurted. "I said I'd call and I got super busy and didn't do it. I owe you one big apology, and I'd like to tell you how sorry I am in person. Any chance of that happening?"

"Well if we set a date, you're not going to stand me up again, are you?" she chided. I swore that I would not and even offered to have Al draft an affidavit to document my good intentions. We chuckled and hung up after having arranged a date for a few days later. When we finally did meet face-to-face, I immediately realized what a fool I had been for not meeting Mary Ellen Kisylia when I had the chance one year before. She was not only attractive, with flowing auburn hair, but she also had the most engaging and unflappable personality. After only a short time together I was completely taken with her warm sense of humor and generous openhearted nature.

I overcame my objections to driving the thirty-mile span between Mary Ellen's home and mine, and we began dating each other exclusively. As the relationship matured, we began discussing marriage plans and decided to tie the knot the following year. We celebrated our marriage with one of the largest weddings ever held in Downey. At the time of our nuptials, my sons, RJ and Mike were 19 and 17 years old respectively. They were both attending school and living at home. My daughter, Linda, 25, was living on her own in the area and she, and my granddaughter Marci, were regular visitors.

Mary Ellen had no prior children and so, by marrying me, she was also inheriting a fully functional family. Becoming a bride and a stepmother all in one swoop can be disconcerting, but Mary Ellen took the transition all in stride. She saw at once that our home needed a woman's touch, so she proceeded to quit her job at the bank and devoted herself fulltime to the boys and me.

Our marriage ushered in a golden time for me both personally and professionally. A more stable family situation gave me the ability to focus on my affairs and do some important re-evaluation of my business and personal priorities. It was during this period that Mary Ellen and I satisfied our mutual thirst for adventure and started doing a good deal of world traveling. It was also at this juncture that I eventually sold my company, Mayer Construction Company, in 1980 and moved from Downey to Newport Beach shortly thereafter. By age 54, I had three wonderful grown children, a loving wife, and the financial freedom to enjoy life to the fullest.

I thought that I was ready for retirement and decided to give that a try. My retirement was short-lived, however, since I soon discovered that I sorely missed the excitement and satisfaction found in the high-risk realm of real estate development. I returned to work, founded The Robert Mayer Corporation in the early 1990s and began plans to develop The Waterfront. During the course of our marriage, Mary Ellen and I witnessed our children marry and start their own families. We were truly enjoying the prime time of our lives, living each day to the fullest, and savoring all the sweetness that Southern California living had to offer.

But, as such things sometimes do, my relationship with Mary Ellen began to unravel. I had never envisioned myself going through a divorce. We had been happily married for over twenty years and we clearly loved each other. But as things began to deteriorate over the next few years, divorce turned out to be the only sensible option for us both. We eventually parted and set up separate households in 1997. It took another three years to reach a final divorce settlement. Our marriage officially ended in 2000.

By 2005, Mary Ellen and I had been separated for almost eight years. Over those years we kept in close contact, maintained a cordial relationship, and I continued to watch over her and made sure she was financially secure for the duration of her life. Later that year, in November, at the early age of 68, Mary Ellen passed away after a lengthy illness. Her family and I received hundreds of cards and phone calls from the many well wishers whose lives had been touched by Mary Ellen's kindness and humor. I count myself among them because she touched my life, too, and made a deep impression upon my heart.

I now found myself a widower for the second time in my life. Although I was prepared for Mary Ellen's passing, and although we had been separated for many years, I still experienced a profound sadness and heart-felt grief. At the same time, I also felt a great sense of gratitude for the wonderful memories we had accumulated during our first twenty years of marriage. I will cherish those memories forever.

CHAPTER THIRTY-FOUR

MAYA

You're never too old to become younger.

Mae West

As any real estate developer will tell you, the value of a given piece of commercial property depends mostly upon two things: the quality of the lease and the quality of the tenant. In early 2002, we had finally reached the "ground-breaking" moment at our Waterfront Project in Huntington Beach, thanks to successfully completing the land lease for our second hotel, the Hyatt Regency Resort and Spa. While the 99-year lease was with the City, we, at the same time, entered a joint venture with the Hyatt organization, wherein they would become a partner in the project and operate the hotel upon completion.

I was in high spirits and in high gear as the project moved closer to reality after so many years of frustration and struggle. But the Hyatt deal wasn't the only thing I was excited about. My six-way bypass heart surgery the year before had been a total success and I felt as though I had been awarded a new "lease on life" as well. My whole world outlook had benefited. I felt invigorated, enthusiastic, energized and ready to tackle anything that came my way. My friends and business associates noticed the change. "You seem like a new man, Bob," many would tell me. And that's just how I felt.

I had gotten into the habit of going to lunch at the Four Seasons Hotel that was located just across the street from my Newport Beach office. On this particular day, as I strode out of the elevator headed for the hotel, I spotted her again. I had no idea who she was, but I presumed she worked in our building since we occasionally rode the elevator together. My attempts at making eye contact during those elevator rides had been rebuffed — a fact that only served to arouse my curiosity. She likewise ignored my further attempts to catch her eye as I tossed a smile her way whenever we passed. She plainly would not give me the time of day. But, the "new" Bob Mayer was not about to be deterred so easily.

Today, she was simply standing on the corner, looking lovely, and waiting for the cars to pass as I approached. I could not contain my silence any longer. My renewed sense of energy gave me the courage to finally break the ice.

"Hi," I said bravely as I whipped out my business card. "Could I give you my card?"

She took it and asked: "What do you want me to do with this?"

I didn't know what else to say. Not being well seasoned in the art of making new female friends, I had done what business people typically do when meeting for the first time. I felt a bit foolish since I appeared to be trying to impress her with my business credentials. Fortunately for me, she quickly understood my predicament and responded with a sympathetic smile.

"Look, is there something I can do for you..." she scrutinized my card. "Mister ...uh...Mayer?"

"Actually, there are two things," I responded quickly, finding my voice and my poise at last. "You can call me Bob and you can tell me your name." Her smile broadened and she said, "It's Maya."

We conversed for a bit and as we parted I asked her to give me a call if I could be of any help to her in any way. She never called, so I decided to do some sleuthing on my own. Maya had mentioned that she was working as an independent contractor for one of the legal firms in our building, so it didn't take long for me to track her down and then call her up.

"Hi, Maya. It's me, Bob," I said. "Remember, we chatted on the corner a few days ago?" She said that she did.

"Great," I went on. "I was wondering if you'd like to have dinner with me tonight. Or tomorrow night? Or any night?"

"Well," she said with a bit of hesitation, "Hmm, all right. I'll try it."

Over dinner we exchanged war stories and offered each other glimpses of our respective life sagas. I learned that Maya had been traveling the western seaboard for almost eighteen months looking for a new home. She was searching for a place that would deliver her from the harsh winters and gloomy climate of the Pacific Northwest where she had been living for several years. Her friends in Huntington Harbor encouraged her to rent a winter apartment just up the street from our Waterfront development while she made her plans for the future. Having been born and raised in Hawaii, she felt at home amid sunshine and sand and she had warmed to Southern California's temperate climate.

"I'm just planning to stay a few months until I thaw out," Maya explained over dinner. She clearly appeared to have her own agenda and didn't want anyone or anything to get in the way of her leaving town when the time came.

The evening was filled with warm words, bits of wisdom, and miles of smiles all around. Feeling my oats, I suggested that we go dancing. I could still cut a pretty mean figure on the dance floor, and Maya certainly seemed like she would make a great partner. As we twirled and swirled around the floor, I came to a clear realization. I was struck by the fact that Maya was just what I needed. I began to envision her as more than just a dance partner and determined that this amazing woman, with her dynamic personality, could easily have a profound influence on the remaining years of my life.

As we got to know one another more fully over the coming months, I learned that Maya was born on Valentine's Day in 1944 on the island of Oahu. Her childhood in pre-statehood Hawaii was shaped by the events of World War II that began for the U.S. with the Japanese bombing of nearby Pearl Harbor in 1941. To put things into perspective concerning our relative ages, I had graduated from Huntington Park High School a few months after Maya was born.

Maya impressed me greatly with her insights and clarity. Although she was eighteen years my junior, she seemed wise beyond her years and firmly down to earth. She had never married. Instead, she went to school, educated herself, traveled the world, and over the years worked through several careers. In contrast to her well-grounded worldview, Maya had elected to live life as something of a free spirit and I found this combination to be utterly delightful.

It did not take me long to discover that I had entered the digital age thanks to my developing relationship with Maya. Among her many skills is her adeptness with computers and electronics. She enjoys an uncanny ability to fix things and has often amazed me with her technical know how.

"Girls aren't supposed to know how to do that," I commented in amazement as she programmed my garage door openers so I could easily open them at a finger's touch from inside my car.

Prior to meeting Maya I had always appreciated the value of computers in the operation of my business. But little did I realize what a fantastic world awaited me when I learned how to turn on a computer and enter the vast libraries available in the wonderful world of the Internet. As Maya instructed me in the most rudimentary skills, I quickly came to appreciate what I had been missing. While I am certainly not an expert, I now feel comfortable in using a mouse, in finding my way around the keyboard, and in surfing the Web—all skills that I would never have acquired if I had not been encouraged to learn. It's been a wonderful learning experience and it has made me feel younger as I've grown older.

At the time we met, I had been married for a total of forty-eight years, albeit in two separate marriages, and I considered myself to be a traditional family man. Maya's background was much different. Because of her upbringing in Hawaii where she saw so many families torn apart because of the war, she had nurtured a highly independent spirit. She had charted her own course and felt she was responsible for her own destiny. Yet despite these differences in our individual histories, we felt very comfortable with each other. What accounts for this bond is our mutually held set of values. We share a common morality and a shared sense of what's truly important in life. Maya brought to our relationship those qualities that I admire: love, loyalty, support, commitment, and selflessness, all combined with a highly creative work ethic. I have come to rely upon these valued qualities of hers in many aspects of my life today.

After dating for several years, we became engaged. Maya asked that I take her home to Hawaii so that we could marry on the sand at the ocean's edge. In October of 2006, we were married on the island of Maui.

CHAPTER THIRTY-FIVE

THE MAGNIFICENT
MAYER BROTHERS

Regardless of circumstances, each man lives in a world of his own making.

Josepha Murphy Emms

January 1st, 2008 was a national holiday that most people set aside to usher in the new year. Or, more likely, to sleep in after the prior night's celebrations and then settle back to enjoy some college football. But on this date, exactly one hundred years before, for some of the industrious residents of Mankato, Minnesota, January 1st, 1908 was just another day of work. My grandfather, Lorenz Mayer, along with his two brothers, Conrad and Louis, were counted among these industrious mid-westerners who reported on the job that day. But I'm sure that even my father, who was only seven years old at the time, could sense that there was something special, something out-of-the-ordinary, about this particular New Year's Day. As indeed there was.

As my grandfather Lorenz joined my two great-uncles on Vine Street at the Mayer Bros. Foundry—the successful iron fabrication plant they had opened in 1894—the trio quickly got to the business at hand. This was the day that they were to ship out their newest, and most technologically advanced product: the 25-pound trip hammer they had dubbed "The Little Giant." The six-foot tall upright machine had been ordered by a metal shop operator in Ralston, Oklahoma in response to the printed circulars the brothers regularly mailed out. The trip hammer bore a nameplate engraved with its identifying data: The Little Giant Power Hammer; Mayer Bros. Foundry; Mankato, Minnesota; Jan. 1, 1908; Serial No.1.

Over the course of the next eight decades, more than 18,000 trip hammers of this type would be produced and shipped to every state in the nation and more than thirty other countries. The Little Giant Power Hammer was destined to become the best-selling mechanical hammer ever made. Thousands are still in use today and early models are often restored and prized by collectors. Serial No. 1, known as "Model Alpha," has been restored to its original condition and is on display at a Nebraska City museum dedicated to the transformation of metal.

A trip hammer, sometimes called a power hammer, is an essential tool in the shaping and fabrication of metal. For my uncle Louis, credited as the inventor of the device, necessity truly was the mother of the machine. Louis, born in Germany in 1867, was the eldest of the three Mayer Brothers and arrived in America via Ellis Island in 1871. He and his five younger siblings, including the youngest, eleven-month old Conrad, had been brought to the new world by their parents, Lorenz, Sr. and Catherine. The family had set sail from the port of Hamburg as part of the massive wave of immigrants arriving at America's shores seeking political freedom and economic opportunity. A skilled blacksmith, it was the latter reason that pushed Lorenz, Sr. to gather his family and head for America's golden shore. The German economy was nearing collapse due to war, military conscription, and the influx of Irish immigrants flooding the labor pool as a result of the potato famine.

The family settled among one of the ethnic German communities that sprung up rapidly across the Minnesota prairie and soon thereafter, in 1874, Catherine gave birth to the first member of the Mayer family to be born in America. This was my grandfather, Lorenz Lucas Mayer.

The prosperity the family encountered in the boomtown that was Mankato in those days was in stark contrast to the deprivations they had known back in Germany. The newly opened rail line that delivered raw materials and carried away finished goods to distant markets fueled the industrial and economic development of the town. Great-grandpa Lorenz went to work immediately, carrying his anvil and smithy tools in a knapsack on his back as he went door-to-door, peddler-style, offering his services to homes and businesses alike.

At first his income was barely enough to feed his swiftly growing family, but he trudged on diligently, forging horseshoes and new pump handles and eventually started to enjoy the benefits of boomtown Mankato. Finally, during the centennial year of his adopted homeland, great-grandpa Lorenz was earning enough to send his children to Mankato's newly established parochial school. But it was amid the fiery heat and prairie dust of Lorenz' blacksmith business that something more than bits of iron were being forged for his three young sons. After learning their father's trade, the Mayer Brothers opened a blacksmith shop on busy Vine Street and forged their own business. Their tempered steel characters, that would soon propel them down the road to great accomplishment and financial success, were also being hammered into shape.

For Louis, the eldest, the blacksmith shop represented a grand stage upon which to audition the fruits of his rapidly evolving ingenuity. He would observe, first-hand, how his father would call upon one of his sons to lend a "third hand" as he bent and twisted a malleable piece of metal into the correct shape. "Why not," thought Louis, "devise a machine that could bring down the hammer while the smith held the metal in position?" Louis was aware of trip hammers that had been used for centuries for just such a purpose. Typically they were powered by water wheels that would, through a series of cams and pulleys, raise the hammer and then release it to fall against the metal under the force of gravity. Such devices had been used in Europe since the 12th century to manufacture armor plating, for example. Why not apply the tools of the Industrial Revolution to this task? Louis set out to do just that and in 1895 he succeeded in producing a prototype for the world's first powered trip hammer. It was just one year before that the brothers had expanded the blacksmith shop to launch the Mayer Brothers Foundry. Louis's revolutionary invention would become their premier product.

As the brothers' enterprise grew, they made it a practice to live simply and plow their profits back into the family business. Their new shop was a modern brick and steel structure that included an engine room, a storage building and a stone and brick boiler area. The foundry was well equipped and served as fertile breeding ground for the brothers' new product research and development efforts.

During the early 1900s, in addition to Louis' invention, dubbed "The Power Hammer," the Mayer Brothers Foundry vastly expanded their product line and began producing a wide variety of metal goods. The printed catalogue that the company put out each year during this period promoted products of "only the highest quality" including hoists, ditching and grading equipment, steam engines, boiler machinery, road graders, drill presses, architectural ironwork, manifolds, circular saws, lathes, and many more. While most of the products listed in the Mayer Brothers catalog were produced for only a short time, the Little Giant Power Hammer endured across the entire span of the twentieth century. The longevity of such tools is difficult to fathom, but the fact remains that there are thousands of pieces of equipment still in use today that were originally manufactured at the Mayer Brothers Foundry up to 100 years ago. Most well known, particularly among machinists and mechanical engineers, is the Little Giant Power Hammer, which was manufactured in five different sizes by the Mayer Brothers and their successors from 1908 until 1984.

It was not long after that New Year's Day shipment of Little Giant No.1, that my great-uncle Conrad left the company to pursue his own interests. My grandfather, Lorenz, stayed on and, thanks to his studies in finance and accounting, became the company treasurer while his older brother, Louis, was the engineering genius and ran the day-to-day operations. Louis held dozens of patents in a wide number of fields, but his true love was the foundry business.

There was also something of an automotive boom underway during this period in Mankato. Ever the inventor, Louis produced one of America's first V-8 internal combustion engines in 1903. The Mayer Brothers Foundry built the chassis and the engine, but they imported the car's massive wooden body from Detroit. The huge enclosure, that they lacquered with twenty coats of black paint before mounting it onto the chassis, seated eight passengers comfortably. The Mayer roadster was an elegant looking vehicle with ample horsepower that allowed it to easily motor up steep Main Street hill. I sometimes wonder if my great-uncle Louis or my grandfather Lorenz had been more devoted to their automobile enterprise, instead of their foundry, could our family have founded a business empire to compete with Ford, Chrysler, and General Motors? As a matter of fact, Henry Ford did contact the brothers about a possible acquisition, but it was not their autos he was interested in. Although the deal never materialized, Ford wanted to know about another product that came rolling out of the Mayer Brothers foundry: farm tractors.

The Mayer Brothers used a straight four-cylinder block in a new line of tractors that they also branded with the Little Giant moniker in 1910. Sporting a unique cast aluminum fan and steering wheel and an advanced spring-loaded hitch, the Little Giant tractor ran on a fuel blend of kerosene and water that served to deliver a powerful performance punch. The advertising copy contained in the company's 1914 catalogue extolled the virtues of the Mayer Brothers tractor:

"It will make farming so interesting that your boys will rather stay on the farm than leave for the city!" read the headline, and then went on to proclaim:

"Our work has been completed and cannot be improved upon. In design, we have created a tractor that is good to look upon. In material, we have used high-grade metals with prodigality heretofore unknown in tractor manufacturing. In workmanship, we have called to our side labor most skilled. In practical durability, we have produced an article that will outlive and outwork the horse and the ox."

The description, in the mannered style of that era that had been popularized by the Sears & Roebuck catalogue, gushes on for several more paragraphs. Unfortunately, the tractor's power could not overcome the enormous financial challenges the company was about to face. Although 500 tractors were produced, they did not sell well since they shared a price tag with the most lavish luxury automobiles of the day. As the war clouds loomed, the supply of "labor most skilled" mentioned in the catalogue began to dry up. Because of this, one out of four orders for their key product, the Little Giant Power Hammer, were left unfilled. This situation arose just as the company announced in Farm Implement News in 1914 that it planned to triple the size of its factory facilities. Consistent with the brothers' practice of re-investing their profits, these plans never materialized as profits began to dwindle. Clearly over-extended, the failure to meet demand for their most successful product threw the company into a shaky financial footing.

In order to finance their factory expansion plans, the Mayer Brothers had previously offered company stock to local investors. This move succeeded in raising needed capital, but it forced the brothers to yield control of the company to a non-family Board of Directors.

As the foundry faced mounting financial challenges, and as Mankato's dreams of becoming the automobile producing capital of America were ceded to Detroit, it was time to make a change. The Board, in 1916, asked the brothers to step down. The brothers did so and it was at this point that my grandfather, Lorenz, along with my father-to-be, Bert, and the rest of the family, moved to Kaukauna, Wisconsin. He was joined there by his brother Louis and, for a short time, they produced and marketed a slightly modified trip hammer that has been labeled the "Wisconsin Hammer" by historians and collectors.

After the departure of the Mayer Brothers, the company, now being operated primarily by its creditors, changed its name to Little Giant and focused its activities on producing its best-selling namesake, the mechanical trip hammer. The new company president, L.J. Fazendin, took charge in 1923 and quickly discontinued the production of tractors and other unprofitable products. Fazendin did attempt to diversify the product line into such areas as plumbing parts and potato picking equipment, but these, too, proved unsuccessful.

In 1937, as the Great Depression swept America's heartland, the Little Giant Company found it could no longer persevere and filed for bankruptcy. Mr. Fazendin, who bought the assets of the company at bargain basement prices, continued its operations. During World War II, Fazendin's son-in-law, Jerry Dotson, joined the company just as the nation's industrial output was placed on a war footing. By this time the name Little Giant was well established and all U.S. military procurement contracts for power hammers specified "Little Giant or equal." After the war, and under Dotson's leadership, the foundry grew, through merger and expansion, from a small captive manufacturer to a sizable jobbing foundry. In 1955, at the death of Mr. Fazendin, the Dotson Company name was adopted.

Dotson reinvigorated the foundry, which remains in his family's hands to this day. The production of The Little Giant trip hammer ended in 1984 and the brand name was sold in 1991 to a couple from Nebraska City, Nebraska, Sid and Mary Suedmeier. The Suedmeirs picked up what was left of the Little Giant Power Hammer: blueprints, foundry patterns, and a library of hand-written sales records. Under the name LittleGiant.com, the couple maintains a spare parts line, conducts repair services, and operates as a clearinghouse for information about the Little Giant that serves a worldwide community of collectors, machinists, and blacksmiths. Visitors to their facility in Nebraska City are today able to view on display the Alpha machine; the 25-pound Little Giant Power Hammer No. 1 that my grandfather first shipped on January 1, 1908.

The first half of the twentieth century saw the rise to fame of numerous extraordinary brother teams. The Wright Brothers, the Warner Brothers and the Marx Brothers come to mind most easily. Despite never having reached the same level of celebrity, I feel it is not merely family pride that prompts me to include the accomplishments of the Mayer Brothers into this same fraternal fraternity.

The Mayer Brothers, and the breakthrough products they created, helped to change the face of American industry. But beyond their specific accomplishments, it is the enduring audacity of their entrepreneurial spirit that has inspired me time and again throughout the course of my own business career. It is my hope that by chronicling a bit of their history on these pages, I can serve to pass on that inspired spirit to my own descendents.

I have included, in the Mayer Brothers Album at the end of this book, a collection of articles that provide more details about the life and times of the amazing Mayer Brothers. I hope you will find them to be of interest.

CONCLUSION

*For what is a man's life if it is not linked with
the life of future generations by memories of the past?*

Marcus Tullius Cicero

I'd like to wrap things up by expressing my thanks to each of you for taking the time to explore this book and letting me share some of the more memorable moments of my life with you in this way.

If you are member of our family, I hope that by reading these pages you have come away with a little deeper appreciation for those who have preceded us. If, in the coming years, you were to employ this book to educate your children and grandchildren about their family heritage, I would feel humbled and deeply honored.

To other readers, it is my hope that you found wandering through the "stories" of my personal history high-rise to be an enjoyable and, at times, an amusing journey. There is obviously much more that could have been written on the topics and about the personalities discussed in this book. But one of my over-riding goals was to make each chapter concise and to the point. I also tried to make each chapter stand on its own and not dependent upon your reading of any of the prior chapters. I hope you agree that I succeeded in achieving these objectives.

So whether you read the entire book, front to back in order, or if you skipped around from story to story, it is my devout hope that you came away with a somewhat clearer sense of who I am and how I've lived my life. The truth is that I too gained a greater understanding of who I am as a person through the act of writing this book. In order to provide the accounts you find on the preceding pages, I was required to come face-to-face with issues that had, over the comfort of the years, remained more or less buried. The writing experience was a cathartic and enlightening one and I would not have missed it for the world.

Do I recommend the writing of a book like this to others as a form of psychic therapy? The answer is yes, if you're ready. If you are prepared to confront the ghosts of loved ones and to relive past conquests and defeats and if you are not put off by the literary exposure of your private thoughts and memories, then, by all means, head straight to the word processor and get to work. You will not regret it, I promise you.

Perhaps the most profound revelation I encountered during the production of this book is this: I have led a very fortunate existence. While not without its share of challenges, when looking at the sum of my personal and professional experiences, I am struck by what a lucky and fun-filled life I've led. And the most fortunate aspect is this: While this is the Conclusion of my book, it is by no means the conclusion of my life's journey. I am blessed with good health, a wonderful wife, a loving family, and a thriving business enterprise. It's my desire to keep right on building a bright future atop the foundation described in these pages.

Whether it's bouncing off the walls of the Zero-G Force One aircraft or negotiating our next hotel deal at The Waterfront, I intend to keep adding more amazing stories to the ones in this collection. Keep on the alert for *Without Risk There's No Reward Volume II*. It should be a doozy!

One disclaiming note: While I, and the team of people involved in the production of this book, worked diligently to assure the accuracy of its contents, the possibility of factual error, nevertheless exists. If you discover any such goofs or gaffes, I would urge you to contact me, or the publisher, and let us know. Every effort will be extended to correct any such errors in the next printing.

It is customary, when concluding books of this sort, for the author to indulge in some prognostication and apply the wisdom of his years towards projecting what the future may hold. Unfortunately, I don't own a crystal ball and I don't see myself as any sort of oracle or visionary. While certain current trends can be identified and then extrapolated, what the future actually holds is anybody's guess.

I have found it much more advisable, in my business dealings, to honestly focus on one key aspect and then attempt to honestly project which way things are heading. For example, I always made it a practice to study population patterns and demographics when putting together a new residential project or hotel deal. Any time a person accepts the risk involved in such a deal, he or she is attempting to accurately predict the future. When we launched the first extended stay hotels in the Southwest, we were accurately predicting that a demand for this type of lodging was on the horizon. As I have said repeatedly in these pages, such risk-taking is essential to any and every type of business success. The key point to remember is that in order to accurately anticipate the future for financial gain, one must fully and deeply understand the present.

The demographic landscape of America is undergoing monumental change. As baby boomers reach retirement age in the coming two decades, the housing market will be dramatically altered. As our nation in short order achieves the distinction of possessing the largest foreign-born population percentage in the world, vast economic consequences will certainly arise. Those who today are able to accurately base their plans on these, and other major trends, will be in a position to take the risks necessary to achieve future success. There simply is no other way.

To sum it up, permit me to thank you for also accepting a risk. When you decided to invest your most precious commodity, your time, into the reading of this book, you, in effect, were taking a risk. It is my position that in order to acquire the reward, you are required to take the risk. I sincerely hope that you feel you have been rewarded in some small way for your investment and that you agree when I point out that without the risk, there really is no reward.

—**Bob Mayer**
Spring 2008

ANCESTRY PROFILES

MAYER FAMILY

Great-Grandfather Lorenz

Great-Grandmother Catherine

Lorenz Mayer, Sr.
1831-1916

Catherine (Ruder) Mayer
1832-1890

GREAT-GRANDFATHER LORENZ was born in Bingen near the Rhine River. He was thirty-nine years old when he left his native Germany with his wife, Catherine, and their six children. Of the six children, the eldest was Anna, age ten, and Conrad the youngest, an infant of only eleven months. Although the family left Hamburg on a ship named Cambria, they would sail on several other ships before arriving at their final destination at Ellis Island in New York City on January 6, 1871. Shortly after arriving in America, Lorenz took his family to settle in Mankato, Minnesota, where he worked his trade as a blacksmith. While his sons, Louis, Conrad and Lorenz (my grandfather), were growing up in Mankato he taught them his blacksmith trade. The brothers would eventually form several businesses of their own. They first opened a blacksmith shop, and then a machine shop and several years later added a foundry under the collective name of The Mayer Bros. Lorenz, Sr. and Catherine would remain in Mankato for the rest of their lives. Great-grandpa Lorenz passed away at the age of eighty-five.

GREAT-GRANDMOTHER CATHERINE was also born in Germany and was of Austrian descent. She had been married twice. Her maiden name was Ruder and her first husband's name was Joerg. Great-grandmother Catherine lived to the age of fifty-four.

THE MAYER BROTHERS

Great-Uncle Louis
1867-1942

Great-Uncle Conrad
1870-1948

Grandfather Lorenz
1874-1934

THE MAYER BROTHERS' story is an entrepreneurial dream. They were the first generation to grow up in America after their parents, my great-grandparents, Lorenz, Sr. and Catherine, left their native Germany in 1871 and settled in Mankato, Minnesota. Louis was the eldest brother, born in Germany in 1867. Conrad was only eleven months old when the family set sail for New York's Ellis Island, and grandfather Lorenz was the first to be born in America. The Mayer Brothers grew up in Mankato, and like their father, became blacksmiths. Later, they opened their own blacksmith shop and several other businesses that included a machine shop and one of the largest foundries in the country. Uncle Louis was a prolific inventor and well known for his many inventions, among them was a 100-horsepower 8-cylinder automobile and the "Little Giant Power Hammer."

HUETTL FAMILY

Great-Grandfather	Great-Grandmother
Joseph	Maximiliana

Joseph B. Huettl	Maximiliana (Magel) Huettl
1839-1922	1845-1929

GREAT-GRANDFATHER JOSEPH who was born in Roshaupt, Austria arrived in New York City in 1869 at the age of 30 and settled in Mankato, Minnesota with his family. He and Maximiliana had four daughters and two sons. He was 88 years old when he died of complications of old age. Maximiliana, his six children, twenty-eight grandchildren and nineteen great-grandchildren survived Joseph.

GREAT-GRANDMOTHER MAXIMILIANA was also born in Roshaupt, Austria and settled in Mankato with Joseph and their two children who had been born in Austria. They had four more children who were all born in Mankato. She survived my great-grandfather by seven years and died at the age of 84 after a short illness brought on by complications of the flu.

Circa 1888 – Huettl Family
Theresa, Margaret, Joseph, Mary and Anna (my grandmother)
Seated: Joseph, Sr., Harry and Maximiliana

MARRIAGE OF
MAYER AND HUETTL FAMILY

Grandfather Lorenz

Grandmother Anna

Lorenz Lucas Mayer
1874-1934

Anna Huettl Mayer
1878-1958

GRANDFATHER LORENZ was born several years after his parents, Lorenz and Catherine, left their native country of Germany. Lorenz was their seventh child and the first to be born in America. He went to school in Mankato and later entered business college. He married Anna Huettl and they had seven children. Together with his brothers, Louis and Conrad, they founded a blacksmith shop, the Mayer Machine Shop, the Little Giant Company and one of the largest foundries in the United States. Lorenz resided in Mankato for almost forty years. The balance of his life was spent in Kaukauna, Wisconsin, where he worked as an accountant for the Kaukauna Machine Shop and the Moloch Foundry. He was a member of the Catholic Order of Foresters and of the Knights of Columbus. Grandpa Lorenz had been ailing almost two weeks before he succumbed to a stroke at the age of sixty.

GRANDMOTHER ANNA was born in Mankato, Minnesota and was of Austrian decent. She married Grandfather Lorenz on August 21, 1900 at the age of twenty-two. They lived in Mankato until 1915, when the family moved to Kaukauna. She survived Lorenz by twenty-four years. She died at the Kaukauna Community Hospital after a long illness at the age of seventy-nine. A requiem mass was held for her as a former resident of Mankato.

1900
Lorenz and Anna's Wedding

Circa 1911
Lorenz Mayer Family at a Young Age
Marie, Catherine, Cornelius, Clotilda, Bertram (my father)

1918
Lorenz Mayer Family All Grown Up
Top Row: Catherine, Cornelius, Bertram, Clotilda
Seated: Marie, Anna, Lorenz, Lorenz, Sr. and Charlotte

1933
Grandparents Anna and Lorenz
Kaukauna, Wisconsin

PIZZO FAMILY

Grandfather Fred	Grandmother Juanina

Ferdinando (Fred) Pizzo 1856-1934	**Juanina Cotita Pizzo** 1867-1963

1932
Grandparents
Fred and Juanina
in Later Years

GRANDFATHER FRED was born in 1856 in the small town of Zisola near Palermo, Sicily. He left Zisola by ship and traveled to Africa and France, finally making his way to New York City. He later lived in New Orleans where he met and married Juanina, and then moved to Chicago. From Chicago he ultimately settled his family in Madison, Wisconsin where he ran a repair shop sharpening knives and repairing bicycles. In 1923, my grandparents moved to California for Juanina's health. Fred passed away in Los Angeles at the age of seventy-eight.

GRANDMOTHER JUANINA was also born in Sicily. She married Grandfather Fred in December of 1890. During their 44-year marriage, Fred and Juanina had seventeen children. Four died at birth and three by accident. She survived Fred by eighteen years. Grandmother Juanina passed away in Alhambra, California at the age of ninety-six.

GRANDFATHER FRED
MAKES HEADLINES

December 19, 1933 – The Capital Times, Madison

Fred Pizzo to Fly to Home in California; Walked Twice

Once Kept Repair Shop Here; Well Known in Madison

By A. O. BARTON
(Of The Capital Times Staff)

Over the route which in his earlier years he twice trudged on foot and back, Fred Pizzo, one of Madison's first Italian residents, expects on Saturday to fly to his far-off California home at Los Angeles.

Mr. Pizzo left Madison 11 years ago for California, but for the past four months he has been staying at the home of his daughter, Mrs. Bertram Mayer, 16 N. Bassett St. while receiving treatment for a cataract on one of his eyes. He is now 77 years old, but otherwise hale and hearty.

Mr. Pizzo will be remembered by the older residents of Madison as the keeper of a repair shop in the 300 block on State St. He mended bicycles, clocks, umbrellas and similar articles. Previous to that time he had a shop on N. Pinckney St. He also frequently acted as interpreter for the courts and for his Italian countrymen in their business deals.

Mr. Pizzo is also the father of Tony Pizzo, who in 1928 staged an auto endurance drive of 174 hours in Madison chained to his steering wheel. Tony Pizzo is still giving endurance exhibitions and is now in Florida.

Mr. Pizzo was a man of political

Fred Pizzo
– Baron Bros. Studio

influence among his countrymen and in the presidential campaigns of McKinley and Theodore Roosevelt he traveled about the state in the interests of these candidates, working among his countrymen in Madison, Milwaukee, Racine and other cities.

He was also an early friend and supporter of the late Sen. LaFollette while governor. Before the days of safety razors he used to sharpen razors for LaFol-

Man to Fly
Over Route He
Walked Twice

(Continued from Page 1)

lette and thus early formed his acquaintance.

It was from the sunny climate of southern Italy that Mr. Pizzo and his wife both came. Mr. Pizzo likes California because it reminds him somewhat of the old home, earthquakes and all.

Had 10 Children

Mr. Pizzo's wife is still living. Of their 10 children, seven are in the West and three in Madison. Those in Madison being Mrs. Mayer, Mrs. Theodore Speros, 1208 Spaight St., and Joseph Pizzo, 16 N. Bassett St. Mrs. Mayer was Miss Benerita Pizzo before her marriage. She attended the Madison High School, entering in 1919 as one of the first Italian girls in that school. There are also 17 grandchildren of the Pizzos. The Pizzos were married in New Orleans, where Mrs. Pizzo came as a girl with her people.

Mr. and Mrs. Pizzo came to Madison in 1892 from Chicago, where they had previously lived. Before leaving Italy, Mr. Pizzo had traveled extensively there and in North Africa, making his way with his repair kit. He did the same after coming to Chicago.

His daughter says he walked to New Orleans and back four times and to California and back twice. This was before he was married. While on these trips he had visited Madison and later decided to locate here, partly on account of the beauty of the place.

Finds Changes Here

He finds great changes in Madison in the past 11 years and still greater in the 40 years since he first came here. Then the city had wooden sidewalks and unimproved streets. Many fine new buildings have gone up since and many old landmarks have disappeared. While the Pizzo children were growing up the family home was for years at 536 W. Dayton St., opposite what is now Barry playground. Eleven years ago Mr. and Mrs. Pizzo went to Los Angeles, largely for the benefit of Mrs. Pizzo's health. They were in the midst of the recent earthquake shock, but escaped unharmed.

Will Fly Home

Mr. Pizzo's eyesight has been almost entirely restored since coming to Madison. The Mayers will take him to Chicago Saturday by auto, after which he will board a plane for his first air trip, bound for Los Angeles.

In the meantime, he would be pleased to have any of his old friends call on him.

MARRIAGE OF
MAYER AND PIZZO FAMILY

Father Bert

Mother Betty

Bertram Joseph Mayer
1901-1996

Benerita Mary Pizzo
1904-1991

MY FATHER BERT was born in Mankato, Minnesota. He lived in Mankato until he was 14 years old when his father, Lorenz, moved the family to Kaukauna, Wisconsin. After graduation from high school, Bert worked for the State of Wisconsin in the engineering department. After marrying my mother, Betty, in 1923, they resided in Madison, Wisconsin where Dolores and I were born. When I was eleven and Dolores nine, Dad moved our family to Huntington Park, California. There he worked for several companies between 1938 and 1947, and finally at the C. F. Braun Company until he retired. He passed away from complications of old age in San Gabriel, California at the age of ninety-five, five years after my mother died.

MY MOTHER BETTY was born in Madison, Wisconsin. She married my father, Bert, when she was nineteen. After our move to California, Betty became a working mother. She first worked for The Rabun Bronze Company as a secretary, and on Sunday sold war bonds in front of our church. Later, she studied for and eventually obtained her real estate license and became a realtor. At the time of her death, she was married to my Dad for over sixty years. She passed away in 1991 in Los Angeles at the age of eighty-seven.

CORREA FAMILY

Father-in-Law Andre
Marcie's Father

Mother-in-Law Sarah
Marcie's Mother

Andre Correa
1899-1969

Sarah Correa
1888-1968

MARCIE'S FATHER ANDRE was a fisherman from Portugal who, at a young age of 19, boarded a ship and migrated to America arriving in New York City in 1918. He roamed across the United States where he eventually settled in a small town east of the San Francisco Bay, where he bought a gas station. It was here that he met Marcie's mother, Sarah. He died in San Pablo, California in 1969 at the age of 68.

SARAH was a feisty independent woman, who was born in San Leandro, California, and lived most of her life in Berkeley. She already had several children of her own when she met Andre. Although there were other children in the family, Marcie was the only daughter born from the marriage between Andre and Sarah. Sarah died in San Pablo, California at the age of 80.

1948
Andre Holding Linda

1948
Sarah With Linda

MARRIAGE OF
THE MAYER AND CORREA FAMILY

Robert Lawrence Mayer
1926-

Marceline Ann Correa
1927-1967

I WAS BORN IN MADISON, Wisconsin and lived there until I was eleven years old when my father moved our family to Huntington Park, California. After graduation from high school, I joined the Air Corps and served a tour of duty where I developed a passion for flying. In 1946, after the war, I returned home, attended junior college, met Marcie and married. As we started our family, I began work in the construction business. The field of construction lead me to my second passion in real estate development, and then to the formation of my first company. I've been thrown many curve balls, but at eighty-two, as I approach my winter years, I feel fortunate to have experienced the life I've lived with all of its trials and tribulations.

MARCIE WAS BORN IN OAKLAND, California and spent most of her early years outside of Berkeley. She later moved to Los Angeles and began working at a bank in her late teens. Shortly after I returned from tour duty, we were introduced, dated a short time and married in 1947 when Marcie was twenty years old and I was twenty-one. We had three children together. We lived in Downey, California during most of our marriage where our children grew up and went to school. We were married twenty years when she was involved in a car accident that took her young life at thirty-nine, a few months before her fortieth birthday. Today, Marcie would have been a grandmother of ten and a great-grandmother of eighteen children.

THE MAYER and CORREA CHILDREN

Linda Dolores Mayer
1947–

Robert Lawrence Mayer, Jr. (RJ)
1953–

Michael David Mayer
1955–

THE CHILDREN'S MARRIAGES

August 1992
Linda and Michael Howit
Linda has a child, Marci.
Michael has two children, Matthew and Kimberly.
They have three children and seven grandchildren.

June 1986
Rhonda and RJ Mayer
RJ has two children,
Bob III and Samantha.
Rhonda has two children,
Stacy and Ryan.
They have four children
and six grandchildren.

April 1992
Michael and Mary Mayer
Michael has a child, Amanda.
Mary has two children,
Dawna and Deen.
They have three children
and five grandchildren.

Mary Ellen and Bob

I WAS A WIDOWER ALMOST FOUR YEARS when I met Mary Ellen. At the time, Mary Ellen was 34 and I was 45 years of age. Mary Ellen had a wonderful personality, a great sense of humor and an enormously generous nature. We lived in Downey after our marriage before moving to Newport Beach. Although we divorced after 28 years of marriage, we kept in contact and maintained a friendship over the years. In November of 2005, at the young age of 68, Mary Ellen passed away after a long illness.

Bob and Maya

I MET MAYA IN NEWPORT BEACH just before my 75th birthday, when she was turning 58. She was wintering here and ready to return to Northern California where she felt most at home, although she is originally from Hawaii. Down to earth, with an independent nature, she possesses the creative ability to make things happen. She has not only encouraged me to expand my horizons, she has been my mentor in taking me through the digital age. In October 2006, several years after we met, we were married on the island of Maui.

DOLORES AND JAMIE CALVA

I WAS TWO YEARS OLD WHEN MY SISTER DOLORES THERESA arrived in Madison, Wisconsin on May 24, 1928. Later, when I was older, my parents, Bert and Betty, told me that they were just as excited waiting for their new bundle of joy as they had been when I was born. This time, it would be a girl and I would have a sister to play with. Dolores was a wonderful playmate during our formative years in Madison, and I have always had a great affection for her. When I was 11, and Dolores only 9, our parents moved our family to Huntington Park, California where Dolores and I finished our schooling. After our teenage years and graduation from high school, I went into the service and Dolores went to work in the banking industry. While working for the Bank of America she met Marcie Correa, and introduced us. In 1950, at the age of 22, Dolores met and married Jaime Calva, whose family was originally from Spain, and who had a young son from a prior marriage named Danny. Jaime was a general contractor who was involved in framing quite a number of the apartment projects our company built over the years in Southern California, plus he was one of the original partners in my first aircraft adventure. Their marriage would produce three more children, Maureen, Tom and Eileen. Jaime passed away at the age of 73 in 2000. Today, at the spry age of 80, Dolores is in good health and lives in Covina in the same home I built for her and Jaime in 1978. She is now the grandmother of eleven grandchildren and seven great-grandchildren, with one more on the way. Still active, she is part of a group of traveling widows who are involved in a number of social functions. She's also a volunteer with her local hospital auxiliary, working in admissions, and jokes that she is usually older than most of them on the list. Written with a great sense of humor and warmth, each year we await Dolores' "yearly Christmas letter" that is chock-full of funny stories of the many travels and activities she's done over the past year with her group of friends and her growing family.

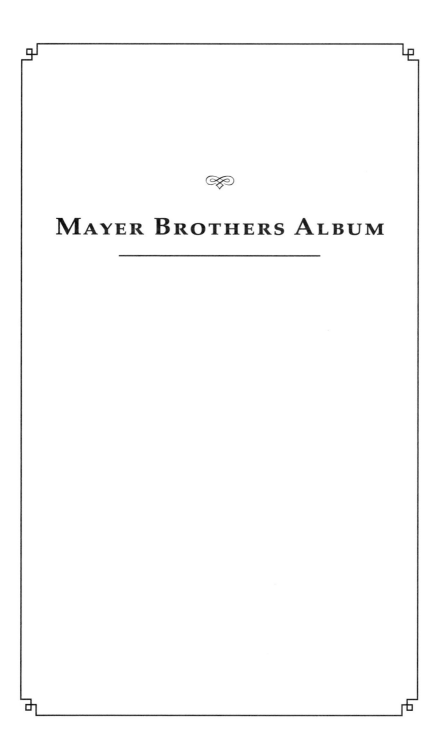

MAYER BROTHERS ALBUM

Great-grandfather Lorenz Mayer (right)
Mankato, Minnesota

Circa 1891 – The Mayer Brothers
Conrad, Lorenz and Louis

Mayer Brothers Foundry
The office was in the front of the building on the left.
Above the office to the back of this building was a large 2-story shop.
Center of the photo is the old city mill building that was
remodeled into a foundry, and to the right is the Boiler Works.

Mayer Brothers Boiler Works

Inside Mayer Brothers Foundry

Foundry Workers

Little Giant Rotary Grader

Conrad Mayer's Blacksmith Shop

PROPOSED NEW FACTORY
MAYER BROTHERS COMPANY

New Million Dollar Plant will be Built in the North Part of the City and will Cover Fifteen Acres of Ground

Located at the junction of Omaha and Northwestern railways in Mankato, near new stock yards and fair ground, on ground formerly occupied by sheep barns. Total site occupies fifteen acres.

Above picture is on scale of about 250 feet to an inch. The front building will be 80x400, and the rear building 80x500, while the long building on left connecting up the five wing buildings will be 125x800. The detached building in foreground is the general offices and garage.

THE DIFFERENT BUILDINGS.

The third building from front, with two stacks, is the iron foundry. The building to rear of foundry will be occupied by drop forging and crucible steel plant. The large building with tall smoke stack is the power plant, from which power will will be transferred in form of electric current to other buildings. The entire factory, including offices, will be heated by exhaust steam from power plant.

Entire construction will be of steel and concrete, including roofs, with sides of all buildings of glass with steel window frames. The factory will be as nearly fireproof as human ingenuity can plan.

COMPLETE PART THIS YEAR.

It is hoped to complete the front building, 80x400 feet, this year, and add others as business grows until the entire factory will be completed as shown in picture. Such a plant will mean an investment of about one million dollars for buildings and equipment, with as much or more invested in material and working capital.

The completion of this factory as shown means the employment of some fifteen hundred men, whose pay roll will be more than $100,000 monthly. When finally all buildings have been completed, if the business grows to an extent warranting same, the entire factory will be a harmonious whole blending into a perfectly planned and constructed manufacturing plant, second to none of its size and capacity in the United States or elsewhere.

TEN-TON ELECTRIC CRANES.

Ten-ton electric cranes will travel in the top of each building, and from one building to another, like a cash carrier in a store, or a hay carrier in a barn, which will save handling of raw or finished material. As will be noted from picture, the railway switch will run through each one of the wings, and cars can be loaded or unloaded by electric crane economically. Cars also run between power plant and foundry, and fuel and raw iron can be unloaded with little handling.

A track, a little over half a mile long, runs around the entire plant on which tractors can be tried out until all mechanism has been perfectly smoothed out.

EMPLOYED BEST EXPERTS.

In planning of this plant the Mayer Bros. Co. have availed themselves of the best talent and advice obtainable for it is their desire to give Mankato something that will be a real show place for visitors, while it is gathering up the dollars from all parts of the world and bringing them to Mankato to help make the city and surrounding community more prosperous than ever before.

THIS WAS A PROPOSED MAYER BROTHERS FACTORY.

Only a portion of the building was ultimately built.

VF Mankato Industry, March 14, 1915

310

ADS WERE RUN TO PROMOTE THE SALE OF COMPANY STOCK
TO ADD ON TO THE EXISTING FACTORY.
$30,000 was raised.

THE MAYER BROTHERS' NEW PLAN

One of the Leading Industries in Mankato...Trip Hammers and all Kinds of Structural Steel Work, etc., Manufactured.

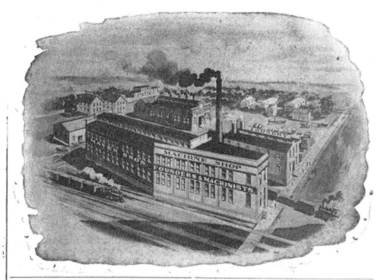

The above is a half tone of Mayer Bros.' new plant. The main building is 60 by 200 feet, two stories high, and cost $10,000. J. B. Nelsen & Co., secured the contract for the labor, and the big structure will be completed next week, when the work of moving in the machinery will begin.

The front part of the building is devoted to an office on the first floor and a drafting room above, with a two story vault. A. Anderson is the firm's capable draughtsman, and he puts in his forenoons to that work. A large two-story shop is back of this, and in the rear is the big machine shop, occupying the entire main part of the building, 60x180 feet. There is also a large new building for the boiler works, and the old City mill building has been rebuilt as a foundry.

Mayer Bros. will put in a large amount of heavy and costly new machinery including a forty-inch by twelve foot planer, a twenty-four inch engine lathe, and a five ton traveling crane. The latter can be used for first and second floor.

The engine lathe has already arrived and is in operation in the old shop. A pneumatic hammer has been placed in the boiler works, that strikes 500 blows a minute and drives rivets into boilers and structural work in almost no time. A pneumatic drill that also rolls the flues of boilers has also been put in. With the aid of this improved machinery, work is turned out quickly.

The three brothers started in business in 1891 with one small lathe, and have worked up a large and profitable business. From that small beginning, they now have a shop that has but one equal in the state, and that is located in St. Paul. If anybody wants to see the kind of structureal steel work that the firm does, it can find it in the interior of the new machine shop.

The firm now consists of Louis and Lawrence Mayer. They employ a large number of skilled mechanics. They have invented and patented a trip hammer that is being sold to small blacksmiths all over the United States. A number of orders have recently been coming in from California. Thus far this year 110 of the hammers have been manufactured and sold, and the orders are increasing from year to year.

Our citizens hardly appreciate the magnitude of Mayer Bros.' plant and business. To get some idea of it, a visit should be made to the plant, on Rock street, near North Front.

THE MAYER BROTHERS FACTORY THAT WAS ACTUALLY BUILT.

18

The 8 Cylinder 1903 Mayer Automobile

By Allie Mayer

The (1903) Mayer 8-cylinder car as it appeared in 1910 after many modifications.

In 1903 there was a remarkable car being assembled in the Mayer Brothers (Louis and Lawrence) machine shop at Mankato, Minnesota. The auto was far beyond what anyone else at that time had ever dreamed. In 1903, most of the auto industry was satisfied with building one or two cylinder engined cars, a few were dreaming of as many as four cylinders — but eight cylinders was unbelievable!

The idea, as conceived by my father Louis Mayer was to build an eight cylinder engine car, and more fantastic a V-bank with four cylinders on each side (bank of 2 split) made of cast iron. It would be able to seat seven passengers with jump seats. Dad decided for the rough roads at that time, to use coil springs. He would use gears, instead of a chain drive, to get the car moving on its wheels. People told Dad his ideas were not practical. But Dad did not let the people distract him from his project. Whenever time permitted from the machine shop, he had his workmen turn their talents to his car.

Joe Marka helped design the car, Hank Guth assembled it. Mr. Bennett helped in designing and making the carburator and ignition. George Huettl and Ole Dedrickson also remember the year the car was built. The crankcase and transmission were made of aluminum. It had a Bosch swiveling magneto. The steel body was made in

Detroit, according to Dad's design. The radiator was built in North Milwaukee. These were the only two parts of the car that were manufactured outside the Mankato plant. The engine was four feet long, and had a covered gear box, and hand shift system. The rear end universal was almost like those in our cars of today. The wheels had 37 x 5 tires. The frame was riveted. The horsepower was about 100.

Dad called on his old friend John Theissen to paint the car black with yellow wheels. Now the people who thought Dad was impractical, were convinced it could run.

In 1907, Dad took it for a test run and the car soared through Main Street of Mankato with grandeur. Proven to himself that he could invent such a thing, Dad turned his talents to the invention of a tractor. He also built two more V-type engines. He hooked the two V-type engines together and installed them in a motorboat to be used on Lake Minnehaha at 65 mph — which everyone again thought was something that was unheard of.

In 1915, Dad and his brother Lawrence left Mankato for Wisconsin and they took the 1903 Mayer car with them. In 1922, Mother insisted Dad junk the car and it was done . . . The only remnant I have of Dad's car is the four cylinder tire pump.

Note: The name Lawrence should be Lorenz

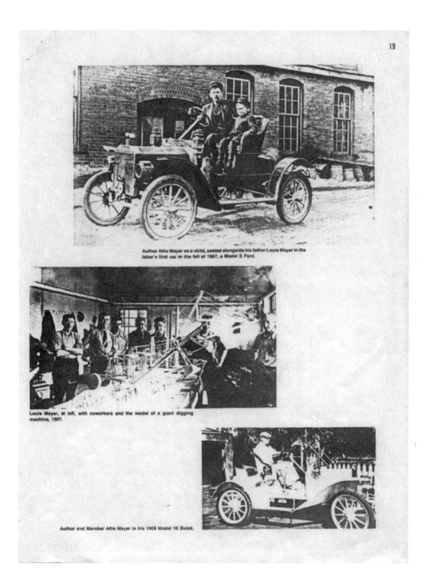

19

Author Allie Mayer as a child, seated alongside his father Louie Mayer in the latter's first car in the fall of 1907, a Model S Ford.

Louie Mayer, at left, with coworkers and the model of a giant digging machine, 1907.

Author and Member Allie Mayer in his 1908 Model 10 Buick.

Page 2 of The Horseless Carriage Gazette

Auto Built In Mankato In 1903 Had 8 Cylinders, Coiled Springs

By DON SPAVIN
Staff Writer

"The darn thing'll never work, Louie," the kibitzer declared with the certainty characteristic of all his type. "Who ever heard of a car with an eight-cylinder engine?"

The "thing" referred to by the hanger-on was a car being assembled in the smoke-stained machine shop of Louis Mayer at Mankato. But, such a car no one in Mankato had ever seen before. For that was 1903 and while some had heard of the new-fangled horseless carriage that was being built, mostly in the East, few had ever seen a vehicle that ran without horses.

So, when the kibitzer expressed his opinion he was only reflecting the general attitude of Mankatoans. For, the auto Louie Mayer was building was so far beyond what anyone else at that time had even dreamed that even the builder wondered at times if he wasn't the "crackpot" he was often called.

SANITY QUESTIONED

In 1903 the infant auto industry, for the most part, was content with building one or two cylinder engine cars, in appearance only a shade away from the buggies and carriages the public had known so long. A few daring experimenters were beginning to dream of as many as four cylinders, but eight cylinders—that was fantasy.

So it's no wonder that those who learned of Louie Mayer's plans for a car began to wonder about his sanity. How, they asked, could an uneducated blacksmith do what he proposed to do when even the best brains in the business would shy away from such ideas.

Louie's idea was to build an eight-cylinder engine car—not just eight cylinders in a row but even more far-fetched, a V-bank with four cylinders on each side. Louie's dreams didn't end there.

His car, he planned, would resemble no other in existence. It would be able to seat eight persons comfortably and even as many as 11 with a little crowding. In design it would depart a long way from the well-known buggy. For the rough roads of the time, Louie had a solution for his car.

PLANNED COIL SPRINGS

He'd have no brittle leaf springs to break when his vehicle hit a bump. He'd suspend each on its own spring, and the coils, he decided, would be a

SEVERAL YEARS after Mayer built his car, Henry Ford came out with this model —1909. In appearance it resembles the Mankato car with the exception of the front door. The picture was taken in St. Paul in 1947. The car was driven here by Sidney M. Strong of Atwater, Minn. He is at the front of the car with his wife and mother-in-law, Mrs. Grace Koerner of Litchfiel...

TYPICAL of the cars of the early 1900's was this 1904 one-cylinder Reo. The Mayer, a year earlier, was far advanced.

the biggest single attraction this city had ever seen."

The rest was an anticlimax.

wasn't there," said Mr. Theissen, "but there were many among the passengers who won-

Missing text… story will finish on next page
St. Paul Pioneer Press March 30, 1952

the same guy who advised the Mankato blacksmith that his auto-building ideas were not practical. But, Louie, a stubborn German, let the advice roll off his broad back and began transfering his "radical" ideas from his head to iron, steel and wood.

During the cold winter months, whenever time could be spared from other work, Louie turned his skilled workmen loose on his pet project—the car.

George Huettl, still working at the machinist trade, was one who helped build Mayer's dream.

"I started to work for the Mayer firm in 1902," George said, "and in 190? did considerable work on the car. I helped turn out the pistons on a lathe in the shop."

George J. Hodapp and Ole Dedrickson also remember the year the car was born. Although none were automobile builders they could follow the orders that flowed from the agile brain of Louie Mayer.

YEARS AHEAD

Thus, details of construction have been forgotten, but many of the car's outstanding features are still remembered. For instance, these machinist midwives remember the giant engine was four feet long; it had two crankshafts; was gear driven, had covered gear boxes and had a shift system similar to the present standard type. The rear-end universal was almost a duplicate of today's vehicles. The wheels wore 30-inch tires. The car had a riveted frame. Its horsepower was rated at 100.

For nearly a year workmen in Mayer's shop put odd minutes and hours on the car and at last the chassis and motor stood ready to receive the body. This portion of the car—made of wood to a design drawn by Louie—was purchased from a body factory in Detroit and arrived at Mankato unpainted. After it was bolted onto the chassis, the vehicle stood ready for painting.

Although the car was an experiment there was no skimping and for the painting Louie called in his old friend, John P. Theissen, a master at his trade.

20 COATS OF PAINT

Mr. Theissen, now curator of the Blue Earth county museum at Mankato, used all the skill at his command to make the car as beautiful as possible.

"We put on 20 coats of paint," he said, "each by hand. After each coat was dry it was rubbed down with pumice stone. When finished the vehicle had a shiny black finish on the body with sparkling yellow wheels. She was sure a sight to behold and equalled until in recent years.

Agency hill, now known as Main street hill, today soars up extremely steep grade. In 1903 it was even worse and as an added hazard there was no hard surfacing on the street. Climbing it in one of the 1903 vintage autos was out of the question, but to Louie Mayer it presented the proper challenge for his car.

UP IT GOES!

John Theissen was one of those taken along for ballast the day the test was made. With Louie at the wheel the vehicle rolled out of the shop, down Front street a few blocks to Main, then turned left. For several blocks the street was nearly level then began a gradual climb that developed into what seemed an almost verticle ascent.

As Louie turned the corner at Front and Main he poured the gasoline to the eight hungry cylinders and the car sprang to life. With its hundred horses roaring, the Mayer Special took off in a cloud of dust on a historic test that would be the talk of Mankato for years to come.

"We made the hill like it of the car he had created, even time was considered one of the worst in the state.

George Hodapp, who often drove the big Special, said he made 65 miles an hour in short spurts. No one among those associated with the car dared drive it wide open for any length of time.

HE TIRED OF IT

Far ahead of its time, the Special was far from perfect and oldtimers remember many times it broke down and had to be pulled in. But by 1903 standards, or for that matter standards of even a later date, the car could be considered a real success.

Mayer, who had built the car partly as a hobby but more to prove he could do it, soon tired of the Special and turned his talents to the invention and manufacture of other items, including a tractor.

Just to prove it wasn't beginner's luck, Mayer built two more of the V-type engines. A friend installed them in a motorboat he used on Lake Minnetonka many years.

The Mankato man built only the one car and after the novelty had worn off eventually sold it to a couple of his workmen. When they left the Minnesota city they took the car with them to Wisconsin.

Page 2 - St. Paul Pioneer Press March 30, 1952

Local carmaker's near misfire

Mayer's 1903 model had mighty engine but wasn't marketed

By MARK FISCHENICH
Free Press Staff Writer

MANKATO — If the car had been marketed as well as it was engineered, Mankato might have been another Flint, Mich., and people across the world might be driving Mayer Mustangs.

But the turn-of-the-century car wasn't sold. The designer and builder of the Mayer Special didn't even try to manufacture his revolutionary design. He built it to show that he could, he put it through the testing wringer and then he moved on to other things.

The Mayer Special, one of the first cars with a V-8 engine, passed test after test. With power well beyond the one-, two- or four-cylinder vehicles that others were building, the Mayer allegedly hit a speed of 65 mph on one occasion.

Designed in 1903 by Louis Mayer of Mankato, the engine was built in 1906 and the machine was believed to have been on the road by 1907. It was fabricated at the Mayer Bros. foundry, the forerunner of the Little Giant Co. and later the Dotson Co.

"These guys were just marvelous tinkerers and inventors and were way ahead of their time in many of the things that they did," said Denny Dotson, owner of the Dotson Co.

Louis Mayer, the son of a German immigrant, was greeted with skepticism when he talked of the car he was building. It passed the ultimate test in the Mankato area, however, when Mayer started the vehicle at the corner of Front and Main streets and drove straight up the unpaved street to the top of the Main Street hill.

The car cruised up the steep hill "without a quiver," according to records at the Blue Earth County Historical Society. "That satisfied Louis for a while, but in the next few weeks he was seen attacking every hill in southern Minnesota out to prove his point."

Bert Burns, a former Mankato State University professor and a member of the historical

'That must have been a remarkable automobile. The gear system apparently was far advanced and the suspension system, too. What a shame that he didn't pursue it.'

Bert Burns,
Blue Earth County
Historical Society

work.

"That must have been a remarkable automobile," Burns said. "The gear system apparently was far advanced and the suspension system, too. What a shame that he didn't pursue it."

The car got mixed reactions from locals who were still getting used to the idea of a buggy without a horse — especially one the size of the Mayer Special.

"They dubbed it the 'Titanic' because it was so big, but they would run to the curbs to stare whenever Louis drove by," according to the historical society document.

The machine could carry seven passengers. It had two forward gears and one reverse and ran for several years with a makeshift body that was eventually replaced with a spiffy, wooden body ordered from Detroit.

Louis apparently never showed

Power to burn

Above: The Mayer Special, designed and built by a group of Mankato foundry men, was a remarkable performer, but no effort was ever made to mass-produce it. Below: The 'Kato' truck, such as one purchased by Hubbard Milling, was built from 1906 to 1913.

Little Giant Tractor. He built a four-wheel-drive truck, another innovative vehicle at the time, for local candy manufacturer Ernest Reminberger, who produced several dozen "Kato" cars and trucks.

Despite the creation of numerous remarkable inventions that included the tractor, a highly touted trip hammer and hand saws that Dotson said still work well today, the Mayer Bros.

out of town on a rail because of the number of people they [were indebted to]," Dotson said.

Louis Mayer ended up in Wisconsin in 1915, and the car's fate was believed to be as scrap at a Kaukauna, Wis., junkyard. The Mayer brothers' only apparent flaw, their lack of business acumen, might be the only thing that kept them from becoming one of the giant names in manufacturing, Dotson said.

A FEW OF THE MAYER BROTHERS LOGOS

THE MAYER BROTHERS LITTLE GIANT POWER HAMMER

THE MAYER BROTHERS LITTLE GIANT TRACTOR

1917 Mayer Bros Little Giant

Thornbury Vintage Tractor & Implement Club Inc

Foster Road,
Thornbury,
Southland,
New Zealand

Little Giant in the Field

THE MAYER BROTHERS STRADDLE DITCHER

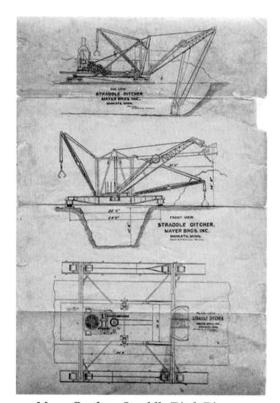

Mayer Brothers Straddle Ditch Diagram

Straddle Ditcher in the Field

THE MAYER BROTHERS IN THEIR LATER YEARS

Great-Uncle Louis

Great-Uncle Conrad

Grandpa Lorenz

GRANDMOTHERS IN THEIR LATER YEARS

Great-grandma Maximiliana (third from left)

Grandma Anna   **Grandma Juanina**

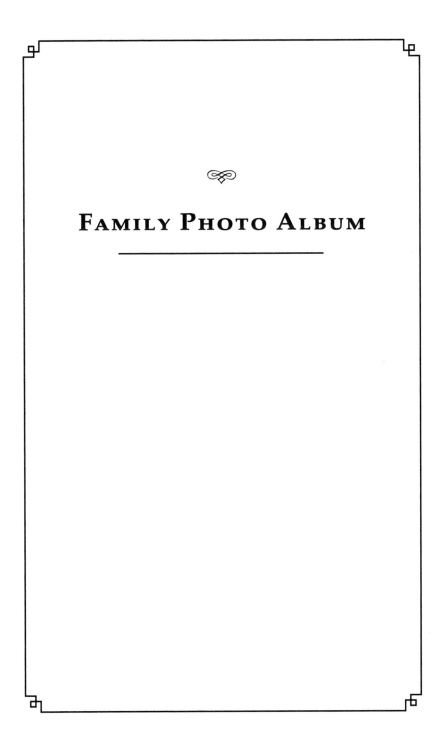

FAMILY PHOTO ALBUM

1922
Betty and Bert

1923
Betty and Bert in Madison

1923
Bert and Betty's Wedding

1926
Bob at 4 Months

1927
Prize Wining Picture

1927
Betty

1932
Uncle Joe and Margaret

1930
Our New Chevy

1932
Bob and Dolores in the Snow

1933
Bob and Dolores

1932
On Vacation Driving from Madison to Los Angeles
Visiting the Great Salt Lake in Utah

1932
On Vacation From Los Angeles Back to Madison
Camping at Lake Tahoe

1941
A Young Man at Age 15

1940
Dad, Mom, Bob and Dolores

1942
With the Family All Grown Up
Bob, Mom, Uncle Joe in Back, Dad, Dolores and Sailor Friends

1944
Huntington Park Home

1944
Joins Army Air Force

1944
Army Air Force

1944
With Dad in Uniform

1944
Ready for Combat

1945
Gunnery Training in Florida

1945
A Young Aviator
Fort Meyers, Florida

1945
Sheppard Field Flying

1947
Marcie and Bob's Wedding

1948
Bob and Baby Linda

1952
Linda at Age 5

1953
Bob, Marcie, Linda and Baby RJ

1953
Linda with Dad on the Bike

1953
Linda in Lynwood

1955
Fishing in Acapulco

1962
Bob and Marcie in Las Vegas

1962
Bob, Marcie, Rosalie and John Nisser

1963
Mike, Dad and RJ

DESTINATION HAWAII

For the Robert Mayer family of 10538 Briarbush, the
last few weeks before the opening of the 1966-67
school year were devoted to a visit to the Hawaiian
Islands, where they enjoyed the traditional aloha welcome on their arrival in Honolulu Harbor aboard the
SS Lurline. Mr. and Mrs. Mayer are pictured, foreground, with their two sons, Robert and Michael,
prior to their departure from Los Angeles Harbor.

1966
Mike, RJ, Marcie and Bob

1966
Bob, RJ, Mike and Marcie Aboard the Lurline Sailing to Hawaii

1966
Marcie with Lloyd and Jeanne Cox

1972
Nancy, RJ, Mary Ellen, Bob, Joe, Linda and Mike

Dolores and Jamie

Tom, Eileen, Dolores Jaime, Maureen, Danny

Calva Family All Grown Up

1972
Mary Ellen and Bob

1973
Bert and Betty's 50th Anniversary
Bob, Mary Ellen, Mom, Dad, Dolores, Jamie, Nancy, RJ

Mom and Dad

1923

1983

Mom and Dad
Celebrating Their 60th Anniversary In 1983

1980
Buying the Rolls Royce at a Charity Event

1980
The Rolls…It Looked Great…But…

Halloween Was a Costume Party Every Year

Jamie and Bob

Dolores and Bob

Bob and Mary Ellen

Bob as Yellow Bird

Jeanne and Lloyd Cox

John and Rosalie Nisser

1988
Mary Ellen and Bob in the Desert

1992
Mary Ellen, President Bush
and Bob

1995
Restoring the Huntington
Beach Pier After the Big Storm

2002
Bob and Maya on the Island of Kauai

2003
Downey Hospital Man of the Year
Bob, Maya and Jack Campbell

2003
Downey Hospital Event, Bob and Johnny Nisser

2003
The Nisser Family
Alanna, Mary Lee, John and Denise

Key Largo Casino and Quality Inn offers a unique
experience in Las Vegas. Nowhere else can you
find such a friendly, casual atmosphere. Whether
you're visiting the casino or staying in one of our
newly refurbished rooms, you'll discover Key Largo
is your home away from home.

Free shuttle service to and from
the airport and Las Vegas Strip.

377 E. Flamingo Rd.
Las Vegas, Nevada 89109
Phone 702.733.7777
        800.634.6617
Fax   702.369.6911

© copyright 1997, Ambassador Gaming, Inc.

Key Largo Casino and Quality Inn

Steve Wynn and Bob
Orange County, California

2004
Congressman Dana Rohrabacher, Bob, Maya
and Govenor Schwarzenegger

2005
Mediterranean Cruise

2005
Mykonos, Greece

2006 – Maui
Bob and Maya's Wedding Photo

Wedding Party
Mike, Mary, Mike, Bob, Maya, Peggy, Jack, Rhonda, RJ and Linda

With the Kids
Mary, Mike, Bob, Linda, Mike, Rhonda and RJ

2004
Christmas
Bob and Dolores

2006
Three Generations
Bob III, Bob and RJ

2008
Las Vegas, Nevada, Zero Gravity

Ready to Board the Zero-G Aircraft

Experiencing Zero-G
Zero Gravity with Bob III Upside Down on Left

Zero-G – We Made It!

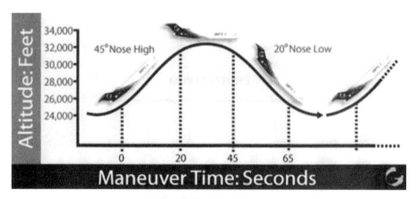

Parabolic Diagram

Cessna 340—Palm Springs

Cessna 421—Palm Springs

36' S.S. Naughtiness

THE CLÉNET COLLECTION

The Red Clénet– Series I, No. 23

The Red Clénet – Series I, No. 223

The Blue Clénet – Series II, No. 23

1972
Palm Springs, California

2008
Golfing in the Desert

THE WATERFRONT PROJECT

2004
50-Acre Site of The Waterfront Project
Hilton Waterfront Beach Resort
Hyatt Regency Resort and Spa
Residential Communities Sea Colony and Sea Cove

1978
50-Acre Site Before Development of The Waterfront Project
Huntington Beach, California

Hilton Waterfront Beach Resort
Bob and Steve Cutting the Ribbon

1990
The Hilton Waterfront Beach Resort
Huntington Beach, California

Portecochere at Night
Hilton Waterfront Beach Resort

2002
Hyatt Construction – the Hilton Waterfront in Background

2003
Hyatt Regency Opening Ceremonies

2003
Hyatt Regency Resort and Spa
Huntington Beach, California

Fountain Courtyard at Night
Hyatt Regency Resort and Spa

VOL. 27 NO. 34   AUGUST 23-29, 2004

ORANGE COUNTY BUSINESS JOURNAL

A Profile in Excellence

The Robert Mayer Corporation Helps Shape Southern California with a Legacy of Success

From modest beginnings in post WWII Downey, California, to the state's most spectacular oceanfront development in Huntington Beach, Robert Mayer has led his namesake company on an inspiring journey of success over the past 50 years. Before founding what is now the Robert Mayer Corporation in 1955, he learned his trade literally from the ground up as Los Angeles and all of Southern California experienced unprecedented growth and welcome prosperity in the late 1940s.

Bob was a young man when he was honorably discharged from the Army Air Corps. He immediately found work with a local developer building apartments to house the burgeoning population in Los Angeles County. He began as an apprentice pushing wheelbarrows, worked hard, put in long hours and quickly learned all the various trades of the construction industry. By the early 1950s, he was serving as general manager of the company. By then, the company had become the largest developer of apartment buildings in the Los Angeles area.

In the mid-1950s, Bob left the relative security of his prior employer, electing to put his life savings and expertise to work by founding his own company, Mayer Construction Company. Initially, Bob and his young company handled residential remodeling projects, which were easy to come by and quick to complete. Open land was more plentiful in the region at that time, and demand for housing seemed unlimited. One day, he found an ideal lot in southeast Los Angeles, and with the sponsorship of an investor, Mayer Construction built a two-unit duplex. With a business model designed to simply repeat success, the company grew from there, completing larger projects.

As the Southland grew, so did the company, building housing tracts, apartment complexes and other residential projects throughout Southern California. By 1960, Bob had again earned the position as the largest developer of apartment projects in Southern California, but this time as an owner and entrepreneur, not a general manager working for someone else.

THE ROBERT MAYER CORPORATION

Robert L. Mayer, Chairman,
The Robert Mayer Corporation

A New Vision in Hospitality

In the 1970s, the concept of an extended stay hotel was virtually unheard of. With his unique vision, Bob recognized an opportunity to create transitional housing for individuals and families as they arrived in certain communities. The first in a chain of hotels known as Ambassador Inns of America was opened in Las Vegas, Nevada. Over the next few years, the chain expanded to twelve cities within California, Nevada and Arizona. Although the balance of the chain has been sold, Bob continues to operate the original location currently known as the Key Largo Hotel and Casino in Las Vegas, Nevada. Bob is understandably proud of the fact that he and key executives within the organization are licensed by the Nevada Gaming Authority to operate any casino on an unrestricted basis.

Expanding into Related Businesses

Bob Mayer has used his experience and financial strength to expand into related industries. In 1979, he co-founded Metro Bank, a financial institution focused on business development, which Comerica Bank purchased in 1996. Following that success, Bob joined with various colleagues in the industry to participate in the founding of Prime Bank, another business bank, which was later purchased by East/West Bank, a major financial institution based in Southern California.

Retiring from Retirement

By 1980, Bob Mayer felt satisfied with his accomplishments, but wished to step back from the day-to-day management of over 1,000 employees and construction projects in three states. He elected to sell the business and planned to retire to Newport Beach, where he intended to live and manage a small real estate-based investment firm. However, in a decision that could be described as either shrewd or fortuitous, he held on to several parcels of land he believed were underutilized and undervalued. His vision for one parcel of oceanfront property would later transform a city and become the crown jewel of Bob Mayer's remarkable career.

Retirement did not last long for Bob. His drive, his vision and his passion for his work soon coaxed him back toward the business of land development full time. Bob recognized that the city of Huntington Beach was ready for a renaissance, and his land could be the catalyst that would preserve the charm of Surf City U.S.A. while elevating the quality of life

for residents, merchants and visitors.

Bob Mayer soon partnered with Stephen K. Bone for the purpose of bringing his vision of a world-class destination resort complex to life along Pacific Coast Highway. The new organization was small by design, comprised of a team of impressive industry leaders and specialists that Bob admired and trusted. Today, many of those founding experts remain an integral part of the company's day-to-day operations.

Bob led that team throughout the 25-year process of creating what is now simply referred to as "The Waterfront," consisting of the Hilton Waterfront Beach Resort, the Hyatt Regency Resort and Spa, Sea Cove and Sea Colony, a residential community of 184 new homes. This spectacular destination resort and residential community serves as the anchor for the city's downtown redevelopment, an enormous success that has established Huntington Beach as a world-class tourist destination. The Hyatt Regency is home to the largest oceanfront conference facility in the state. A third hotel is planned and has been tentatively approved for the site, meaning the entire development process for the Waterfront project will likely span 30 years.

The Robert Mayer Corporation Today ... and Tomorrow

Rather than focusing on construction, The Robert Mayer Corporation concentrates on what is considered the most challenging and high-risk aspect of land development: the acquisition and entitlement of unique opportunities. Bob's philosophy has always been to go after the difficult projects — the properties where others have failed to recognize value, or refused to touch, due to complexities and perceived obstacles.

Over the past 50 years, Bob has built his family business by surrounding himself with dedicated and brilliant senior executives who have the patience, tenacity and expertise to navigate complex layers of government requirements and delicate waters of community relations. Integrating redevelopment into existing neighborhoods is a very complicated process and generally is much more difficult than new homes in brand new subdivisions. Bob and his team understand the need for acute sensitivity to the desires and concerns of

the existing property owners. These issues must be carefully considered during countless meetings to solicit their opinions and earn their support, and clear communication is essential. If current property owners do not understand and embrace the benefits that a project will bring to their neighborhood, then their reluctance and opposition can delay or even halt the entire project. Bob credits his team's understanding of these dynamics, and its practice of addressing such issues proactively with respect and sensitivity, to the firm's remarkable record of success.

When asked to discuss his vision for the future of The Robert Mayer Corporation, Bob Mayer replied, "With the lack of available land in the highly concentrated areas of Southern California, our organization should become one of the leaders in the redevelopment of 'underutilized' residential and commercial sites in local markets. The expertise developed over these past many years will provide a very strong foundation for future development, where so many impediments to 'rebuilding' now exist."

Today, Bob serves as chairman of the company, providing vision and guidance to a team led by President Stephen K. Bone and Bob's eldest son, Vice Chairman Robert L. Mayer, Jr. (RJ). Steve Bone is responsible for the day-to-day operations for nearly all Mayer entities. Steve joined the company in 1986 as a partner during the development of the Waterfront project. A graduate of Columbia Law School, Steve's legal expertise and extensive background in real estate and tourism development bring an important dimension to the leadership of the company. As Vice Chairman, RJ follows in the footsteps of his father in moving the company forward by navigating through today's complex challenges. He also spearheads the company's philanthropic efforts. Bob's grandson, Robert L. Mayer, III, is the most recent addition to the family business, bringing three generations of the Mayer family together on a daily basis.

For further information contact: Robert L. Mayer Jr., Vice Chair, The Robert Mayer Corporation, 660 Newport Center Dr., Suite 1050, Newport Beach, CA 92660.